reel spirituality

Engaging Culture

WILLIAM A. DYRNESS
AND ROBERT K. JOHNSTON,
SERIES EDITORS

The Engaging Culture series is designed to help Christians respond with theological discernment to our contemporary culture. Each volume explores particular cultural expressions, seeking to discover God's presence in the world and to involve readers in sympathetic dialogue and active discipleship. These books encourage neither an uninformed rejection nor an uncritical embrace of culture, but active engagement informed by theological reflection.

reel spirituality

theology and film in dialogue

robert k. johnston

Baker Academic
A Division of Baker Book House Co
Grand Rapids, Michigan 49516

Published by Baker Academic
a division of Baker Book House Company
P.O. Box 6287, Grand Rapids, MI 49516-6287

Printed in the United States of America

Library of Congress Cataloging-in-Publication Data

Johnston, Robert K., 1945–
    Reel spirituality : theology and film in dialogue / Robert K. Johnston.
        p.   cm. — (Engaging culture)
    Includes bibliographical references and index.
    ISBN 0-8010-2241-X (paper)
    1. Motion pictures—Religious aspects. I. Title. II. Series.
PN1995.5. J59 2000
791.43′682—dc21   00-041358

Unless otherwise indicated, all Scripture quotations are from the New Revised Standard Version of the Bible, copyright © 1989 by the Division of Christian Education of the National Council of the Churches of Christ in the United States of America. Used by permission.

All photographs appearing in this book were supplied by Photofest, New York, New York.

For information about academic books, resources for Christian leaders, and all new releases available from Baker Book House, visit our web site:

http://www.bakerbooks.com

For Cathy

Everything you need to know about life is in the movies.

—Travis, *Grand Canyon*

contents

illustrations

Photos

Figures

acknowledgments

Reel Spirituality has been shaped and formed by the five classes in theology and film that I have taught at Fuller Theological Seminary. The first three of these were co-taught with Robert Banks. Much of what is written on these pages developed in dialogue with Rob and our students. It is impossible to credit (or even know) all that were originally Rob's ideas. Suffice it to say, I am deeply in debt to my former colleague for his creativity, his stimulation, and his encouragement.

Many of the film descriptions in this book first appeared as reviews in the pages of *The Covenant Companion*, a monthly publication of the Evangelical Covenant Church. I am thankful to Jane Swanson-Nystrom, managing editor of the *Companion*, for asking my wife and me to be regular contributors to that magazine. The reviews were co-written with my wife, Catherine Barsotti. It is with Cathy that I have seen most of the movies described in this book, and it is with her that I have had my fullest discussions about them. Her insights have consistently stretched my thinking and broadened my experience. It is to her that I dedicate this book.

In one of the film columns that we co-wrote, we asked readers to suggest titles for this book. Among the suggestions we received were

> *Rumors of Glory*
> *God in Hollywood: Resident Alien?*
> *Action! Hearing God's Voice in the Midst of the Movies*
> *Why I Am Not Afraid to Share My Popcorn with Jesus*
> *Jesus the Film Critic*
> *Movies That Changed My Life*

However, the title I chose, *Reel Spirituality*, comes from another source. It is borrowed from a conference I co-chaired in 1998 with Hollywood producer Ralph

Winter (*Star Trek IV and VI; Mighty Joe Young; X-Men*). We brought fifty pastors and church leaders together with fifty Hollywood writers and directors to discuss "Storytelling as Common Ground." I am indebted to Ralph and to those on the planning committee for teaching me much about storytelling in the movies.

I am also indebted to a number of individuals who read a draft of this book and offered helpful suggestions as to how I might improve it: Ken Gire, who has written widely on the spirituality of everyday life; screenwriter Craig Detweiler; Fuller Theological Seminary colleagues Rob Banks and Bill Dyrness; and students Ginger Arnold, Chad Pecknold, and Neal Johnson. I am thankful as well to students in my class on Theology and Film, which I taught in the fall of 1999. All forty students were given a copy of the manuscript and asked to write a response to it. Their criticisms and encouragements have helped shape this book as well.

introduction

The task I'm trying to achieve is above all to make you see.

D. W. Griffith

Barry Taylor, a musician who also pastors a church for those in the Hollywood entertainment industry, was asked by a producer friend to go to the Warner Sound Studios for a test screening of a new movie. It was a rough cut, that is, one with temporary music, unedited sound, and some special effects missing. Over one hundred people were invited that evening in order to provide the producers and directors feedback about the film, which has since been released with the title *The Third Miracle* (d.[1] Holland, 1999). Barry provided music for the movie.

The movie's story is about Frank Shore, a Catholic priest who has lost his faith and is living a dissolute life. The lapsed priest has a gift no one else has, however—one that is needed by the church. He can expose fraudulent miracles. As the story unfolds, the diocese calls on Shore to help with an investigation of a series of apparent miracles. The source of the unexplainable phenomena seems to be a mysterious woman, now deceased, whom some people consider a saint. When Shore meets the woman's daughter, there begins for him a journey toward the recovery of faith and hope.

After the screening, the producers tried to elicit from the audience their opinion about technical aspects of the film. Specifically, they wanted to know whether or not the story held up, the characters were compelling, the scenes made sense, and so on. But, recounted Taylor, "They didn't get the information they were looking for. Instead they got an hour-long discussion that they had to forcibly stop about God, faith, and miracles. And apart from my friend, I was the only person in the room who had set foot in the church in the last five years." Barry said he sat in a theater that night and heard people arguing about the nature of

13

faith, and whether miracles could happen. They were asking, What makes a saint? Who is part of the church? And who are we as human beings? The conversation simply erupted, and it was theological to the core. Taylor concluded his remarks to a group of faculty and fellow-students at Fuller Theological Seminary by saying that "there is a very, very serious conversation going on in our culture, in Western culture at the end of the twentieth century, about God. And the church is not a part of it. We're not invited to the conversation most of the time . . . and we are not aware."[2]

Conversation about God—what we have traditionally called theology—is increasingly found outside the church as well as within it. One of the chief venues for such conversation is the movie theater with its adjacent cafes. With attendance at church stagnating and with movie viewing at theaters and through video stores at an all-time high, Christians find themselves wanting to get back into the conversation but often are not able to do so effectively.

This book is intended to help the Christian moviegoer enter into theological conversation with film. As image, film assumes an artist and a viewer. As story, film assumes a speaker and a hearer. That is, although we might be watching a movie while sitting silently in a theater, we are still part of a dialogue. For movies seek to engage us, their viewers, as whole human beings. They invite—we might almost say, demand—our response. And it is easily given. After seeing a film, we go with friends to Starbucks or a restaurant to have a cup of coffee and to talk about whether we liked the film or not. We want to share our reactions and response.

For many Christians, however, this conversation with film remains partial, both naive in its judgments and disconnected from our faith and beliefs. How can we enter into the conversation with Hollywood in a way that goes beyond bumper stickers and sloganeering? How can we engage this alternate form of storytelling, both emotionally and intellectually?

Too few of us have developed the skills of movie watching, let alone of film criticism, so as to make authentic dialogue from a Christian perspective possible. Even fewer have reflected theologically on how God might be using film to reveal something of the divine to us. Many Christians assume that movies are neither the context for theological discussion nor the occasion for revelatory event. When they go into a theater, they do not expect to see anything but celluloid and therefore are not disappointed! But they are impoverished. Moreover, they are increasingly out of step with those outside the church who resonate strongly with Hollywood's spiritual fare.

Many people in our society are seeking spirituality, even if they have little interest in organized religion. The situation is not entirely new, but it is surely more pronounced of late. In an introduction to his classic book, *Basic Christianity* (1971), John R. W. Stott states that "large numbers of people, especially young people" are "hostile to the church, [but] friendly to Jesus Christ."[3]

They believe what Annie Savoy did in the movie *Bull Durham* (1988), that the church produces too much guilt and is boring, and thus they reject it. But many today, particularly young adults, are willing to examine their spirituality and the spirituality of others. They even "believe" in Jesus. If religious ideas or experience can be put into an irreverent or interesting package, so much the better. Here is the appeal of Kevin Smith's edgy but God-affirming movie *Dogma* (1999).

Wanting to help Christians better connect with Hollywood—wanting, that is, to help Christians get back into the conversation on that which concerns us most—this book risks being one-sided. If film is a powerful tool for engaging its viewers spiritually, surely it can be used for bad as well as good. If it can be the occasion for divine encounter, can it not also undercut and destroy belief? Must not Christians be selective in what they see? The answer is, "Of course." The violence that was integral to *Saving Private Ryan* (1998) and *Schindler's List* (1993) helped viewers discover the horror of war and the Holocaust. It is easily distinguished from *Nightmare on Elm Street* (1984). But what of *Pulp Fiction* (1994) or *Unforgiven* (1992)? The sexuality of *The Thomas Crown Affair* (1999) can be distinguished from *Caged Heat* (1974) or *Frankenhooker* (1990). But do viewers understand the larger intention of these movies, or are they all just occasions for many in the audience to engage in murder and sex from the safety of their seats? From the typical applause at showings of these movies, it is safe to say that most of the irony and subtlety of these films is lost on the average viewer. Christian discrimination is called for, but in two senses of that word. Not only should Christian moviegoers be at times selective, but they must become knowledgeable filmviewers as well.

Though discrimination is called for, something that will vary depending on an individual's personal and spiritual maturity, the church has swung the pendulum so far in that direction for so long that another danger seems the bigger problem today. Currently, the church risks irrelevancy without its walls and complacency within. We have boxed in God and the results are proving disastrous. New eyes are called for as we attempt to see God anew.

Henry David Thoreau wrote in his journal, "The question is not what you look at, but what you see."[4] *Reel Spirituality* is a book about "seeing." And "responding." Again I take my cue from another of our great nineteenth century humanists, John Ruskin: "The greatest thing a human soul ever does in this world is to see something, and tell what it saw in a plain way."[5]

The focus of *Reel Spirituality* is on *film* and *theology*, two words that demand clarification from the outset. Movies were invented just over one hundred years ago. Yet they are one of our most popular art forms. For this reason, perhaps, movies have not been taken seriously either by art critics or by theologians. In an attempt to help legitimate their discipline, film critics in the fifties and sixties turned from Hollywood "movies" to European "films" in order to concentrate on the more serious fare of directors like Fellini and Bergman. As a result, the early seventies evidenced a spate of books on the theological significance of serious and non-commercial European films. While American movies were thought to put entertainment first and soul-searching second, if at all, foreign films were considered to be just the opposite. Now, almost fifty years later, such distinctions seem artificial, though they are occasionally still voiced.[6] By *film* I mean *movies*, whether seen in theaters, on video, or on TV; whether produced in Hollywood or Europe, by a major studio or the independents.[7]

While writing much of this book, I was on sabbatical living near Malaga, Spain. When it was time for the Oscars, I was amazed. Hollywood's premier event is now a world event. For two days, the Spanish news, both on television and in the papers, was filled with Oscar discussion. It is estimated that in 1999, over one billion viewers in 117 nations watched the awards ceremony live, many getting up in the middle of the night to do so. In 1999, the Best Picture Award was given to the English movie *Shakespeare in Love* (1998); Best Actor went to the Italian Roberto Benigni for *Life Is Beautiful* (1998), a film he also wrote and directed; and the American Steven Spielberg won Best Director for his movie *Saving Private Ryan* (1998). European "films" are Hollywood "movies," and Hollywood movies are film. This book is about Hollywood and its worldwide industry. It is, after all, the movie that became the twentieth century's major form of storytelling, and nothing yet, not even video games or the web, seems ready to supplant it.

The word *theology* is at least as ambiguous as *film*. For some, it means an academic, and perhaps arcane, discipline that systematically discusses the doctrines of Christianity. It is the equivalent of academic discussions of European "art house" films in the sixties—something best left to the critics. But what has become a technical subdiscipline in the study of Christianity, abstract and for many lifeless, has a much broader history. In the early centuries of the church, theology meant simply the study *of* God. It was first-order reflection, much closer to what a word like *spirituality* might mean today. Edward Farley notes that in the early centuries after Christ's birth, theology meant a habit of the human soul, a way of knowing God and what God reveals. Theology had to do with "a personal knowledge of God and the things of God in the context of salvation. Hence, the study of divinity (theology) was an exercise of piety, a dimension of the life of faith." To be interested in theology was to be interested in knowing God directly.[8]

With the rise of the universities, theology came chiefly to mean study *about* God. Theology was now understood as second-order reflection, though it was still viewed comprehensively and holistically. In the words of Farley, *theology* in this second sense "refers to a cognitive enterprise using appropriate methods and issuing in a body of teaching."[9] Theology, that is, was to be seen not first of all as an experiential enterprise but as a critical task—a discipline whose end was an integrated knowledge about God.

It is in both of these two original senses of the term that I will use the word *theology* in this book. For movies, like other art forms, help us not only to know about God, but to actually experience God as well. And they do so with an artistic power unique to their medium.

the power of film

In the movie *Smoke* (1995), Paul Benjamin stops in one evening at the tobacco shop of Auggie Wren, located on a street corner in Brooklyn.[1] Paul is a writer, but his pen has been silenced by the senseless death of his pregnant wife from random gunfire. Whiling away the time, Paul notices Auggie's camera sitting there. Auggie explains that he uses it every day and invites Paul to look through his photo album. What Paul discovers seems odd to him—picture after picture of the same scene, people passing by Auggie's corner store. The photographs were all taken from the same spot, at the same time—8 A.M., one each morning—and there are several thousand. As Auggie explains, "It's my corner. Just a small part of the world, but things happen here, too." Paul, however, sees nothing except the same picture!

As Paul leafs through the pages, Auggie says to him, "Slow down. You'll never get it if you don't slow down, my friend." And as Paul does, he begins to see small differences in each of the photos. The light changes; the seasons pass. There are bright mornings and dark mornings, summer light and autumn light. There are weekdays and weekends. Different people pass through the photographs, some repeatedly. In several pictures, Paul even discovers his wife walking to work. The pictures bring tears to his eyes as he begins to see life afresh. He discovers the variety and vitality of life once again, this time through a small slice of Brooklyn.

This scene from *Smoke* is both a metaphor for what can happen when one watches a movie and a movie clip capable of evoking from those in its audience what it itself portrays. For movies help you to "see." They focus life for the viewer, giving us a richer variety of experience than would otherwise be possible. Carl Sandburg, the poet laureate, once commented,

> I meet people occasionally who think motion pictures, the product Hollywood makes, is merely entertainment, has nothing to do with education. That's one of the darnd-

est fool fallacies that is current. . . . Anything that brings you to tears by way of drama does something to the deepest roots of our personality. All movies, good or bad, are educational and Hollywood is the foremost educational institution on earth. What, Hollywood more important than Harvard? The answer is not as clean as Harvard, but nevertheless farther reaching.[2]

For some, going to the movies is what we do when we have a free evening. A video is what we rent for our children when we are going out. A few of my friends who are over forty consider film a waste of time, or at best one leisure-time option among many. It is hardly a staple of their lives. But for increasing numbers of people, movie watching is as natural to their daily routine as eating, sleeping, or using the computer. When I ask my students how many movies they have seen in the theater or on video in the last month, the typical response is eight or nine. Even among senior citizens, many regularly go to matinees in order to get senior discounts and even more watch movies on television. Yet though we watch movies, we seldom try to relate what we have seen to our Christian faith, and particularly to our theology. After all, theology is one thing, and film, another.

This book attempts to bridge the chasm that exists for many Christians between movie viewing and faith. The rift is deep and historic. For while early motion pictures showed the passion play of Oberammergau (1898)[3] and the temptation of St. Anthony (1898),[4] the growth of the film industry was so dramatic that the church and Hollywood soon came into conflict. Between 1913 and 1916, twenty-one thousand theaters opened in the United States. One of the most engaging portrayals of this early confrontation is John Updike's *In the Beauty of the Lilies*,[5] a novel about America in the twentieth century; thus the title's allusion to the "Battle Hymn of the Republic."

As the story opens, we are in Patterson, New Jersey. It is the spring of 1910. D. W. Griffith is filming *The Call to Arms* with Mary Pickford, his teenage star. As the actress faints in the heat, across town the Reverend Clarence Wilmot stands in the pulpit of Fourth Presbyterian Church, feeling "the last particle of faith leave him." Both Hollywood and the church are struggling, but the trajectory that the book will take is clear from the outset. As the church grows old and loses its faith amidst the onslaught of culture, film is destined to grow. After all, Mary Pickford is only seventeen. Clarence eventually must resign and is reduced to selling encyclopedias. His son, Teddy, stops going to church. Later, when he is an adult, Teddy will find that his daughter Essie, even as a little girl, wants most to go to the theater, where she is enraptured by what she sees on the screen.

As the novel proceeds through four generations of the Wilmots, Essie becomes the Hollywood star Alma DeMott. Life is not easy for her, however. Hollywood is a wilderness that invites moral compromise. Her son, Clark, thus pays the price for her profligacy. Clark ends up in a cult similar to the Branch

Davidians. He is not so much a believer as someone searching for life's meaning. With a plot that spans most of the twentieth century, John Updike has chronicled modern American life in terms of the conflict between the church and Hollywood, the sanctuary and the movie theater. Neither side really "wins" the war, but the secularization of society is clearly evident.

In Updike's fictional world, we used to have giants of the faith. Now we have merely struggling artists. In an earlier novel, *The Centaur*, Updike recounts the conversation of the narrator, Peter, with his mistress, as he lies with her in his painter's loft in Greenwich Village. He is trying to tell her how life was good in his childhood, despite the fact that his grandfather had lost his faith as a Lutheran minister, and his father had struggled with self-doubt about the meaningfulness of his vocation as a high-school teacher. Nevertheless, Peter had felt a sense of place. Now as a poor artist, he confesses his rootlessness—his lack of a firm foundation on which to stand—and comments, "Priest, teacher, artist: the classic degeneration."[6] Again Updike confronts us with the question, Is the movie theater simply a poor substitute for the church? He leaves the answer ambiguous, but the gap between art and faith seems increasingly wide.

The Power of Film

If the theater and the church are simply in competition, or if movies represent the "classic degeneration," then why bother watching movies at all? The question is nonsensical to many, particularly those under thirty. Movies are simply part of contemporary life. But to others, the seriousness and relevance of film is still an issue. As we begin this study, therefore, perhaps several testimonials can provide a perspective for any who would doubt the importance of film.

The screenwriter and *maggid* (ordained Jewish storyteller who teaches people about God) Paul Woolf tells of growing up Jewish in Brooklyn. He had a strong feeling about Judaism even as a young boy, but the rabbis did not connect with him. The spiritual experiences that he had were more often the result of simple things. He remembers walking down the street when he was four, holding his mother's hand and realizing that he was in the presence of God. His consciousness seemed enlarged to the point that he could hear every bird singing and every leaf rustling. A similar experience happened when he was ten, as he stayed out playing with fireflies late into the summer evening. He says, "Here were these creatures twinkling their lights, and the summer had breath. I could hear everything. The faraway tinkling bells of an ice-cream truck, dogs barking, my friends laughing. Again, it was a shift of awareness, away from the self to a wider awareness."[7]

The next time this happened, Woolf was fourteen. It was the days of movie roadshows, and he got dressed up to go into Manhattan to see *Spartacus* (1960). Woolf sat transfixed as he watched Kirk Douglas, the gladiator Spartacus, say to his wife, played by Jean Simmons, "Anyone can kill, can be taught to fight; I'm not interested in that. I want to know where the wind comes from . . . why we are here." Woolf describes that all of a sudden there was this "incredible flight of questioning about life. In a film, no less."[8] As the movie ended the audience just sat there, stunned by what it had seen. Woolf concludes: "On the train ride back to Brooklyn, I kept thinking, how can this be? Why had I never experienced this in a house of worship? That's when I made my decision. I said to myself, I'm going to Hollywood to make movies."[9]

Woolf's story is told repeatedly. Methodist pastor William Willimon tells of growing up in Greenville, South Carolina. One Sunday evening in 1963, in defiance of the state's blue laws, the Fox Theater opened its doors. Willimon, together with six of his buddies, entered the front door of their church as if to go to the Methodist Youth Fellowship, but then slipped out the back to join John Wayne at the Fox. He says that evening was "a watershed in the history of Christendom, South Carolina style":

> On that night, Greenville, South Carolina—the last pocket of resistance to secularity in the Western world—served notice that it would no longer be a prop for the church. There would be no more free passes for the church, no more free rides. The Fox Theater went head to head with the church over who would provide the world view for the young. That night in 1963, the Fox Theater won the opening skirmish.[10]

The power of film extends well beyond impressionable youth, however. When a cartoonist named Walt Disney created the character Bambi, deer hunting nose-dived in one year from a $5.7 million business to $1 million. In 1984 Jessica Lange, Sissy Spacek, and Sally Field were all invited to testify before congressional subcommittees on agricultural matters(!) because of their supposed expertise stemming from the roles they played that year in *Country, The River,* and *Places in the Heart*.[11] Felicity Shagwell's Corvette Stingray from the *Austin Powers* sequel sold in 1999 for $121,000. In 1934 after the opening of the movie *It Happened One Night* sales of men's undershirts dropped dramatically. The movie's star, Clark Gable, was dressed sans undershirt in order better to show off his manliness. As a result, it was not until World War II, when men were retrained to wear undershirts by the military, that sales were reestablished.

In a different arena, observers have noted that increasingly the public learns history from film. It is *Platoon* (1986), *Born on the Fourth of July* (1989), and *The Deer Hunter* (1978) that give us our understanding of Vietnam and *Mississippi Burning* (1988) that shows us the civil rights struggle. Some have even argued that a film such as *M*A*S*H* (1970), though ostensibly about the Korean War, was meant to teach its contemporary viewers about the irrationality and inhumanity of the Vietnam War that was then being waged. And through its humor, it did a good job. But if such an interpretation is open to differing opinions, no one harbors any illusion about Steven Spielberg's intention in his film *Saving Private Ryan* (1998). As he hoped, it has become a primary shaper of opinion concerning World War II. Tom Hanks, the lead actor, has taken up the cause of veterans as a result of his experience. For some whose fathers and mothers fought in these wars but came home silent about the horrors they experienced, the film has brought new dialogue and healing. Several weeks after the film came out, the *Los Angeles Times* ran an article describing how some younger people were saying that they understood for the first time something of the sacrifices that were made. After seeing the film, some twenty-year-olds were even going up to people in their seventies and thanking them for what they had done.[12]

The power of film is not limited to congressional hearings, merchandising, or history lessons. In his provocative book *Life the Movie,* Neal Gabler goes so far as to see American culture itself as taking on the characteristics of a movie. Life has become show business, where we each play a role and long for our moment of celebrity. Gabler argues that it is not politics or economics, but entertainment "that is arguably the most pervasive, powerful, and ineluctable force of our time—a force so overwhelming that it has finally metastasized into life."[13] Fun, accessible to everyone, sensuous, and providing a release from order and authority, motion picture entertainment has captured the American spirit. For many Americans, life is now played out as if it were a movie. Our fantasies are more real than reality. It doesn't matter how celebrity is achieved, only that it is. Think of Kato Kaelin, or the technician on *The Tonight Show with Jay Leno* who strips to his bikini shorts and shakes his oversized gut for the laughter of the audience, or guests on *The Jerry Springer Show.*

The conversion of life into an entertainment medium is pervasive. We are coached on our roles by Martha Stewart. Our costume designer is Ralph Lauren. Our makeup artists are plastic surgeons. In the words of Andre Agassi in a commercial for Canon cameras, "Image is everything." Theme restaurants sell atmosphere more than food. Stores like Niketown have become entertainment centers. Ideas have become sound bites. Our president is "entertainer-in-chief." Athletic events are often subordinated to the athlete's story. Books need promotional tours if they are to sell. News programming is for our enjoyment; it is prime-time fare. Recall the televising of the Gulf War in 1991, where each network had its title card, its logo, and even its musical signature for the nightly broadcasts. Hard news is increasingly written using the techniques of fiction, so that it can be read at Starbucks.

Today everyone seems to own a camcorder. Our concern to capture it all on film causes many to experience life primarily through the lens of their camera. Brides and grooms, for example, videotape their weddings, so that they can play the tape at their wedding receptions (as if the real event is the showing, and the ceremony the taping). Images of John F. Kennedy Jr. and Princess Diana have allowed these individuals to become not only icons but personal friends to be mourned. The latest Internet idea has twenty-four-hour videocams in dorm rooms, allowing viewers to see the "lifies" that others are playing—this just months after the release of the movies *The Truman Show* (1998) and *Edtv* (1999). If life is not a cabaret, it is at least a movie!

Even if Gabler overstates his case, the fact that movies play an increasingly significant role in defining both ourselves and our society seems beyond dispute. Movies broaden our exposure to life and provide alternate readings of life's meaning and significance. Values and images are formed in response to life's experiences, with movies providing the data of countless new stories. In fact, as society's major means of telling its stories, movies have become a type of lingua franca. Who doesn't know the story of *Titanic* (1997)? Think of the millions of children who have seen *The Lion King* (1994). When one goes to a party and must make conversation with new people, is it not a recent movie that provides the smile of recognition and the conversation starter? Even in the church, theological discussion is often more likely to happen following a movie than a sermon.[14] Movies cannot be dismissed as mere entertainment and diversion. Rather, they are life stories that both interpret us and are being interpreted by us. As Elia Kazan, the controversial filmmaker of the fifties, sixties, and seventies (*On the Waterfront* [1954], *A Streetcar Named Desire* [1951], *The Last Tycoon* [1976]) said, film is now "the language of mankind."[15]

Is it any wonder, then, that film has created fear in wide segments of the church? Many Christians grew up in homes that believed that if all movies were not sinful (though surely many were), the cinema was at least not morally uplifting or a good use of leisure time. It should thus be avoided. The father of one of my friends worried, for example, about what would happen if he were in a theater when Jesus returned. Surely Jesus would not approve! It was only with the advent of television that abstinence proved an unworkable policy. Nonetheless, suspicion and fear continued in many quarters. For it was recognized, rightly, that movies are as "dangerous" as life itself.

But rather than recounting the suspicion and fear that has sometimes prevailed in the church as it has considered the power of film on our lives, I need to tell the other side of the story as well. For movies have also proven to be a force for healing and insight. The power of film can change lives and communicate truth; it can reveal and redeem. Consider the following examples.

Oskar Schindler (Liam Neeson) welcomes workers to his factory. *Schindler's List* (d. Spielberg, 1993). Photo by David James. ©1993 Universal City Studios Inc. and Amblin Entertainment, Inc. All rights reserved.

Schindler's List (1993)

Schindler's List tells the story of a group of Jews condemned to the Krakow ghetto by the Nazis during World War II. Threatened with annihilation, they are saved by a German businessman and munitions manufacturer named Oskar Schindler. At first more interested in obtaining cheap labor, Schindler comes to care about his Jewish co-workers. They become his family, and he goes to extraordinary lengths to rescue them. As the war winds down, Schindler must flee, for he is a war criminal. In a moving sequence, we see his Jewish workers gather around him as he is about to drive off from the factory. They hand him a signed letter telling of all he has done for them, hoping that the Allies will read it if Schindler is picked up. They also give him a gold ring made from the fillings of their teeth on which is engraved in Hebrew a Talmudic saying, "Whoever saves one life, saves the world in time." Schindler is overcome with emotion as he reflects on how his gold lapel pin might have been bartered for a Jewish life and his car for ten or more people. "I could have got more," he cries.

Toward the end of the movie, we are fast-forwarded to the present. We see some of the actual survivors from Schindler's factory, along with the actors who played their parts in the movie, gathering almost fifty years later in

the power of film——— 25

Jerusalem at Schindler's grave to pay homage to him. While the survivors move past his gravestone, two sentences are superimposed on the screen: "There are fewer than four thousand Jews left alive in Poland today." "There are more than six thousand descendants of the Schindler Jews." Just as his Jewish foreman said, there are generations because of what Oskar Schindler did.

Though the movie ends this way, it is not the end of the story. The scene now shifts to Switzerland, October 1996, and Christoph Meili has just seen *Schindler's List* at a local theater. He realizes that he does not know a single Jew personally. After all, there are very few Jews living in Switzerland today. Three months pass, and Meili is making his routine rounds as a young security guard at the bank in Zurich where he works. Passing by the room where the paper shredders are located, he sees two large containers filled with old books. He has never seen anything like this before. Looking more closely, he discovers that the books contain records dating to World War II. Stuffing one book under his clothing, Meili completes his rounds. Taking the book home, he finds that it is a ledger documenting Jewish-owned property that had been confiscated in Berlin and turned over to the Nazis.

What should Meili do? He remembered scenes in *Schindler's List* of Nazis stealing valuables from Jews, and he remembered that Schindler did something. In a later newspaper account, Meili said, "I have the feeling I also have to do something." And do something he did. The next day he found two more oversized ledgers in the garbage that had been too big to fit through the shredder. He then tried to contact a Zurich newspaper but was put off. When he spoke to a Jewish cultural organization in town, they told him that they would not do anything. As they put it, "This is dynamite, too hot to handle." Finally, Meili contacted a small Jewish newspaper, and at a press conference the next day, the story exploded around the world.

Meili was soon accused by his fellow Swiss citizens of being an Israeli spy. Others threatened his life. After all, Swiss banks are a national institution and considered sacrosanct. A police investigation was instigated because it was said that he "stole" bank secrets. Even his father asked him, "Are you crazy? Why are you helping the Jews?" Ironically, Meili was forced to become the first Swiss in history to ask for and receive political asylum in the United States. As a result of his action, however, the Swiss banks were forced to reach a settlement with Holocaust survivors, their families, and Jewish groups. The amount was one and a quarter billion dollars! Could the Jewish director Steven Spielberg, who had owned the rights to the movie for ten years before making it, have dreamed of a better response to his film story? Here is the power of film.[16]

Belle, a beautiful and independent teenager, sings of her desire to lead a full life. *Beauty and the Beast* (d. Trousdale and Wise, 1991) ©The Walt Disney Company. All rights reserved.

Beauty and the Beast (1991)

Disney's animated fable *Beauty and the Beast* tells the story of Belle, a teenager living in an eighteenth-century French village. Belle loves books and is not interested in the romantic advances of the muscular Gaston. As the opening sequence of the movie reveals, Belle is compassionate, intelligent, and liberated. She is not one to be easily outsmarted, having a clear mind of her own. After her father is imprisoned in the forest in the castle of a ferocious beast, Belle sets off to rescue him. She too becomes a prisoner of the beast in his crumbling but formidable castle. We know from an earlier sequence that the beast is actually a young, handsome prince who has been cursed because he was unkind. Unless someone loves him, he will be a beast forever. As you can guess, after great adventures, the two young people eventually fall in love, and the results are magical.

What does this children's movie have to do with a book on theology and film? The film is one of Disney's best animated features. Roger Ebert, writing in the *Chicago Sun-Times* (22 November 1991), says, "Watching the movie, I found myself caught up in a direct and joyous way. I wasn't reviewing an 'animated film.' I was being told a story, I was hearing terrific music, and I was having fun." Here is a film to take you back to your childhood. But that is not why I describe the film. I tell the story because of a book by Gerry Sittser titled *A*

Grace Disguised. Gerry is a religion professor at Whitworth College in Spokane, Washington. The book relates his response to the catastrophic loss of his wife, his mother, and one of his daughters in a car crash in 1991. The van he was driving was hit by a drunk driver, and only Gerry and three of his other young children survived. Five years later he wrote his book, reflecting on how a person might grow through loss.

Sittser shares that among the things that helped him and his children to cope were the stories of countless others—whether friends, strangers who wrote to him, or even those they read or saw on the screen. After commenting on those stories that had helped him personally, Sittser turns to reflect on what stories were meaningful to his children, Catherine (8 years old at the time), David (7), and John (only 2). Let me quote Sittser:

> The children read books and watched movies that somehow touched on the theme of loss. John asked me to read *Bambi* dozens of times after the accident. He made me pause every time we came to the section that told the story of the death of Bambi's mother. Sometimes he said nothing, and the two of us sat in a sad silence. Sometimes he cried. He talked about the similarity between Bambi's story and his own. "Bambi lost his mommy too," he said on several occasions. Then he added, "And Bambi became the Prince of the Forest." . . . Catherine found comfort in Disney's movie version of *Beauty and the Beast* because the main character, Belle, grew up without a mother and, as Catherine has observed, became an independent, intelligent, beautiful person.[17]

If the compelling power of *Schindler's List* was in the scope of its revelation concerning the value of all persons, and particularly the Jews, here a movie story spoke more personally, helping to redeem the life of one small girl. And who could ask for more?[18]

Becket (1964)

Nominated for twelve Academy Awards and starring Richard Burton and Peter O'Toole, the film *Becket* tells the story of Henry II, the Norman King of England, and his drinking buddy, Thomas à Becket. King Henry wanted free rein to live and act as he chose, to whore and wage war and tax the citizenry as he saw fit. His one obstacle to complete license was the archbishop of Canterbury, who had his own independent authority as leader of the Church of England. The archbishop often frustrated Henry's designs. In order to solve his problem, King Henry ingeniously decided to appoint his companion in "wine, women, and song," Thomas, as archbishop. Brilliant, except for one problem. Thomas decided to take his new vocation—his calling to be God's servant— seriously and to serve God rather than the king. King Henry tried to persuade him to compromise and accommodate to his old friend's (and king's!) wishes.

King Henry II (Peter O'Toole) tries to persuade Becket (Richard Burton) to compromise his position as archbishop. *Becket* (d. Glenville, 1964). Courtesy of Photofest, New York, New York.

But Thomas remained steadfast. As a result of his faithfulness Thomas was martyred in Canterbury Cathedral on the altar steps.

When I saw this film as a freshman in college, I did not much identify with Thomas's martyrdom (or with his subsequent sainthood!). But I did hear God calling me to the Christian ministry. My struggle with accepting my call to become a minister was with my image of the pastor as needing *first* to be a holy person. My Young Life leader, who had ministered to me when I was in high school, was such a person, as was my church counselor. I knew I was presently no saint. In the film, however, I heard God saying to me through his Spirit, "You need not be holy. Thomas was not. You only have to be obedient to my call." And I responded like Thomas and said, "God, I will be loyal to you with all my being." Here again is the power of film. Not only can it reveal and redeem, but also it can be the occasion for God to speak to the viewer.

I told of my call into the ministry at the conference entitled "Reel Spirituality," which several of us organized in the fall of 1998 and from which the title of this book is taken. Fifty Hollywood screenwriters and directors and fifty leading pastors and church leaders had gathered to discuss "Storytelling as Common Ground: The Church and Hollywood." When I was finished, one of the other speakers, Father Gregory Elmer, a Benedictine monk, commented that he too had heard God speak to him, calling him into the monastic life, while watching the same movie! We could even identify the different scenes in the film where God had made himself known to us.

What is noteworthy in this "coincidence" is that the two of us saw the same movie, *Becket*, yet heard God's call in unique ways. For me, the issue was obedience to the call to active service in the world, and I became a Protestant minister who teaches theology and culture. For Father Elmer, the call was to purity of heart and single-minded devotion, and he became a Catholic mystic. In the chapters to come, we will consider the importance of the viewer in understanding what makes a film work. We will also consider film as the occasion not only to know about God but to know God. At this point it is enough to note again that a movie's story has the power to transform life.

2

a brief history
of the church
and hollywood

Critics debate about when the first movie was shown. Some claim its origin to be October 6, 1889, when Thomas Edison and his associate William Dickson, working with film from George Eastman, projected moving pictures across a screen. Edison later linked the images up to a phonograph. But Edison did not secure an international patent for his invention, a machine that by 1896 allowed a single viewer a "peep show" for thirty seconds. Soon there were a variety of rivals to Edison's Kinetograph camera and Kinetoscope machine, with such exotic names as Zoëtrope, Cinématographe, and Bioscope. All provided the lucky few with magical demonstrations of flickering pictures.

The more usual date for the beginning of the cinema, however, is December 28, 1895, when the first paid exhibition was put on by the Lumière brothers at the Grand Café in Paris. Earlier that year, Louis and Auguste had patented their projector, which used a strip of celluloid with perforations down the center. With it, they could easily transport their moving pictures. For a time, Lumière projections were offered in special showings for the rich, but very soon the cinema moved to the fairgrounds of Europe and the nickelodeons of America's cities.

Mutual Experimentation

Early movies showed a train arriving at a station, a man sneezing, a gardener being squirted with his own hose, or a staged fistfight. Some early patrons were so perplexed by these moving images that they ducked the ocean waves that crashed on the screen and jumped out of the way of the oncoming train. The novelty of seeing uninterpreted reality soon wore off, and filmmakers began to record theatrical plays and to develop their own tableaus. Many of these early "movies" had religious themes.[1] *The Horitz Passion Play* (d. Klaw and Erlanger) was shot in 1897 on a vacant lot in Paris; the more popular *Passion Play of Ober-ammergau,* a nineteen-minute movie filmed in the snow in New York City(!), but claiming to be an authentic version of the German passion play, premiered in 1898.

Some of these early religious movies were even made by evangelists. Just after the turn of the century, Herbert Booth, son of Salvation Army founders William and Catherine Booth, was appointed Commandant for Australia. In order to interest people in coming to the Sunday night lectures and prayer meetings, he experimented with the use of slides and film. Booth, with the help of Joseph Perry, produced a multimedia show titled *Soldiers of the Cross,* which combined short films with slides, hymns, sermons, and prayers. The production used a Lumière machine to show film sequences done by nonprofessional actors chosen from Salvation Army personnel. The shorts depicted martyrs burning at the stake, Stephen being stoned to death, Christ in agony on the cross, and Christian women jumping into vats of lime rather than forsaking their Lord. Both the secular and the religious press gave the performance high praise.

Not all movies were religious in theme, however, and not all the religious films were reverent. *The Great Train Robbery* (d. Porter, 1903) was an instant success. Some one-reel short subjects poked fun at clerics, showing them drinking and being involved with women. But many movies continued to portray religious life with reverence, and churches were often used as movie theaters. Soon the adaptation of Lew Wallace's novel *Ben Hur* (d. Olcott, 1907), the Jesus story *From the Manger to the Cross* (d. Olcott, 1912), and the Italian religious epic *Quo Vadis* (d. Guazzoni, 1912) all made it to the big screen and were widely successful as feature films. *Quo Vadis* even opened on Broadway and went head to head with traditional theater.

Almost from the start, motion pictures were wildly successful with the public. By 1907 the American market for movies had grown so large that the gross income of the movie industry was larger than the combined receipts of vaudeville and traditional theater. Ronald Holloway calls these early years of the twentieth century "the inventive age of cinema."[2] Developing techniques as they went, many of these first-generation moviemakers also had a deep mystical sense. As the poet Vachel Lindsay wrote in 1915 concerning the new cinema: "The real death in the photoplay is the ritualistic death, the real birth is the ritualistic birth, and the cathedral mood of the motion picture which goes with these and is close to these in many of its phases, is an inexhaustible resource."[3] The church and Hollywood seemed to be mutually reinforcing each other's needs and values.

Growing Criticism

After the First World War, however, things began to change. Commercialism and a reaction in the larger culture against nineteenth-century attitudes began to alter the motion picture landscape. The star system was born as Mary Pickford and Charlie Chaplin received salaries of over ten thousand dollars per week. One estimate suggests that during these years over 80 percent of the paying public went to a movie in order to see a particular star. Movie magazines were produced showcasing Rudolph Valentino and Greta Garbo.

Paralleling the growth of the star system was the evolution of the movie theater. Its architecture no longer resembled nineteenth-century neoclassical churches, but dream palaces, expressing the romantic and exotic. In Hollywood, two of these "theme" palaces, the Egyptian and the Chinese, attracted huge crowds, as did the Roxy in New York, with seating for six thousand in its "royal" hall.

Increasingly, movies became escapist fare. Gangsters and monsters, intrigue and romance filled the screen. But instead of risking a fresh, imaginative portrayal of life, whether through fantasy or realism, movies reverted to formulas. Although large studios and chains of theaters had created financial health for the industry, the artistic heart of the motion picture business was put in jeopardy, as was its cordial relationship with the church.

Perhaps the key figure during the period between World War I and the Depression was Cecil B. DeMille, who recognized in the increasingly secular culture a growing market for the illicit. Religious himself, DeMille nevertheless understood the new morality of the flapper era and gave the public what they wanted—a religious gloss over salacious scenes. After viewing one of DeMille's movies, D. W. Griffith was reportedly so upset with DeMille's tactics that he said to his star Lillian Gish, "I'll never use the Bible as a chance to undress a woman!"[4] DeMille's "bathtub" and "bathrobe" epics all had a similar shape and feel to them. Based on the rationalization that indiscretion could be presented on the screen as long as the sin was eventually corrected, his spectacles were little more than glorified melodramas that included an effective combination of debauchery and piety. They were, however, hits with the public.

In *The Ten Commandments* (1923), which was produced for the then-astronomical figure of one and a half million dollars, DeMille housed his portrayals of orgies within a larger moral framework of the giving of the Law. In his next film, on the life of Christ, DeMille realized that he was on even more sensitive ground, so he used Protestant, Catholic, and Jewish clergy as advisors (perhaps to co-opt the opposition!). He even had Mass celebrated on the set each morning. But DeMille also turned to the best-selling author Bruce Barton, who had written his life of Christ as if Jesus were a Madison Avenue executive. Again, the formula of biblical veneer (some of the heroic postures are held so long that they bring to mind a religious painting) and contemporary recasting is evident. *The King of Kings* (1927) opened with DeMille's usual formula of sex and piety, this time beginning with an apocryphal scene in Mary Magdalene's lavish pleasure palace where she is expressing anger about the loss of her boyfriend, Judas, who has forsaken her to follow a preacher from Nazareth. Leaving her guests in the middle of the party, Mary rides off on her chariot to get Judas back and is converted upon meeting Jesus. And so the biblical story is not only retold but rewritten.

Confrontation

It was the continuing excesses of DeMille's orgies that finally ushered in a period of direct confrontation with churches. This was particularly true of the Roman Catholic Church, which realized the power of film to shape opinion. DeMille's *The Sign of the Cross* (1932) portrayed both pagans and Christians in Nero's Rome. Again, DeMille gave his viewers an "immoral morality play."[5] It is Nero's fiddle that sounds most loudly as the camera pauses voyeuristically to capture the pagan excesses. The movie's most famous scene shows the empress Poppea, played by Claudia Colbert, bathing in milk and saying to the Christian Dacia, "Take off your clothes, get in here and tell me all about it." The camera shows Colbert's back and legs, while not quite exposing her breasts. But it was enough; the sensual effect accomplished its intention. So, too, did the scenes of torture and suffering. Many, in fact, when looking at the film today, think DeMille was almost obsessed by cruelty. There was in the film such a heavy dose of sex and sadism that a growing number of leaders, both in the Protestant and in the Catholic Church, found it offensive.

Public opposition to Hollywood had been growing since the early twenties. Coming hard on the back of the Chicago White Sox baseball scandal in 1919, when several of the sport's idols were accused of game-fixing, several high profile scandals involving Hollywood people caused a popular backlash. Mary Pickford, "America's Sweetheart," proved not quite the innocent that she was portrayed to be on screen as she divorced her husband to marry her lover, Douglas Fairbanks. Then, in 1922, "Fatty" Arbuckle was accused of rape and contributing to the death of an actress. Though he was never convicted, the lurid stories in the press ruined his successful career. Just as the baseball establishment had looked for a "czar" to bring back into the game a perception of morality, so the movie industry moved quickly to appoint a head of their association whose character was beyond reproach.

The industry already had a loosely rendered list of thirteen prohibitions that included proscriptions of such subjects as drunkenness, nudity, crime, gambling, and illicit love. But the vague and omnibus quality of these standards, plus the lack of any enforcement tool, made them ineffective. Faced with the threat of government censorship, the industry organized itself as the Motion Picture Producers and Distributors of America (MPPDA) and appointed Will Hays to develop and supervise a self-censorship program. An elder in the Presbyterian Church, the Postmaster General of the United States, and the chairman of the Republican Party, Hays brought prestige to the office. His new production guidelines were approved in 1927. Similar to the earlier attempt, they included a ban on swearing, any suggestive nudity, ridicule of the clergy, antipatriotism, and so on. But Hays made the standards more effective than the previous effort. Through his office, over one hundred scripts were rejected between 1924 and 1930. Self-control seemed to be working.

With the rise in production costs and the loss of editing flexibility given the advent of sound in movies, a greater codification of the rules seemed necessary, however. Studios were unwilling to modify their product once it was largely finished. Martin Quigley, a Catholic film journal publisher, and Daniel Lord, a Jesuit priest who had consulted with DeMille on *The King of Kings*, were brought in. After a series of meetings with Hays and with representatives of the studios, a new Production Code was adopted in 1930.

But the start of the Depression quickly changed matters with regard to Hollywood's willingness to live by the Code. Faced with growing red ink, the studios turned to sensationalism—to sex and violence—to lure back the public. As James Skinner opines, "Nothing succeeds like excess."[6] Gangster films such as *Public Enemy* (1931) with James Cagney and *Little Caesar* (1930) starring Edward G. Robinson and Douglas Fairbanks Jr., were thought by many to glorify crime. *Blonde Venus* (1932), starring Marlene Dietrich, took prostitution as a theme, even if the star became a hooker for the sake of her child. Neither the Hays Office nor its Production Code Administration, which was created to grant a seal of approval, could stem the tide of the sensational and seductive. It was perhaps the production of *The Sign of the Cross* (1932) that best symbolized that a voluntary system of restraint would no longer work. When Will Hays asked Cecil B. DeMille what he was going to do about a provocative dance scene in the movie, DeMille replied, "Not a damned thing." And the scene was left in the final cut. But if Hollywood would not do something itself, then the church felt it had to step into the void.

The response of the Catholic Church was the creation of the Legion of Decency. In 1933, the Vatican's Apostolic Delegate in the United States announced that "Catholics are called by God, the Pope, the bishops and the priests to a united and vigorous campaign for the purification of the cinema, which has become a deadly menace to morals."[7] This was followed later in the year by the appointment of an Episcopal Committee on Motion Pictures, which was charged with coming up with a plan to stem the tide of Hollywood excess. Bishops around the country were also beginning to act unilaterally. In 1934

Cardinal Dougherty of Philadelphia instructed his faithful with regard to movies to "stay away from all of them. . . . [T]his is not merely a counsel but a positive command, binding all in conscience under pain of sin."[8] As a result, attendance in theaters in Philadelphia quickly fell off by 40 percent. Flush with a new sense of power, the Episcopal Committee came up with the idea of a pledge of decency that it would ask Catholics to abide by.

The Legion of Decency asked its members to "remain away from all motion pictures except those which do not offend decency and Christian morality."[9] Within a few months, seven to nine million Catholics had taken the pledge. With the Legion of Decency providing the strong arm, the Production Code got a new lease on life. Joseph Breen was appointed to administer the Code, and he began working with both producers and the Legion to insure that acceptable movies were screened. The Code's "first principle" set the tone for its twelve(!) commandments: "No picture shall be produced which will lower the moral standards of those who see it. Hence the sympathy of the audience shall never be thrown to the side of wrong-doing, evil or sin." Its eighth restriction stated, "No film or episode may throw ridicule on any religious faith."[10]

Though the Code was only advisory, teeth for it were provided by the Legion with its threat of boycott. But, to be effective, the Legion needed a standardized system for rating what was unacceptable for viewing by members in the church. Thus, the bishops turned to the International Federation of Catholic Alumnae, a film reviewing group of the Catholic Church which dated back to 1924 and which was located in New York City, away from the pressure of Hollywood. While this group of educated women had heretofore only rated acceptable movies by placing them in two categories—suitable for church halls and suitable for mature audiences but not for church and school settings—they now were asked to rate unsuitable movies as well. And their power in influencing the Code for well over two decades is legend.

The initial results of the Hays Office, working in conjunction with the Legion, were impressive. By 1936, 91 percent of the movies that the Legion reviewed were given an "A" (approved) rating, and only 13 out of 1,271 movies were labeled "C" (condemned). The stories of how various film projects were altered to avoid the wrath of the censors makes interesting, if dated, reading. If producers accepted the advice of Joseph Breen in the Hays Office, then the Legion usually followed with the granting of acceptable ratings.

Again, however, larger pressures from society intervened. With the advent of World War II, two-piece swimsuits were justified on the patriotic grounds of saving fabric! Women became common in the workplace, and pinup calendars were everywhere. Standards with regard to sexuality in the movies seemed hopelessly dated. The Hays Office responded by subtly easing its code, but the Legion of Decency remained adamant that morality would be preserved. Howard Hughes's movie *The Outlaw* (1943), publicized with pictures of Jane Russell wearing a cantilevered bra that enabled her breasts to be maximized regardless of her posture, became a focal point. When in 1940 the Production Code warned Hughes that Rio (Jane Russell) was not to be leaning over in her peasant blouse in front of the screen, Hughes ignored the warning. Approval was therefore denied pending thirty-seven cuts. Hughes was not through, however, and he went to the Appeals Board. The result was a capitulation by the Production Code Office and the ordering of cuts of only one minute. Breen had lost most of the battle. Though the wrangling over this film would last for six years more before *The Outlaw* went into national release, and though the Legion's own censors were eventually able to extract another twenty minutes of cuts, the tide was turning.[11]

By the fifties, the system of censorship was clearly failing. Society's standards had changed concerning what was deemed acceptable. In 1956 the Code was revised, but to no avail. The Catholic Church, on the other hand, tried to stand firm. For example, when the Broadway play *The Moon Is Blue* was adapted for the screen by Otto Preminger in 1953, the Legion opposed its easy posture toward girls being seduced, even though the heroine herself remained a virgin. Although the Legion condemned the movie with a "C" rating and Cardinal Spellman warned Catholics against attendance, *Life, Variety*, and *Newsweek* gave the movie strong reviews, and the courts insured that theaters could not ban films from being shown without better reason. Over ten thousand theaters screened the movie, and it proved a box office success, with Catholics attending in the same proportion as the general population.

The Catholic rating systems worldwide were proving to be inconsistent. For example, the International Catholic Film Office awarded Fellini's *La Strada* a major prize only for the Legion to rate it unacceptable for the general public. On the other hand, when Fellini's *La Dolce Vita* came out in 1960, there was a papal condemnation of the film, but this was not enough to keep the Legion from dividing into two camps with regard to the acceptability of the movie. In the film, Christ is symbolized as out of touch with the people. The opening scene has a large granite statue of Christ being carried over the people by helicopter for installation at St. Peter's Square. Moreover, hedonism and immorality among the rich make up the bulk of the story. Nevertheless, the artistic strength of the movie caused the Legion ultimately to deem it acceptable for mature audiences. The era of the Code and the Legion was over.

A New Rating System

In the sixties, society's standards and Hollywood's tastes changed even more quickly. *The Pawnbroker* (1965), *Who's Afraid of Virginia Woolf?* (1966), and *Alfie* (1966) appeared and—with their flashbacks of concentration camp memories, vitriolic domestic argument, and immoral and abusive seduction—set new standards of openness in Hollywood. The Production Code was now largely ineffective, and the Legion was increasingly ignored. In one year, the Legion's listing of objectionable movies rose from 15 to 24 percent. A means of providing more nuanced ratings was clearly necessary.

The growing popularity of international films was as important to the changing context as was the Code's demise. Students were flocking to cinemas to see the "artistic" films of European and Asian directors. How could the Legion give their highest rating to *Godzilla versus Mothra* (d. Honda, 1964) and condemn Antonioni's *Blowup* (1966)? The wide popularity of serious, subtitled films in the late fifties and early sixties—movies by Kurosawa, Bergman, Bunuel, and Fellini—together with the ineffectiveness of the Production Code caused Hollywood to scrap the old system of self-regulation.

In its place, there was adopted in 1966 a variant of the current ratings system. The code was developed under the direction of Jack Valenti and the Motion Picture Association of America, beginning just prior to the release of *The Graduate* (1967) and *Bonnie and Clyde* (1967). Things had changed forever in Hollywood. Sympathy could now be thrown to the side of wrongdoing and sin. Movie critic Pauline Kael noted that by the end of the seventies, the "old mock innocence" had too often been replaced by "the sentimentalization of defeat" and a movie culture that seemed to "thrive on moral chaos."[12] It is understandable, as well, that in some movies a backlash against the church and its clerics was portrayed. After all, Hollywood had not been able to present anything but pietistic glosses on Christianity for most of its existence. Michael Medved is no doubt right that some in Hollywood swung the pendulum too far. But there was surely that within clergy and church practices deserving of criticism.

If theologians and church-related film critics were to have any voice at all in this new situation, they would need a broader and more informed approach to a Christian understanding and interpretation of film than the traditional rhetoric of caution or even abstinence. Dialogue, not censorship, was being called for. It was in this changing context that the church began to interact theologically in a new way with Hollywood.

The Current Rating System

Increasingly, the Motion Picture Association of America's rating system is also coming under attack. For those like movie critic Roger Ebert, it seems "hypocritical and broken down." Ebert has judged MPAA President Jack Valenti to be lacking "the slightest understanding of film as an art form." How can *American Pie* (1999; whose raunch is clearly intended for teenagers) and John Sayles's small but engaging story *Limbo* (1999; with no clearly discernible reason for its rating) both be rated "R"? And what is the criteria for garnering a PG-13 rating? If a movie is given a PG-13 rating, it seems reasonable that parents should not have to worry about their teenagers seeing it. But *Blue Streak* (1999) was given a PG-13 rating even though it is extremely violent, with the bad guys getting away with the crime. Not surprisingly, Valenti is so far resisting any changes. He admits to some broadening of the PG-13 category, but he believes that this is in line with changes in the society.

The issue is a difficult one. How are parents to be given guidance on a film's content while still preserving a filmmaker's freedom to create? The current system, critics say, fails on both counts. Ratings battles over films like *South Park: Bigger, Longer and Uncut* (1999) and *Eyes Wide Shut* (1999) have forced artistic cuts or computer generated insertions to maintain "R" ratings while not really protecting teenagers from seeing the final versions. With over 65 percent of all movies being given an "R" rating and theater owners largely unwilling to exclude teenagers, the system is no longer able to discriminate effectively. More violence and sex are allowed into the "R" rating than many high schoolers should see (to say nothing of those younger). At the same time, the system is not able to allow full artistic freedom to those filmmakers wanting to create a truly adult movie without having the prurient label "NC-17" attached. Are there not truly adult movies that are not pornographic? To give a famous (infamous?) example, the movie *Midnight Cowboy* (1969) won the Oscar for best picture, despite being given an "X" rating by Valenti's rating board. After being judged to have artistic merit by winning an Oscar, the movie was re-rated by the MPAA and reassigned an "R," even though not one frame was altered. Such inconsistency is simply confusing for all involved.[13]

theological
approaches
to film criticism

Since the invention of motion pictures a century ago, one can observe five differing theological responses that the church has made to film as it has learned from and has sought to influence Hollywood. In the class on "Theology and Film," which I taught with Robert Banks, we labeled these avoidance, caution, dialogue, appropriation, and divine encounter.[1]

These theological responses by the church to moviegoing can be shown graphically on a linear timeline:

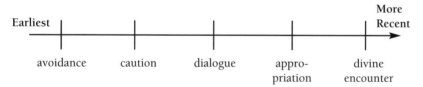

Figure 3.1 The Theologian/Critic's Posture

Although these approaches developed more or less chronologically over the last seventy-five years or so, one can still find good contemporary representatives of all five of these types of theologian/critic. Moreover, as each approach is more a type than a firm category, some theologians have adopted over time multiple perspectives, while others have proven somewhat eclectic in their approach. Despite this fluidity, these options are nonetheless identifiable.

These same five theological approaches to Hollywood can also be graphed, using a matrix in order to show whether a given theologian/critic begins his or her reflection with the movie itself or with a theological position, and whether a given response centers on the movie ethically or aesthetically:

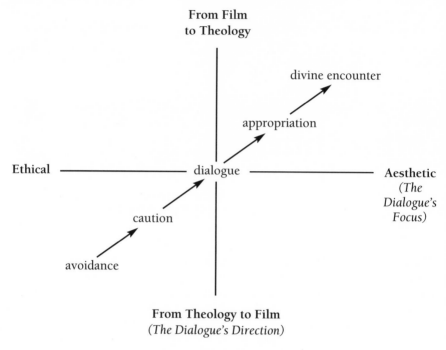

Figure 3.2 The Theologian/Critic's Approach

Theologians who articulate an avoidance strategy do so from an ethical posture (often their books even have words like "morality" and "values" in their titles) and always move from their given theological perspective to the film under consideration, not vice versa. On the other hand, those interested in exploring a divine encounter through film begin with the film itself and only in light of the film attempt to make theological judgments. When they do, moreover, the criticism is first of all aesthetic, not ethical, in nature.

Spread out along the diagonal that one can draw between these contrasting approaches are the three other positions. Those expressing caution take the film as film more seriously but still focus their responses on the film's ethical stance, beginning their deliberations from a biblical/theological posture. Those wishing for theological dialogue want theology to inform their filmviewing and filmviewing to inform their theology in a lively two-way conversation that is *both* ethical *and* aesthetic in nature. Those wanting to appropriate the movie's meaning start in their deliberations with the movie itself but bring their outside theological perspective more strongly into the conversation than those who would explore divine encounters. Both Jewish and Christian theologians/critics have often proven more eclectic in their approach than the graph might suggest. They have in practice made use of more than one of these approaches depending on the films being considered and the audience intended. (That not all persons fit neatly into a given category is typical of any typology, for these are simply artificial constructs to help organize data.) But many have tended in their theological criticism to use a dominant perspective toward the movies.

It is worth looking at each of these positions in some detail, for they will inform the remainder of our reflection in this book.

Avoidance

The stance of some Christians has been to continue the boycott mentality that characterized conservative Protestantism and Roman Catholicism of an earlier era. Writing in the forties in an introduction to Herbert Miles's book *Movies and Morals*, Hyman Appelman labeled movies to be "next to liquor, the outstanding menace to America and to the world."[2] Miles, if anything, was even stronger in his condemnation: "They [movies] are the organ of the devil, the idol of sinners, the sink of infamy, the stumbling block to human progress, the moral cancer of civilization, the Number One Enemy of Jesus Christ."[3] The best that Miles could say about Hollywood was, "There are some good teachings in the movies. Yes. And there is some good paper in the waste basket, but it is only to be used when it is impossible to secure paper from any other source."[4]

Such rhetoric seems to come from a bygone day, certainly one before the advent of television. But Carl McClain, writing for a Nazarene publishing house in 1970, expressed a similar sentiment: "I submit that a frequenter of the theatre or movie house cannot at the same time be a spiritual force for good, a vital Christian leader or Sunday school teacher."[5]

More typical today than such blanket condemnation, however, is the argument for a selective boycott of films judged morally objectionable. For example, writing to the organizers of the City of Angels Film Festival, Dr. Ted Baehr, chairman of the Christian Film and Television Commission, complained that the Festival had chosen to show Peter Weir's *The Year of Living Dangerously* (1982) and Martin Scorsese's *Taxi Driver* (1976). He attached to his memorandum several pages from the *Communist Manifesto* and complained that Weir's film "takes the side of the Communists in the Indonesian struggle for freedom from Communism. I was there at the time," he writes, "and can tell you firsthand that the communists were killing thousands of people, particularly Christians, and were not the good guys as portrayed in the film." He continues, "My question for *Taxi Driver* would be: What was it about the movie that influenced John Hinkley to shoot President Reagan? When you start to answer that question you will start to understand the spiritual significance of the movie, as you well know."[6] For Baehr, there is a great divide between much of Hollywood and the church. The religion portrayed is not Christianity but "materialism, consumerism, eroticism, hedonism, . . . humanism, . . . the cult of violence."[7] Many films should just not be shown, thinks Baehr. Or if they are, Christians should protest by not going to movie theaters and instead relying on videotapes, which they can selectively choose.

Similarly, Larry Poland has written of his leadership in boycotting *The Last Temptation of Christ* (1988). In his book *The Last Temptation of Hollywood*, which was rushed to press just months after the release of Martin Scorsese's film, Poland chronicles what he calls "this century's most passionate conflict between Christians and Hollywood."[8] What he calls "the hideous distortions of the person and work of Jesus," both in the novel by Nikos Kazantzakis[9] and in the screenplay by Paul Schrader, caused Poland and a small group of other concerned Christians eventually to organize a boycott that was partially effective.

There is no question that Universal Studios was duplicitous in trying to quiet those like Poland whom they thought would criticize their interpretation of the Christ event. They lied, were purposely deceptive, and tried to use their power and influence to cover up their high-handedness. Their marketing attempts and damage-control plans lacked ethical conviction. Poland, for his part, tries to avoid the "C" word (censorship) which was used by the press to characterize his efforts. But the boycott that he, Bill Bright, James Dobson, Donald Wildmon, and other Christian leaders organized, together with their publicly announced attempt to buy all copies of the film from the studio in order to destroy them, had much the same feel to much of the American public. For Poland, Hollywood, like other businesses, must be morally accountable for its actions or accept the consequences: "If there is no 'chilling effect' for film and TV producers from the deeply religious majority in America, we will be seeing child molesting, cannibalism, sado-masochism, bestiality, and even 'snuff' films soon accepted as 'art' on the major movie screens of America."[10]

Not everyone is convinced by Poland's logic, but the use of boycott as a strategy by some in the church continues. When Kevin Smith's irreverent yet God-affirming movie *Dogma* opened at the New York Film Festival in October of 1999, it did so over the objections of Cardinal John O'Connor and Mayor Rudolph Giuliani. That the movie exuberantly affirms the existence of God and tells the story of a woman's recovery of faith, or that Smith is a practicing Catholic, was thought irrelevant. It was enough that organized Christianity was mocked and theology questioned.

In *Dogma*, a thirteenth apostle (played by Chris Rock) claims to have been cut out of the Bible because he is black! There are pot-smoking prophets, the crucifix is replaced by the statue of a "Buddy Christ" winking and giving the thumbs-up, and scatological and sexual humor abounds. The plot revolves around two fallen angels, banished from heaven and now living in Wisconsin, who seek to enter heaven again against God's wishes through a loophole in church dogma. A plenary indulgence has been granted to any who pass through the arch of a particular Catholic church in New Jersey, allowing them to be readmitted to heaven.[11] The story, like the jokes in the movie, is irreverent, but it also affirms the importance of faith, the benevolence of God, and the divinity of Christ. Here is a movie that is not agnostic or un-Christian in viewpoint, even if it is sacrilegious and sexy in design. After all, as Smith commented, if he were to talk about God to his generation, he wouldn't make *The Song of Bernadette* (1943). Instead, he wanted "to do something full of faith that was entertaining enough to keep them [viewers] in their seats."[12]

A spokesperson for the Catholic League for Religious and Civil Rights, however, wrote that "the entire plot is one situation after another of making fun of the Catholic faith."[13] It mattered not that when the criticism of *Dogma* was made, no one had yet seen the movie. Reading an early version of the script with its assorted vulgarities and anti-religious jibes and noting that George Carlin was cast as the cardinal and Alanis Morissette as God was enough for the League to institute a letter-writing campaign and for the United States Catholic Conference to give the film its worst rating of "O" ("morally offensive"). Smith has said that the idea for the movie came as he sat in church and listened to homilies that condemned sinners rather than invigorated the faithful. As one of the characters in the movie says, "I have issues with anyone who treats God as a burden, not a blessing." Such theology was lost on many churchgoers, but not on the wider public. As the headline in the *Los Angeles Times* announced following the movie's opening, "*Dogma* Opens in New York to Protesters' Jeers, Audience Cheers."[14]

Caution

A more common attitude among contemporary conservative Christians is that of caution, not avoidance. With the advent of television, few Christians continued to argue for abstinence as a viable strategy. But many remained worried over the entertainment industry's influence. Writing in 1974 for InterVarsity Press, Donald Drew asked whether a Christian should even go to movies. He answered with a cautious affirmative: "It is my conviction that a Christian, providing that his foundations are firm, should see films and become involved in the arts and other forms of knowledge. The Lordship of God in Christ must be seen to extend into all areas of life."[15] Having said this, Drew also advised his readers that "a Christian should enter the cinema with a solid grasp of who man is and what truth is."[16] The Christian viewer can watch movies, but carefully, from a clearly defined ethical and religious stance.

Lloyd Billingsley's book's title, *The Seductive Image*, suggests its content and approach. He writes that his "expectations of film are low" and rarely disappointed: "My basic posture toward film as a medium is increasingly skeptical, and any list of all-time favorites I could put together would be rather short. That said, I stress the medium's power, and add that to ignore it would be folly."[17] John Butler is similarly cynical and introduces his discussion of movies by saying that "the second part [of the book] goes to the movies with a look at some of the moral issues served up in between the popcorn and candy bars. Tips on choosing a movie and possibly saving up to five dollars by skipping that new movie, depending on where you live, are examined in chapter ten."[18]

In their arguments, Billingsley and Butler stay tightly within the Christian sphere, but their skeptical rhetoric is self-defeating with regard to influencing any serious moviegoer. I say this despite the obvious strength of their position in arguing for a necessary moral discrimination when it comes to critiquing a movie. Their books remind me of the pastor who wrote a letter to the editor about an article I wrote putting the movie *The Shawshank Redemption* (1994) into conversation with the Old Testament Book of Ecclesiastes. On the strength of my recommendation, he said he had taken his preteen daughters to see the movie and was horrified by the prison rape scenes and the disgusting language. Only at the end of the letter did he admit that he hadn't really taken his daughters, but he might have (and how could a Christian recommend an "R" rated movie?). My answer is twofold. First, most adults will find the portrayal of hope, friendship, and justice in *The Shawshank Redemption* moral to the core, despite its realistic prison setting. And second, what is suitable for a twenty-eight-year-old viewer is not necessarily appropriate for an eight-year-old. Just as with other of the arts, cultural exposure must always be correlated with personal and spiritual maturity.

Viewer discrimination is obviously necessary for Christians of all ages. One of my single students in her mid-thirties explained to me that although she understood why I had assigned *Bull Durham* (1988) for those in the class, its glorification of casual sex was so well done that it was a temptation to her as she struggled to live a Christian life. She said she would not ordinarily go to such a movie. She did not need it. I said I agreed. Not everyone should see all movies. Discrimination is called for, but so too is sensitivity and maturity in filmviewing.

Michael Medved serves as a good example of a cautious but thoughtful critic of Hollywood's values. Although a faithful Jew, Medved does not assume a Jewish readership as he argues that by constantly pushing the ethical envelope, the entertainment world "encourages" (even if it does not cause) antisocial activity.[19] Though moviemaking might function within a contemporary cultural consensus of values, Hollywood also seeks to transform it. In chapter after chapter of his book *Hollywood vs. America* (1992), Medved wages war with Hollywood because he sees that movies promote promiscuity, malign marriage, encourage illegitimacy, and belittle parents. They are hostile to heroes, bash America, use foul language, often offend, and gravitate toward violence.

In his section entitled "The Attack on Religion," Medved argues that there is today a one-sided vicious stereotyping of the church. In the thirties and forties we had handsome stars who were lovable priests (e.g., Spencer Tracy in *Boys Town* [1938] and Bing Crosby in *The Bells of St. Mary's* [1945]), and there was a feeling of religious uplift in many movies. In the 1980s, by contrast, it was more typical to see Christians portrayed as crazed killers and the clergy as vicious, morally corrupt, and bizarre looking. Hollywood seems intent on affronting the religious sensibilities of ordinary Americans. Medved asks rhetorically, If movie after movie shows this, will not viewers begin to believe it? Anti-religious movies typically lose money, Medved notes, but moviemakers do not seem to care. They have an axe to grind.

Perhaps Medved has overstated his case. Given that the Hollywood Production Code banned any unfavorable treatment of religion, that clergy and nuns were once portrayed more positively should not surprise anyone. Consider the analysis provided by Mark Hulsether, who notes a study done in 1996 that surveyed top grossing films between 1946 and 1990: "It reports that the portrayal of religious characters moved from being far more sympathetic than that of nonreligious characters to being comparable with nonreligious characters over the period studied." Hulsether asks rhetorically, "Should clergy be alarmed that after 1976 they were heroes only 50 percent of the time . . . about the same as other characters? The religious remained more likely to be good than the nonreligious (56 percent vs. 52 percent) and almost as likely (54 percent vs. 57 percent) to succeed."[20]

Les and Barbara Keyser question Medved's conclusions from another perspective. This is what they have to say concerning the Production Code's ban on portraying clergy in a bad light: "In practice, the sanction against evil or comic ministers became a benediction for virtuous and gleeful clerics. If one couldn't laugh at the religious, one could laugh with them. And if clergy couldn't be evil, they could be supernaturally innocent. The priest became a new unearthly creature, full of smiles and cheery lessons, singing songs of innocence to confound the world of experience; nuns worked their own magic by flying or, at the least, singing in perfect key."[21] Lacking any real spiritual dimension, priests could be interested only in saving their church's architecture.[22]

Just before the Oscars in 1999, Medved wrote an article for *USA Today* in which he refers to a study by Kagan Media Appraisals, a Hollywood consulting firm, which analyzed the return on investment of every film released nationwide between 1988 and 1997: "The resulting study of 2,380 films revealed a consistent and unmistakable public preference for family fare. In fact, the average G-rated film generated eight times greater profit than the average R-rated film, though R-rated films remained 17 times more common than their G-rated counterparts." While PG–13 films drew a 35 percent better return on investment than R, G-rated films earned even more, a 78 percent better return on investment than R-rated movies. Why, then, would studios continue to produce adult-oriented movies? One answer, thinks Medved, is that Oscars typically go to such films. Films for adult audiences might not be as financially successful, but they "disproportionately draw industry acclaim and critical endorsement." Medved concludes:

> Contrary to the cliché, it's not pure greed that drives Hollywood's emphasis on gore, vulgarity and gratuitous sex. Statistics, new and old, show that the public welcomes less-disturbing (and sometimes less-challenging) alternatives. This means that petition campaigns and even boycotts will achieve very limited success, since the big studios already work against their own financial self-interest by defying heartland sensibilities with their emphasis on R-rated entertainment.[23]

In a 1997 essay, Medved recognizes recent positive changes since he wrote *Hollywood vs. America* in 1992. He notes that in the 1990s faithful Christians and Jews assumed prominent positions in Hollywood. After the "relentless religion-bashing of the last fifteen years" there has been a "shift to more supportive on-screen treatment of religious themes and characters." He concludes with this assessment: "Hollywood's current status still leaves vast room for improvement, but an exhilarating spirit of change—if not outright rebirth and revival—is already in the air."[24]

It is not just those on the religious "right" who suggest caution, however. Those on the religious "left" are sometimes equally suspicious. Margaret Miles, the dean of the Graduate Theological Union in Berkeley, seeks to identify and analyze the values imaged in films.[25] Hollywood, Miles recognizes, continues to shape our attitudes toward race, gender, class, and sexual orientation through its patterns, stereotypes, and symbolic markers. For example, it is often the male gaze that is captured by the camera's point of view. Even as a child, Miles understood from movie marquees that fat people were laughable, people of color were subservient, and beautiful heterosexual people were the norm. The portrayal of a set of values in this way is not "accidental or incidental to religious perspectives," she argues, "but, *as a concrete way religious perspectives are articulated*, are central to religious values."[26] Miles also notes, with Medved, that in its direct portrayals of religion, Hollywood is typically hostile to Christianity. A student of iconic art, Miles chides the motion picture industry for its inability to inspire religious devotion through the images it projects. Often, it seems able only to caricature fundamentalism, as in *The Rapture* (1991) and *The Handmaid's Tale* (1990).

Miles, like Medved, comes to film from an ethically driven theological stance, but she also seeks to be a student of the films she considers. Few films escape her critical pen. She understands *Thelma & Louise* (1991) to be a cautionary tale about the consequences of women trying to escape a male-dominated world. She castigates two recent "Jesus" movies, *Last Temptation of Christ* (1988) and *Jesus of Montreal* (1989), for not offering heroes to their audiences. And so on. Hers is a hermeneutics of suspicion. She views movies from her ethical/theological point of view and judges whether or not they fit. Though she seeks to be a student of film, she does not try to see a movie on its own terms.

Miles and Medved have a sense of style and discrimination with regard to their movie judgments, even if this reader finds them overly suspicious and does not always agree with their conclusions on particular movies. Butler and Billingsley, on the other hand, seem overly controlled by dogma. All, however, come to film from a defined theological perspective and see a one-sided imbalance between Hollywood and the church, between movies and theology. For the most part, they see that movies are too often in the business of theological subversion. They thus advise caution for the religious viewer.

Dialogue

My comments about avoidance and caution should have been sufficient to signal the direction I believe Christian film criticism must go. Although theoretically the critical dialogue can begin anywhere along the continuum from avoidance to encounter, the danger of theological imperialism is high enough in practice that I would argue that Christian moviegoers should first view a movie on its own terms before entering into theological dialogue with it. The movie experience, like all play activities, functions best when it is a parenthesis within life's ongoingness. That is, when people enter the theater (or go to the opera or the ballpark, or play handball, or dance), they must, when at play, set aside the issues of the larger world around them and be caught up in the movie experience itself. Whether listening to Mozart or looking at a Woody Allen film, the audience must focus exclusively on the "present" of the experience, if it is to be authentic. In a sense, the real world must for a time "stand still." Moviegoers must give to the screen their "as-if" assent and enter wholeheartedly into the movie's imaginative world, or the experience risks being stillborn. With motion pictures, moreover, this happens naturally, as the darkness of the theater and the community of viewers, not to mention the surround sound and oversized screen, combine with the images and story to capture the audience's attention.

To give movie viewing this epistemological priority in the dialogue between film and theology—to judge it advisable to first look at a movie on its own terms and let the images themselves suggest meaning and direction—is not to make theology of secondary importance. Religious faith is primary. In fact, I argue that the nature of both moviegoing and religious faith demands that filmviewing be completed from a theological perspective. But such theologizing should follow, not precede, the aesthetic experience.

I am reminded of the classic essays on reading literature written by T. S. Eliot and R. W. B. Lewis. Writing in 1932, Eliot argued that "literary criticism [substitute "film criticism"] should be completed by criticism from a definite ethical and theological standpoint." But he also recognized that "whether it is literature or not can be determined only by literary standards."[27] In his 1959 essay, Lewis recalled "the remark made to Emerson by an old Boston lady who, talking about the extreme religious sensibility of an earlier generation, said about those pious folk that 'they had to hold on hard to the huckleberry bushes to hinder themselves from being translated.'" Lewis uses the story to illustrate his point that although people's religious beliefs are fundamental, they should not necessarily begin their criticism there. He writes that "absolutely speaking, as between religion and literature, religion no doubt comes first; but in the actual study of a particular literary text, it probably ought to follow, and follow naturally and organically and without strain—for the sake of the religion as well as the literature."[28] Although theology is the final authority for life, or should be, people are best served in the dialogue between theology and film if the movie's vision of life is first received with a maximum of openness before it is brought to the bar of judgment. J. C. Friedrich von Schiller's *On the Aesthetic Education of Man* is a helpful, even if extravagant, reading on the nature of the experience of play (and thus of moviegoing):

> In the midst of the awful realm of powers, and of the sacred realm of laws, the aesthetic creative impulse is building unawares a third joyous realm of play and of appearance, in which it releases mankind from all the shackles of circumstance and frees him from everything that may be called constraint whether physical or moral. . . . *To grant freedom by means of freedom* is the fundamental law of this kingdom.[29]

We thus turn from those approaches which begin theologically and judge movies from a predetermined norm to those critical perspectives, which first view a movie on its own terms. The first of these options I have labeled "dialogue."

Even those who express caution with regard to filmviewing recognize that there are some movies that have identifiably religious themes or elements and thus invite/demand dialogue with them from a theological perspective. Like *Jesus of Montreal* (1989) they might be about Jesus, or like *Sister Act* (1992) might center their story on the nature of the church. They might portray a preacher's redemption, as in *The Apostle* (1997), or someone going insane out of jealousy at another's gifts, as with *Amadeus* (1984). Their posture can be either that of renunciation, as in *Hardcore* (1979) or *Bull Durham*'s (1988) portrayal of the church, or of affirmation, as in *Chariots of Fire*'s (1981) focus on Christian vocation or *Tender Mercies*' (1983) story of salvation. The religious elements in these films might be thematically central or supportive. Theological critics are not imposing an outside perspective on these movies when they enter into conversation with such films. Rather, the movies themselves explicitly deal with religious matters and thus invite a theological response.

Some movies are simply inexplicable except from a Christian theological perspective. In an analogous discussion of the relationship of theology and literature, Amos Wilder discusses the works of Hawthorne, Emerson, Dickinson, Blake, Henry James, and Dostoyevsky and rightly concludes that "the time is past when literary appreciation (can) slight the theological aspects of the work of art, as though all such elements were external."[30] For certain works of art, Christianity, or religion more broadly, has contributed specifically to their characterizations and symbols and must be taken into account if one's criticism is to be adequate, let alone total. To comment on film theologically in this sense is not to isolate one's theological observations from an artistic critique of the work as a whole. Nor is it to bring in an outside perspective as the lens through which the movie is seen. Rather, there can be real engagement and two-way dialogue between Christian theology and the movie, for the movie itself invites it.

The centrality of religion to characterization and symbol in the movies can be demonstrated by John Cooper's and Carl Skrade's book on film, which includes a number of articles about film written from a theological perspective. The chapter titles are self-explanatory: James Wall wrote on "Biblical Spectaculars and Secular Man"; William Hamilton's title was "Bergman and Polanski on the Death of God"; for Anthony Schillaci, it was "Bergman's Vision of Good and Evil"; and for Harvey Cox, "The Purpose of the Grotesque in Fellini's Films." Cox, for example, specifically addresses the essential role of Christianity in Italian films, especially those of Fellini. Setting the stage for his comments, he writes:

> [T]he Italians I met, and this includes Fellini, are *not*, to put it mildly, indifferent to religion. Some of them, especially the most strident atheists, seem almost obsessed with it. Fellini's pictures include an enormous range of religious themes and personages, from the swindlers dressed like priests in *Il Bidone* and the processions in *La Strada* and *Cabiria*, to the dangling statue of Christ that opens *La Dolce Vita*. Italy is a country where Catholicism resides not in the head but in the entrails. Everybody has not just a strong opinion about Christianity but fevered feelings as well.[31]

Schillaci finds much the same to be the case in Bergman's movies, where religious problems are continuously alive. Bergman might see good and evil as residing together, but there is still a longing for wholeness that is profoundly theological and based on his reaction to Christian theology.

It was such European directors and their films of the fifties and sixties that encouraged many people in the church to enter into theological dialogue with movies for the first time. Skrade sums up his intention in these words:

[I]f the study of theology and films is to be of any value in our attempts to reunite the God-question and the man-question, the church and the world, both the discipline of theology and the art of the cinema must be allowed their freedom. Instead of returning to some form of monologue in which theology would preach to cinema—or vice versa—both the discipline and the art must be allowed to speak their piece: that is, the goal must be dialogue.[32]

Both Cooper and Skrade recognize that it is insufficient and perhaps dishonest simply to use a movie to make a point or illustrate a theological truth. Viewers must let the movie work its "charm" on them, enlighten them, disturb them. Only then can it have a chance to deepen their understanding of reality (and perhaps even Reality itself).

There was a spate of books in the late 1960s and early 1970s that promoted dialogue between theology and cinema. Robert Konzelman's *Marquee Ministry: The Movie Theater as Church and Community Forum* (1971), William Jones's *Dialogue with the World* (1964) and *Sunday Night at the Movies* (1967), Roger Kahle and Robert Lee's *Popcorn and Parable* (1971), James Wall's *Church and Cinema: A Way of Viewing Film* (1971), Stanford Summers's *Secular Films and the Church's Ministry* (1969), and W. R. Robinson's edited collection, *Man and the Movies* (1969), are all examples. Most of these books are written with a practical emphasis and provide help for the person setting up film programs or festivals in local churches, since they view movies as a resource for Christian education programs. But regardless of their goals, the consistent critical stance of these books is that of two-way conversation.

More recently, several New Testament professors have written books on Hollywood movies, again using approaches that can best be understood as dialogical in nature. Bernard Brandon Scott's *Hollywood Dreams and Biblical Stories* (1994) seeks a critical correlation between themes that are embedded in movies and in the Bible. In *Saint Paul at the Movies* (1993) and the more recent *Saint Paul Returns to the Movies* (1999), Robert Jewett brings films and biblical texts into conversation by means of an interpretive arch. This arch is rooted on one end in the ancient world of Paul and on the other in the contemporary situation reflected in a particular film. Jewett provocatively asks, "Could it be that certain movies afford deeper access to the hidden heart of Paul's theology than mainstream theologians like myself have been able to penetrate?"[33] Jewett calls his approach "dialogue in a prophetic mode"[34] and wants to be sure that the films he chooses for correlation with biblical texts "become a full partner in conversation with Paul the apostle."[35] Given his choice to start with the biblical text and given his commitment (one I also share) to have Scripture function authoritatively, as first among equals, Jewett is always in danger of imposing a theological perspective on the films he considers. Not all will agree with him, for example, that *Amadeus* is a movie about sin. But at times, as with his treatment of *Grand Canyon*, he is superb, both in his film analysis and in his theological dialogue.

An interesting subgenre of such dialogical criticism is that which has focused on Jesus and Christ-figures in movies. Peter Malone's *Movie Christs and Antichrists* (1990) and Lloyd Baugh's *Imaging the Divine: Jesus and Christ-Figures in Film* (1997) both consider movies whose interpretive center focuses on Jesus Christ. This is sometimes done discursively by retelling the Jesus story. George Stevens's biblical spectacular *The Greatest Story Ever Told* (1965) and Pasolini's *The Gospel according to St. Matthew* (1964), as well as *Jesus Christ Superstar* (1973) and *The Last Temptation of Christ* (1988), are examples of this approach. James Wall proved prophetic in 1970 when he editorialized on the end of the traditional biblical saga following the disappointing reception for Stevens's movie.[36] Wall suggested that the basic mood of people in Western society today is secular, whether they be churchgoers or not. Lacking the basic religious presuppositions that operated prior to World War II, the pietistic Jesus epic lacks persuasive force. It becomes little more than an audiovisual aid for the already informed. Thus, it is not surprising that more recent attempts at portraying Jesus on cinema turned from the spectacular by seeking an audience through the genre of musicals (e.g., *Jesus Christ Superstar*) or by reinterpreting Jesus in more human and, at times, even shocking terms (e.g., *The Last Temptation of Christ*).

An alternative to the explicit Jesus movie is the movie that makes metaphorical use of a Christ-figure in significant and substantive ways. There is a danger, as anyone teaching in the field of Christianity and the arts knows, in having overenthusiastic viewers find Christ-figures in and behind every crossbar or mysterious origin. This is to trivialize both the Christ-figure and the work of art. But in certain films, the Christ-figure is a primary metaphor or the Christ-story does function significantly as a defining theme giving shape to the narrative. When this is the case, any criticism of the movie that fails to notice this theme is incomplete criticism. *Shane* (1953), *Dead Man Walking* (1995), *Star Wars* (1977), *Cool Hand Luke* (1967), *Babette's Feast* (1987), *The Passion of Joan of Arc* (1928), and *One Flew over the Cuckoo's Nest* (1975) are all examples of such movies. We will discuss many of these films later in the book. Here it is important to note the dialogical posture of such theological criticism. Consider Baugh's analysis:

> The Christ-figure [in film] is a foil to Jesus Christ, and between the two figures there is a reciprocal relationship. On the one hand, the reference to Christ clarifies the situation of the Christ-figure and adds depth to the significance of his actions; on the other hand, the person and situation of the Christ-figure can provide new understanding of who and how Christ is: "Jesus himself is revealed anew in the Christ-figure."[37]

Dialogue between theology and movies can take many forms. It can note the explicit theological themes of given films or dialogue with the motifs embedded both in movies and in the Bible. It can bring film and biblical text into conversation or it can compare and contrast the Christ of the Gospels with the metaphorical use of a Christ-figure to advance the meaning of a given movie. A few movies are even explicit depictions of the Jesus story which invite correlation and critique. But whatever the shape, the common denominator in such approaches is the attempt to bring film and theology into two-way conversation, letting both sides be full partners in the dialogue.

Appropriation

The title of Neil Hurley's book, *Theology through Film* (1970), offers a good example of a book written from the perspective of one seeking to appreciate film's vision of life. Hurley seeks to learn from the religious wisdom and insight that film can offer. Will movies simply confirm our prejudices, he asks, or will they "serve that reason which, after all, is the universal spark of the divine which the Stoic philosophers believed to bind all men together in some mysterious cosmic fraternity?"[38] It is telling that when the book was reissued in 1975, the title was changed to *Toward a New Humanism*.

Those, like Hurley, who see a material overlap between film and theology, believe that film is capable of expanding the theologian's understanding. They see this happening particularly with regard to a religious humanism that is embedded within film itself. Movies can tease out of their viewers greater possibilities for being human and present alternative selves not otherwise available to the moviewatcher. Thus, it is not to theology that the critic must first turn, but to a film itself. And the goal in relating theology and film is not, first of all, to render moral judgments, as was the case with earlier options we considered, but to achieve greater insight. Only in light of a movie's own vision of the nature of the human can the theologian effectively enlarge his or her horizons as movie and critic engage in conversation.

Examples of those who seek a dialogue between theology and film around the nature of the human are commonplace. Writing before the use of inclusive language was widespread, John Cooper explored "The Image of Man in the Recent Cinema" as his contribution to the collection of essays, *Celluloid and Symbols* (1970), which he co-edited. In a more recent collection, *Explorations in Theology and Film* (1997), David Graham argues that film "is one means of presenting themes of religious importance in a striking visual medium."[39] Moreover, he argues, one need not restrict the discussion to what is traditionally labeled "religious" but should "include all the questions which pertain to human experience and destiny."[40] Film's ability to portray what it is to be fully human is no doubt also behind movie critic Roger Ebert's comments about the movie *Simon Birch* (1998). The film's religious humanism causes Ebert to gush: "Two thumbs up, way up! It's a funny and warm-hearted movie and I loved it. My purpose is to give good reviews to movies like 'Simon Birch.' That's what I'm on earth for."[41] Ebert sees his vocation as helping viewers see movies that insightfully deal with questions of human experience and destiny.

James Wall provides us another example of appropriation. He concludes his reflections on "Biblical Spectaculars and Secular Man" by commenting optimistically about the secular person who is no longer interested in pietistic presentations of Jesus: "He will, however, be open to the evocative power of a film which celebrated humanity, and thereby calls us all to receive the gift of life. His openness, I submit, is further indication that secular man is deeply religious, so long as he is permitted to define his religion in terms of meaningful living."[42]

Wall, the editor of *The Christian Century* for more than a quarter of a century, is an advocate for dialogue between Hollywood and the church. This dialogue can take several forms, but chief, perhaps, is his belief that a film's vision "can be said to be 'religious' in the Christian sense if it celebrates humanity or if it exercises with conviction a strong agony over moments where humanity is actually distorted."[43] There is no need for explicitly religious symbols or forms. If a movie speaks to the human situation with an authenticity shared by those who are religious, it is enough. Thus, for Wall, *Who's Afraid of Virginia Woolf?* (1966) was a "religious" movie because it celebrated humanity in a manner compatible with how Wall himself viewed humanity, given his location within the historic Christian community.

Though I understand Wall's intention as he seeks to let a movie's vision of life deepen and extend his theology, I would refrain from calling such a film "religious." Such labeling seems dishonest about the intent of the movie. It is better to describe the film as "religion-like" or simply to say that the film invites dialogue from (or even an appropriation into) a Christian viewpoint, given its portrayal of the nature of the human—given, that is, its informing vision of life.

Joel Martin and Conrad Ostwalt Jr. have been influenced by the judicious perspective of Wesley Kort, and in their book *Screening the Sacred* (1995), they caution against baptizing film as unconsciously Christian. It is enough to say that movies can and do perform religious functions in culture today as they communicate a society's myths, rituals, and symbols and provide a web of fundamental beliefs. They are in agreement with Thomas Martin when he writes that "no story can develop without some underlying construct. . . . [A]ll constructs, even in the most banal of stories, are seen as presenting one with a fundamental option about life. And, therefore, every story one encounters has some effect on or challenge to one's sense of reality."[44] Appropriation is inevitable.

In order for theology to appropriate insight from film, one need not call the beliefs and values embedded in a movie "Christian" or even "religious." Phenomenologically, the point seems self-evident that *Who's Afraid of Virginia Woolf?* is not Christian. Better to make the claim that William Jones does in his book *Sunday Night at the Movies* (1967) that "Christians of our generation are becoming increasingly aware that the contemporary arts are pleading the same question the church is committed to holding before society: the question of the essential meaning of human experience."[45]

In an article about the use of Christ in contemporary movies, Neil Hurley seems to recognize the value of refraining from labeling a film "Christian" just because it rings of "truth." He thus differentiates between movies that have "Christ figures" and those that portray "Jesus transfigurations." Films in the first category affirm, at least implicitly, faith in Christ (i.e., they are authentically religious). Those in the latter group draw on "the universal cultural symbolic value of the Jesus persona" (and are thus only religion-like). Bresson's *Diary of a Country Priest* (1950) is a faith-inspired representation of a Christ figure; *Cool Hand Luke* (1967) is a more humanistic projection, or transformation, of the Jesus persona.[46]

It is not necessary to equate the essence of art with the essence of religion, writes Gerardus van der Leeuw in his masterful study of the sacred in art: "There is only a single art, and it is, first of all, art. There is only a single religion, and it is always and everywhere religion."[47] But though this is true, observes van der Leeuw, we also can discern again and again an essential unity between art and religion, for holiness and beauty appear in the same guise. "Climb up upon this height and you will see how the paths of beauty and holiness approach each other, growing distant, until finally, in the far distance, they can no longer be held apart. . . . We erect no ultimate truths, but remain modestly to one side. We believe that we have noticed something there, and so we point it out."[48] Noting similarities but choosing to remain simply descriptive, van der Leeuw speaks of "mere analogy."[49] The one can be a schema of the other without claiming that they coincide. Applying van der Leeuw's caution to the study of film, it is better to say that film portrays something about life that is religion-like.

Having said this (and it is a significant caution), it is also the case that whether we call a film that celebrates humanity "religious," or "religion-like," or whether we speak of a film's axiological convictions or webs of significance, or of having an informing vision about life, the intention is largely the same. Those who would seek to appropriate a movie's vision of life recognize that movies can offer insight to the Christian viewer about the nature of the human. There is something new that a movie can provide a Christian. More than dialogue is called for. The theologian must be receptive to encountering spirit in a new guise and only then turn to respond from the viewer's own theological point of view.

Divine Encounter

John May has provided a helpful typology of the responses that theologians and Christian film critics have developed, starting from the 1960s. There are differences in his schematic structure from the one I have just presented, but the two overlap. May sketches out five distinct approaches to the religious interpretation of film, which he lists in their order of emergence, recognizing that all five theological approaches continue to be practiced. He labels these "religious discrimination," "religious visibility," "religious dialogue," "religious humanism," and "religious aesthetics."[50]

May sees that over the last forty years there has been a general shift in emphasis in theological discussion of film. From an earlier concern with (1) the morality of films and (2) the explicitly recognizable religious elements in a film, theological critics have turned to (3) a desire for theological conversation with film, and a more recent focusing on the (4) humanistic and (5) aesthetic sensibilities of movies. In particular, May believes that "religious aesthetics,"[51] what Robert Banks and I have called "divine encounter," is the most fruitful arena for current inquiry. Movies have, at times, a sacramental capacity to provide the viewer an experience of transcendence. This was my experience with the movie *Becket*, and so too Father Gregory Elmer's.

The emphasis of May on divine encounter is what you might expect from a leading Roman Catholic scholar in the field. For, as Andrew Greeley writes, "Catholicism has always believed in the sacramentality of creation." The Catholic Church has held that God is known through the experiences, objects, and people we encounter in our lives. Greeley would have us know that "grace is everywhere."[52] For Greeley, moreover, film is especially suited for the making of sacraments and the creating of epiphanies, because of its "inherent power to affect the imagination." Moviemakers might not call their intention the celebration of grace, but that is what Christians recognize it to be. Greeley even goes so far as to posit that the filmmaker as artist can at times disclose God's presence "even more sharply and decisively" than God has chosen to do through creation itself. Be that as it may, "the pure, raw power of the film to capture the person who watches it, both by its vividness and by the tremendous power of the camera to concentrate and change perspectives, is a sacramental potential that is hard for other art forms to match."[53]

Other Catholic theologians and film critics argue in similar ways. Neil Hurley, for example, believes that both theology and motion pictures work with transcendence, the difference being that theology appeals to the elite while movies are oriented to the masses. I am not sure theology should be consigned only to the elite, but Hurley is right when he asserts that "moviewatchers are often exercising transcendental faculties of insight, criticism, and wonder that come remarkably close to what religion has traditionally termed faith, prophecy, and reverence. A wedding of the two is overdue, although, happily, the match-makers are growing in number."[54]

Thomas Martin provides still another supporting voice for this methodological approach as he argues that Christian witness must engage the larger society at a deeper level than that of ideas alone. Film, as "an art of moving pictures," has "a greater ability to produce a total environment than either painting or photography because it can include in its form more of the ingredients of a normal setting."[55] As a visual medium that occupies a large part of the average person's life, it has a tremendous impact on the images that govern one's awareness. Moreover, film as a medium has the ability to dramatize, celebrate, and present experiences that are not open to human experience prior to seeing it. It extends human vision to include that which would otherwise pass unnoticed. In these ways, movies have the "ability to awaken a sense of awe and wonder in the beholder."[56] If he had been writing his book today, Martin might have been thinking of the little boy in *Cinema Paradiso* (1988) or of Essie in John Updike's novel *In the Beauty of the Lilies*. Such wonder, writes Martin, "is necessary in laying the foundation for religious consciousness in a culture which tends to reduce experience to 'one damn thing after another.'"[57]

Screenwriter and director Paul Schrader argues that the revelatory kinship between theology and film is not accidental but is rooted in "two universal contingencies: the desire to express the Transcendent in art and the nature of the film medium."[58] Again, as with other theologian/critics we have considered, Schrader has been influenced in his thinking by van der Leeuw's *Sacred and Profane Beauty: The Holy in Art*. He writes,

> "Art can be religious," the late Gerardus van der Leeuw wrote, "or can appear to be religious; but it can be neither Mohammedan nor Buddhist nor Christian. There is no Christian art, any more than there is a Christian science. There is only art which has stood before the Holy." The proper function of transcendental art is, therefore, to express the Holy itself (the Transcendent), and not to express or illustrate holy feelings.[59]

Though film's transcendental style can be variously interpreted by theologians and others, it can only be demonstrated by critics who analyze "the films, scenes, and frames, hoping to extract the universal from the particular."[60] In analyzing the filmic form of the artistic hierophanies (the expressions of the transcendent in society) of three classic movie directors—Ozu, Bresson, and Dreyer—Schrader believes he has uncovered a universal form of representation. That is, there is a "common expression of the Transcendent in motion pictures."[61] Films which open their viewers to the Transcendent rely on repetition over variation, for example, and eliminate as much as possible those elements expressive of human experience. "Transcendental style, like the [Roman Catholic] mass, transforms experience into a repeatable ritual which can be repeatedly transcended."[62]

A Theological Parallel

Those familiar with H. Richard Niebuhr's *Christ and Culture* will note the similarities between the model presented above and that of Niebuhr.[63] One might, in fact, see the preceding discussion as an application of Niebuhr's classic typology to the medium of film, film being one particular cultural expression. In his volume, Niebuhr presented five orientations that the church has taken as it has sought to understand the relationship between Christian theology (knowing "Christ") and the culture in which it is embedded. These are (along with their contemporary American equivalents): (1) "Christ against culture," the Anabaptist (and fundamentalist) option; (2) "Christ and culture in paradox," the Lutheran (and conservative evangelical) perspective; (3) "Christ the transformer of culture," an understanding of Reformed Christians (and mainstream Protestants and progressive evangelicals); (4) "Christ above culture," the Catholic (and more sacramental mainline and evangelical Protestant) option; and (5) "the Christ of culture," the liberal Protestant understanding.

In order to be more descriptive of the chronological development of theology and film criticism, and in order to represent on a continuum the options with regard to theology or film taking the lead in the dialogue, I have labeled one of the poles in my typology "divine encounter," exchanging the positions of liberal Protestant and Roman Catholic thought in the process. But the similarities should be apparent nonetheless.

Critics of Niebuhr believe his understanding of culture to be too static and monolithic, his presentation biased in favor of the transformative option, and his historical examples to illustrate his typology unfair, particularly with regard to Anabaptists.[64] Are these criticisms also relevant with regard to my model as well? Perhaps we have not given equal weight to the avoidance option, but this is in part because so few currently embrace this position. Most of those who might previously have argued for abstinence, given their more conservative or even fundamentalist theology, now argue for caution instead. Given the advent of the television age, abstinence is less and less a practical (or practiced) option. It is also the case that all the positions except avoidance can be given strong theological support. Escaping society has little biblical warrant, though the church has at times in its history embraced this option.

That I have wrongly pigeonholed critics by placing them in rigid categories while they actually are more fluid in their approach is possible; but typologies are artificial constructs built to help sort out critical options. It is clearly the case that a given theologian/critic might adopt several different approaches to the conversation between movies and theology depending on the film in view or the audience addressed. James Wall, for example, published in 1971 perhaps the classic expression of "theology and film in dialogue" in *Church and Cinema: A Way of Viewing Film*. But just a year earlier, Wall's chapter for the edited vol-

Captain John Miller (Tom Hanks, left) finally meets up with Private James Ryan (Matt Damon). *Saving Private Ryan* (d. Spielberg, 1998). Photo by David James. ©1998 DreamWorks LLC/Paramount Pictures/Amblin Entertainment. All rights reserved.

ume *Celluloid and Symbols* ("Biblical Spectaculars and Secular Man") argued for theological appropriation and response. And his editorials from 1991 to 1997 in *The Christian Century* are published as *Hidden Treasures: Searching for God in Modern Culture* (1997). In this book, Wall argues for a sacramental view where "God is active but often in disguise, and where signs of the spirit are waiting to erupt from novels, movie screens and bully pulpits."[65] We can be eclectic about critical methodology and still find it useful to develop constructs for understanding how we proceed.

An Example

Saving Private Ryan (1998)

In assessing the adequacy of this chapter's typology from the side of movies themselves, it might be helpful to turn concretely to a particular film and consider how each form of criticism might work with reference to it. Steven Spielberg's *Saving Private Ryan* provides a good example. Some people might argue, for example, that the corpses and carnage are so graphic that this R-rated movie should be *avoided*. After all, the Christian is called to think on what is pure and commendable (Phil. 4:8). One of the older men in the church I attend said he did not like the movie, not because of the violence, but because of the foul language. The vulgarities were superfluous and off-putting. Most soldiers would probably question whether the language was in fact superfluous, but that it was off-putting to this viewer is no doubt true. And, as a result, he thought such films should be *avoided*.

Others might recognize the validity of a realistic depiction of World War II but would express *caution* concerning the film, for its graphic twenty-five minute opening sequence seems excessive. They might, however, as I once heard a pastor do, consider Captain Miller to be a Christ-figure. After all, he does arrive from the outside with a group of disciples on an errand of mercy and eventually lays down his life so that another might live. In the process they might begin to cautiously *dialogue* with the film, though the film often in such cases becomes little more than an illustration of a biblical text or theological topic.

Other Christians, however, might argue that the movie does not have a significant and substantial rooting in the Christ story, but is rather an occasion for real *dialogue* about whether war, any war, is just and/or justified. World War II is thought by many people to be the textbook case of a "just war." But can eight lives be risked in order to save one? And how are we to understand Captain Miller's comment, "Every man I kill, the further I feel away from home"?

The "mission" portrayed in the film is not, however, to win the war, but to save a man. It is the value of human life and of a family's continuity that Spielberg shows. Thus, others might use the gripping human portrayals within the inferno of war to appreciate anew the humanity of an older generation of soldiers who came back from World War II too horrified to speak of their experience to their families. In the process of experiencing through Private Ryan their true humanity, the viewer might *appropriate* new insight into the nature of one's own humanity.

Finally, despite the saying "There are no atheists in a foxhole," this movie has little in its portrayal that is potentially sacramental in nature. It is literally mired in the mud. I doubt too many viewers had a sense of awe and wonder that seemed transcendent in nature, though perhaps the sacrifice of human life might have been the occasion for a *divine encounter*. If one were to consider other Spielberg movies, however—*Schindler's List*, *Amistad*, or even *E.T.*, they might better speak with reference to an evident transcendent dimension in the film.

Where is the heart of *Saving Private Ryan*? Some viewers might focus their attention on its portrayal of war and seek theological dialogue here. A theology of war can better be considered in the concrete, where the experience of actual soldiers can be reflected on. It is too easy to get lost in abstract political theory and ignore the praxeological dimension that any adequate theology must have. Here is a movie for a Christian ethics class to discuss.

Although such criticism has its place, the theologian/critic is perhaps better served by letting the movie itself suggest the starting point for critical evaluation and dialogue. In the case of *Saving Private Ryan*, this would be its concern with the value of human life, with saving Private Ryan. The film's portrayal of humanity provides the interpretative center of this movie. I am reminded of the line by William Holden in *The Bridge on the River Kwai* (1957) where he observes that the point is not to die like a gentleman but to live like a human being. What is the nature of the human that so many would be sacrificed for the one? As the film ends, Private Ryan, now an old man, has returned with his family to the grave of the man who saved his life. His question as he begins to cry is whether he has lived a good enough life to justify this other man's death. Was saving his life worth the death of most of those who were sent to rescue him? The viewer is left to ponder.

why look at film?
a theological
perspective

4

In days past, Christians raised the question, "What has Athens to do with Jerusalem?" That is, what value does pagan culture have for people of faith? Today, we might substitute Hollywood for Athens and ask a similar question, "Why should the Christian enter into theological dialogue with popular Hollywood movies?" Aren't movies superficial for the most part and too often questionable in their values? At best aren't they merely entertainment? Aren't there better and more important things to do with one's time? Why should a Christian go regularly to the movie theater?

At the outset we must admit that not all think we should. Writing in 1995, evangelical scholars Mark Noll, Cornelius Plantinga Jr., and David Wells bemoan the fact that theology is largely ignored by the church today—even by evangelicals! Theology seems to have little force or impact. Why is this? Part of the explanation, they admit, is that there is too little good theology actually being written. But chief among the reasons, they think, is the church's aggressive embrace of certain forms of popular culture. Christians are contaminated by worldliness, by "Christian bodybuilding and beautyqueening." We are marginalized by an entertainment culture that glories in self-absorption. They answer that any new interest in theology by laypeople must "await success in getting people to read and think again, getting people to walk over to their TV set [and VCR] and pull an enormous condom over it." Yet, they think getting people "to practice safe TV" (and perhaps movie abstinence?) will prove difficult.[1]

If Christians are to live lives of modesty, reflection, and contentment, then why look at movies that seem to encourage the antithesis? One answer is to say that at their best, movies help viewers to see life more clearly. They help us empathetically understand both others and ourselves. In an increasingly visual culture (something our above theologians bemoan, betraying perhaps their Calvinistic bias), film images are an important source of knowledge. Movies provide viewers "imaginative possibility, without which we would be unable to try new models, new roles, new theories, new combinations of behavior."[2] Because the viewer cannot control the images, they catch us off guard and tell us things about ourselves and others. Viewed in this light, movies are part of the toolbox that many people use as they respond to and give shape to their lives. As such, they can be a significant ingredient in a person's individual formation.

Others note that movies help us understand and critique our culture. It is from movies that we get our "collective" images of ourselves, our values, and our social world. Movies both identify our anxieties and reveal our society's values; they "tell" us something about the age we live in. Like the rabbits in the coal mines in nineteenth-century England that were used to sniff out poisonous gas, movies can smell the currents in our society, exploring dimensions of reality that are there for us as well but which we have not fully perceived. Of course, there is a range of values present, so movies often become the context for presenting these ambiguities and conflicts, and thus enabling dialogue. Margaret Miles summarizes film's cultural influence:

> In the decade 1983–93, issues related to race, age, ecology, family, education, addiction, abortion, violence, gender, class, United States foreign policy, fundamentalist Christianity, the New Right, "family values," reproductive technologies, AIDS—to name only a few—permeated popular films. In short, film supplies the historian of the present with an incomparable resource for describing and prescribing for the problems and struggles of the moment.[3]

Movies can provide their viewers both experiences of life and greater understanding of their culture. But what do these have to do with theology? Until a Christian is convinced theologically that movies are an important resource for faith and life, there is little point in proceeding further with our discussion. Let me suggest six responses to this question, six theological reasons why a Christian should enter into dialogue with film. We need to explore these in some depth if we hope to interest the Christian in serious and ongoing dialogue with film. (1) God's common grace is present throughout human culture. (2) Theology should be concerned with the Spirit's presence and work in the world. (3) God is active within the wider culture and speaks to us through all of life. (4) Image as well as word can help us to encounter God. (5) Theology's narrative shape makes it particularly open to interaction with other stories. And (6) the nature of constructive theology is a dialogue between God's story (Bible, Christian tradition, and a particular worshiping community) and our stories (the surrounding culture and life experiences).

Common Grace and Human Culture

God has blessed all of creation, including human culture. This is clear from the opening chapters of Genesis, where the foundations of culture are sketched out for us. The fourth chapter describes the development of cities, agriculture, the arts, and technology (vv. 17–22). Although human invention can be used wrongly, as the subsequent story of the tower of Babel suggests, there is no negative judgment given against the beginnings of human civilization. Rather, culture is seen as part of life itself, part of that life that God blessed by calling it "good" (Gen. 1:31).

This focus on the goodness of created life takes a secondary place in the biblical text as the narrative of God's mighty acts in history is told. Rainbow, Red Sea, Jericho, five smooth stones—these stories of God's involvement in his own people's lives retain their ability to convict and convince. The Bible tells the story of salvation history; but Scripture's alternate, complementary theology, rooted in creation itself, is not totally absent. The goodness of life—all life— remains central to the Old Testament's wisdom literature—to Job, Proverbs, Ecclesiastes, Song of Songs, and selected Psalms. It was Walther Zimmerli who reminded modern scholarship that biblical wisdom thinks resolutely within the framework of creation theology.[4] In the last thirty-five years, his thesis has become nearly axiomatic.

For example, the Book of Proverbs does not ground its admonitions in the Law. Neither does it mention God's saving actions in the Exodus event. Rather, the authority and power of Proverbs is found in life itself.[5] Occasionally, the Book of Proverbs even borrows its material from non-Israelite sources. There is in its pages an international outlook. The compiler of Proverbs makes use of the thirty sayings of the Egyptian *Instruction of Amenemope*, for example, as he proffers God's wisdom in 22:17–24:22. The sayings are freely adapted and put into the larger context of trust in Yahweh, but a reliance on pagan sources is evident. Alluding to *Amenemope*, the wisdom writer reflects:

> Have I not written for you thirty sayings
>   of admonition and knowledge,
> to show you what is right and true,
>   so that you may give a true answer to those who sent you?
>
> Proverbs 22:20–21

The sage did not himself organize his borrowed thoughts into thirty sayings; but he nevertheless is comfortable with finding in *Amenemope's* thirty sayings God's wisdom. Proverbs' authoritative words can even come verbatim from those outside of Israel, as with the sayings of Agur, son of Jakeh (Prov. 30:1f) and those from the mother of King Lemuel (Prov. 31:1f).

That God would choose to speak his truth to Israel through nonbelievers should not surprise us. The prophets recount just such scenarios. The Book of Habakkuk records the argument between the prophet and his God when Habakkuk learns in a vision that God will use the Chaldeans as his instrument of justice against the wicked in Judah. How could Yahweh who is good and just use an evil nation to judge a "less evil" nation (Hab. 1:13)? Such an unholy alliance could not be, reasons Habakkuk. But he is wrong. God's mysterious ways can be mediated even through evil, human agents.

But lest one wrongly conclude that the non-Israelite cultural agents are always themselves evil, consider Melchizedek and Abimelech, Ruth and Cyrus. Or recall the Book of Jonah. Here it is the non-Israelite sailors who recognize God's possible involvement in their predicament long before Jonah does. Only after the lot fell on Jonah and he is questioned by the sailors as to why he is being divinely punished does Jonah respond: "'I am a Hebrew,' he replied. 'I worship the Lord, the God of heaven, who made the sea and the dry land'" (Jon. 1:9). The emphasis, it should be noted, is on God as Creator and Sustainer. What follows next is full of irony. It is not the believer in Yahweh who acts in a godly way, but the pagan sailors: (1) they are the first to recognize that God is at work in the storm; (2) they consult with Jonah and each other as to the best course; (3) even when Jonah says "Throw me overboard," they seek a more "ethical" solution; (4) they cry out to God for mercy for their contemplated action; and (5) after tossing Jonah overboard, they offer sacrifice to Yahweh and make vows. One would hardly expect the actions of non-Israelite sailors to be wise and godly, but such is the case. Is there any doubt as to whom the writer intends us to see as being models of true humanity? If so, one might note that later in the text it is the people of another non-Israelite culture, the Ninevites, who repent, while Jonah pouts. The irony is comical; the theology, crystal clear. God is involved with all of humankind and uses the wisdom and insight of nonbelievers to communicate his truth to people who believe.

I remember the impact on me of one scene in *One Flew over the Cuckoo's Nest* (1975). Inspired by McMurphy, the Jack Nicholson character, the patients want to see the World Series on television. Nurse Ratched, however, refuses to let them, fearing that a break in their routine will upset them. Nicholson is livid at such patronizing control. Fighting back, he begins to narrate an imaginative World Series game. When Sandy Koufax strikes out Mickey Mantle, there is pandemonium. The men on that mental ward feel a new sense of celebration and camaraderie. Simply by the power of his imagination, McMurphy has created a shared community, breaking the bonds of a society that would falsely restrict. As I watched, I too cheered, realizing as I did that I too have the potential to create that which will help others, if I would but seize the day.

As Christian theology has rightly concentrated its understanding of humankind on our pervasive sin and consequent need of redemption, it has sometimes wrongly emptied human culture both of its actual achievement and of God's ongoing presence. Theology has too often failed to see that God is still at work throughout his creation. In doing so, we have lost the biblical balance, ignoring the prophet's creational counterpoints as well as wisdom's "kerygma" of life in its fullness.[6] We have failed to recognize human culture's strength and possibilities. We have failed to see that God is in all of human culture, both in the way of life of a people and in the expression of that identity through human creativity.

Spirit and spirit

> God is interested in a lot of things besides religion. God is the Lord and Creator of all life, and there are manifestations of the holy in its celebration or in its repudiation—in every aspect of the common life.
>
> Joseph Sittler, *Gravity & Grace*

Christian theologians recognize the truth of Sittler's claim. Yet, they have had trouble expressing the nature of God's "presencing" through his Spirit in the lives of women and men. This is, in part, because no definition of the Spirit is given in Scripture; rather, the Spirit is *"narrated as an event—as happening."*[7] The Spirit becomes known as God reveals his personal presence in creation and recreation, in quickening and sustaining power and wisdom, and in inbreaking expectation. Understood as such, the Spirit is to be identified with the divine presence in all of life. In the words of John Taylor, the Spirit is the "Go-Between God."[8] But how is this to be understood? There are countless witnesses to this "happening" of the Spirit in the spirits of humankind. For our purposes in this book on theology and film, let me offer four examples—three from "real" life that are rooted in artistic experience, and one from "reel" life.

In his autobiography, *Surprised by Joy,* C. S. Lewis describes several experiences of his youth in which he was pointed "to something other and outer." The first such experience occurred when he played with a toy garden his brother made for him in the lid of a biscuit tin. In the years that followed, similar experiences came as he smelled a flowering currant bush, as he discovered autumn in Beatrix Potter's *Squirrel Nutkin,* and when he listened to Wagner's romantic music. This "Joy," as Lewis came to call it, was known primarily as a longing until Lewis chanced to read George MacDonald's *Phantastes.* Lewis writes: "It was as though the voice which had called to me from the world's end were now speaking at my side. It was with me in the room, or in my body, or behind me. If it had once eluded me by its distance, it now eluded me by proximity—something too near to see, too plain to be understood, on this side of knowledge."

Lewis goes on to relate: "That night my imagination was, in a certain sense, baptized."[9] Lewis had encountered the Spirit, the divine presence in all of life.

Paul Tillich's theology of correlation is based autobiographically in a similar "baptismal" experience. Living amidst the horror of war as an army chaplain during World War I, Tillich traveled to Berlin during his last furlough. There he saw a painting by Botticelli entitled *Madonna and Child with Singing Angels*. The experience was transformative of his spirit (he calls it "almost a revelation"), opening him to an element of depth in human experience and providing him a "potent analogue" for talking about religious experience more generally. There was, he relates, a "breakthrough."[10] In a lecture entitled "Human Nature and Art" (1952), Tillich labeled his experience with Botticelli's painting "revelatory ecstasy." He said, "A level of reality opened to me which had been covered up to this moment, although I had some feeling before of its existence." Tillich had, he said, "an encounter with the power of being itself."[11] Here again is the presence of the Spirit in the human spirit, though Tillich uses other language in his description.

Peter Berger has called this same awareness *A Rumor of Angels*. Although some would trumpet the demise of the supernatural in our contemporary world, this need not be the case, Berger argues. (Berger was writing in the 1970s, before the current rebirth of interest in spirituality in American culture.) For "'in, with and under' the immense array of human projections, there are indicators of a reality that is truly 'other' and that the religious imagination . . . ultimately reflects." In short, Berger believes that there is possible an inductive approach to theology, an anchorage in fundamental human experiences—in "prototypical human gestures." There are experiences of the human spirit that point beyond their own reality, that have an "immediacy to God." These include for Berger our propensities for order, play, hope, damnation (for example, of Eichmann, Hitler's henchman), and humor. He writes, "Both in practice and in theoretical thought, human life gains the greatest part of its richness from the capacity for ecstasy, by which I do not mean the alleged experiences of the mystic, but any experience of stepping outside the taken-for-granted reality of everyday life, any openness to the mystery that surrounds us on all sides."[12]

These testimonies of and reflection on experience, particularly the experience of art, offer us an important theological resource for understanding the Holy Spirit's presence within the human spirit through film. But more needs to be said about this experience of "Joy," this witness to a "baptismal" presence, this "rumor" of the divine. If we are to be true to our own dialogical methodology, these human stories must be put into conversation with God's story—with Scripture. Can we take this witness back into the biblical text and find further insight concerning what is the persistent and cross-cultural testimony of people through the ages?

In his book *Saint Paul at the Movies*, New Testament scholar Robert Jewett does just that, finding in the "miracles" (the Joy, the baptismal presence, the rumors of angels) experienced in the daily life of characters portrayed in the movie *Grand Canyon* (1991) an expression of Paul's teaching in Romans 2. Jewett asks, What are we to make of Simon, the black tow-truck driver, who risks his life to rescue a white motorist, caught at night in an all-black section of the city? Or what of Claire, who finds an abandoned infant and convinces her husband they should adopt it? Are these righteous actions not also a work of the Spirit in the human spirit? Can we not see in these individuals an example of people who are "patiently doing good" (Rom. 2:7), who "do instinctively what the law requires" (Rom. 2:14)? Are these not persons "who live obediently in accordance with the revelation they have received"?[13]

And what of the Hollywood producer who in *Grand Canyon* is shot in a random act, only to have a "vision" while in the hospital, suggesting that he stop making films that glorify violence? Later, when the man is healed, he turns away from this "calling," again deciding to make violent movies. Is this not an example, thinks Jewett, of one who has "exchanged the glory of the immortal God" (Rom. 1:23) for (other) images? An example of those who "though they knew God, they did not honor him as God or give thanks to him, but they became futile in their thinking, and their senseless minds were darkened" (Rom. 1:21)?

According to Klyne Snodgrass, whom Jewett references, Paul is not speaking in Romans 1 and 2 of a "works righteousness" by which people make a claim upon God, but of a salvation and a damnation that "are a result of one's actions, taking into consideration the amount of revelation given."[14] Here, thinks Jewett, is a description of the characters in the film *Grand Canyon*. The "obedience" which is portrayed in the film and described in Romans 2:7, 14–15, and 29 is a direct result of God's activity. Romans 2 speaks of the law written on humankind's heart "to which their own conscience [their spirits] also bears witness" (v. 15) and of the circumcision of the heart (v. 29). Both are works of the Spirit. In this biblical passage, Paul seems to have in mind those righteous individuals who lived prior to the coming of Jesus. Their salvation is according to their response to the light they were given, the amount of revelation they received. But his argument would apply equally to all who have experiences of God's Spirit, regardless of time or place, whether they prove salvific or not.

Here is an appeal to the work of the Spirit in our spirits at its most rudimentary, the reach of our spirits that is met by the Spirit. Such is the possibility that books like *Phantastes,* paintings like *Madonna and Child with Singing Angels,* and movies such as *Grand Canyon* offer their readers and viewers. If the Spirit is active in and through the human spirit, then the potential for the sacred is present across our human endeavor. Yet Christian theology continues largely to ignore the mundane, the ordinary experiences of human life. This seems particularly the case among those who define the human in "spirit-ual" terms. In some circles, there has been an unfortunate narrowing of the Spirit's role to the Christian community and a limitation of the Spirit's relation with our spirit to the extraordinary. The result of this constriction of the Holy Spirit's role has been a denial of the human spirit.

Hearing God through Non-Christians

As a college freshman, I heard Robert McAfee Brown ask those of us in his class, "How is it possible to see the hand of God in the work of non-Christian writers?"[15] Though Brown had in mind contemporary novelists, his question is equally applicable to filmmakers. If God is the source of all wisdom and beauty, how is it that unbelievers can create wonderful things and speak wisely? Brown suggests that over the centuries theologians have given three different answers to this question.

The first response claims that non-Christian artists are the unconscious inheritors of the Christian tradition. To the degree that such artists portray truth, goodness and/or beauty, it is because they have been nurtured in a cultural milieu formed by Christian convictions that they have unintentionally absorbed. Following this line of reasoning, one might conclude that when a Peter Weir, a Woody Allen, or a Milos Forman regard humankind with reverence and portray our significance and worth, these filmmakers are covertly affirming a Christian perspective, even if outwardly they disavow that they are Christians. The difficulty with such an argument should be apparent. While Christianity has without doubt influenced our culture, it is disingenuous to say that filmmakers covertly affirm what they overtly deny. I remember a well-known scholar in the field of religion and literature, Nathan Scott Jr., once calling Ernest Hemingway a "Christian writer" because his portrayal of human sin was Christian in viewpoint. But surely that does not merit the descriptor "Christian" for Hemingway, nor would he have wanted it.

There are other problems with falsely "baptizing" filmic truth as well. Though Christians sometimes want to give the Christian faith credit for the good a filmmaker shows, they rarely are willing to take responsibility for those images of life that don't ring true. As we know however, Christians have been responsible through the centuries for much wrong as well as much good. Moreover, it is evident that filmmakers who have grown up in non-Christian societies and who have not been nurtured by the Christian faith at all have still produced masterpieces of cinema. The films by the Japanese master Yasujiro Ozu, for example, who was influenced not by Christianity but by Zen (cf. *Tokyo Story*, 1953), come to mind. In an increasingly post-Christian and multicultural society, few theologians take such an imperialistic approach any longer. It simply seems dishonest to use whatever Christian "remainder" there is in society to whitewash the secular or other-religious as Christian. Any kind of direct Christian influence on film is occasional, the result of a particular Christian filmmaker.

A second theological approach that Brown describes is much more widely subscribed to by contemporary Christians. Recognizing that non-Christian culture has produced much of value, some say, "All truth is God's truth." This argument for the general availability of truth has its roots in Justin Martyr, who claimed, "Whatever has been well said anywhere or by anyone belongs to us Christians."[16] That is, since truth comes from God, truth is to be welcomed in whatever garb it appears. Augustine, and perhaps John Calvin, represent other examples of those who have given voice to this common Christian perspective toward the wider culture. Such a theological stance has much to commend for itself vis-à-vis contemporary film, not the least being the humility and the openness that it evidences toward Hollywood. Christians have applauded such movies as *Chariots of Fire* (1981), *E.T.* (1982), *The Iron Giant* (1999), *Places in the Heart* (1984), and *Tender Mercies* (1983) for the theology they embody. We can learn from these stories more of the Story.

Again there are limitations to this approach, which Brown recognized. Rather than allowing film to expand our understanding of life, the critic comes to movies with the "truth" pretty well in hand. Christian affirmations of the truth contained in a movie will, thus, tend to be selective, a cut-and-paste affair. Since Christians, as they watch a film, already have the "truth," they will be tempted to choose from the movies they watch only those insights that illustrate their independently established viewpoints and to ignore the rest. The result is often a warping of a movie's larger vision or an ignoring of films that do not initially fit their theological grid. While Christians holding this perspective commend a movie like *Tender Mercies*, they avoid other movies like *American Beauty* (1999) or *Thelma & Louise* (1991). But if film is to work its full charm, if it is to enrich and enliven us, then we must approach it as viewers with openness and humility.

A contemporary example of this second theological option is provided by Os Guinness in his book *Dining with the Devil* (1993). He writes:

> We should therefore heed Origen's ancient principle: Christians are free to plunder the Egyptians, but forbidden to set up a golden calf. By all means plunder freely of the treasures of modernity, but in God's name make sure that what comes out of the fire, which will test our life's endeavors, is gold fit for the temple of God and not a late-twentieth century image of a golden calf."[17]

Guinness's suspicion of full involvement in the wider culture is evident. Moviegoers must remain leery of becoming "worldly." And his metaphor of "plundering" pagan culture is a particularly unfortunate one. His warning echoes the overinterpretation of Romans 12:2 by Eugene Peterson, in his best-selling paraphrase of the Bible, *The Message*: "Don't become so well-adjusted to your culture that you fit into it without even thinking. Instead, fix your attention on God. . . . *Unlike the culture around you, always dragging you down to its level of immaturity*, God brings the best out of you . . ." (italics mine).[18] What is not considered in Peterson's interpretation (which adds ideas to the original text) is the possibility that God might attempt to bring the best out of us through the work of our wider culture (including the film industry).

Rather than holding to either of the above two approaches, Brown believes Christians must recognize that "God can use *all* things for the fulfillment of the divine purposes, including the *full* message of non-Christians rather than only selected congenial portions."[19] He reflects on the Christian's conviction that God is able to use all things for his purposes—truth and untruth. Brown turns by way of illustration to the tenth chapter of Isaiah. Just as Isaiah recognized in his day that God could speak a true word to his people, Israel, through the unbelieving, unethical Assyrians, so the Christian should affirm today, argues Brown, that God in his freedom can speak not only through believers, but through "Assyrians in modern dress."[20]

In the tenth chapter of Isaiah, we read that the Israelites (who believed that they were "God's people") were being threatened by the Assyrians (who certainly were not "God's people"). Instead of Isaiah telling his people that God was about to judge these pagans through his people Israel in order that justice might reign, the scenario is reversed. It is the raping, pillaging Assyrians whom Isaiah claims will be God's spokesmen to make known God's way to Israel:

> Ah, Assyria, the rod of my anger—
> the club in their hands is my fury!
> Against a godless nation I send him.
>
> Isaiah 10:5–6a

God's people (here called "a godless nation") will not hear (though they think they do). Thus God will speak through the Assyrians. What makes the Assyrians such a powerful witness, moreover, is precisely their unbelief. Isaiah recognizes that they do not realize they are being used as God's mouthpiece: "But this is not what he intends, nor does he have this in mind" (Isa. 10:7). It does not matter; pagan Assyria is to be the expression of God's revelation to "believing" Israel.

The analogy should not be overdrawn, but its point is clear. Christians need not claim that non-Christian filmmakers are covert Christians or simply appropriate from their movies what is congenial to or congruent with their understanding of the Christian faith. Rather, if viewers will join in community with a film's storyteller, letting the movie's images speak with their full integrity, they might be surprised to discover that they are hearing God as well. If this sounds surprising, it is no more so that Assyria was once God's spokesman to Israel.[21]

While such theologizing will sound preposterous to many, not least of all to many of the filmmakers themselves, I find it (1) not only consistent with Christian theology and (2) supportive of the integrity of the film itself, but also (3) liberating to the human spirit of the viewer. I am reminded in this context of the words of Dietrich Bonhoeffer, written from a Nazi prison:

> I wonder whether it is possible (it almost seems so today) to regain the idea of the Church as providing an understanding of the area of freedom (art, education, friendship, play), so that Kirkegaard's "aesthetic existence" would not be banished from the Church's sphere, but would be reestablished within it? . . . Who is there, for instance, in our times, who can devote himself with an easy mind to music, friendship, games or happiness? Surely not the "ethical" man, but only the Christian.[22]

What Bonhoeffer is suggesting is that such attempts as Brown's to reestablish a creative (playful) place for film within an explicitly theological framework might well provide an optimal context in which community can be actualized, in which filmmaker and viewer can truly and freely meet, in which film can be experienced for what it is. To come "ethically" to a work of art with truth in hand is to destroy its ability to speak freely and powerfully. It is true that all viewers watch movies "presuppositionally," that is, with a hidden or stated agenda that is theirs by virtue of their humanity. But it is only the viewers whose presuppositions enable and encourage them freely to engage the center of power and meaning of a movie on its own ground who are able to be critically free and freely critical.

One such recent experience for me was the viewing of the award-winning movie *American Beauty* (1999). The movie is a dark comedy and not for the easily offended. It portrays the hollowness of suburbia's chase after the American dream—after money, status, youth, and, of course, beauty. The story is gorgeously bleak, the filmic equivalent of a John Updike novel about a hero's midlife crisis. It is also laced with profanity and nudity, adultery and drug use.

As the story unfolds, one might think that the theme of *American Beauty* is going to be, "Eat, drink, and be merry, for tomorrow we die." But the movie is anything but sensational. Its iconoclasm mocks our media-generated illusions without resorting to either a simple fatalism or a perverse cynicism. Lester Burnham, the film's hero, is ignored by his wife, bored by his work, and unloved by his daughter. He is shriveled of soul until an infatuation with his daughter's cheerleader friend shocks him alive. He literally begins to smell the roses. Despite being almost a caricature of middle-class life today, the movie's portrayal of a man who does not know what his role in life is and fears growing old is all too real. "I'll be dead in a year," Lester tells us as the movie opens. "In a way, I'm dead already."

But much like the Book of Ecclesiastes, despair does not have the final word. There is a hard-won serenity that Lester discovers at life's core. Lester is therefore able, even in death, to embrace his life. And through him, so do we. Ultimately, sadness does not have the last word, but compassion and joy. In the fourth century, Evagrius listed sadness as one of the eight chief sins. Under pres-

Lester Burnham (Kevin Spacey) exasperates his wife, Carolyn (Annette Bening), by dropping out of life. *American Beauty* (d. Mendes, 1999). Photo by Lorey Sebastian. ©1999 DreamWorks LLC. All rights reserved.

sure to use the complete number seven, Pope Gregory the Great later dropped sadness from the list of the seven deadly sins. But Evagrius's recognition is an important one for our own day. At its core, and despite its fragility—its mystery, its amorality, and death itself—life has a beauty that is to be cherished. *American Beauty* understands this. The movie can shock us alive to such beauty, however transient. It can overcome our sadness. It did for me.

Encountering God through Image

> Art does not reproduce the visible;
> Rather it makes visible.
>
> Paul Klee

As we have already noted, film gives story a unique shape. It is not enough to understand a movie according to the canons of storytelling that one might apply to a novel, for instance. Movies also have to do with image. And this presents yet another challenge for the Christian who would engage in dialogue with Hollywood. For Christianity—in particular, Protestant Christianity—has not always looked kindly on the use of image, which has most typically been associated with idolatry. For example, under the heading "Image," both the *International Standard Bible Encyclopedia* (revised edition, 1982) and the *Harper's Bible Dictionary* (1985) have "See Idol."

In an otherwise helpful book that has been a perennial best-seller, James Packer's *Knowing God* warns against the use of any image as an aid to worship.[23] For Packer, idolatry consists not only in the worship of false gods but in the worship of the true God through the use of images. As the second commandment states, "Thou shalt not make unto thee any graven image . . . thou shalt not bow down thyself to them, nor serve them." Packer believes this commandment to be categorical. It is not just talking about degrading representations of God, but even pictures and statues of Jesus Christ as a man that are made with reverence.

According to Packer, images obscure God's glory and convey false ideas about God. If we are to know God, it can only come from God's revelation of himself through his holy Word, "and from no other source whatsoever." Why would God make such a generalized prohibition?

> Surely this is in order to make us realize that those who make images and use them in worship, and thus inevitably take their theology from them, will in fact tend to neglect God's revealed will at every point. *The mind that takes up with images is a mind that has not yet learned to love and attend to God's Word.* Those who look to man-made images, material or mental, to lead them to God are not likely to take any part of His revelation as seriously as they should.[24]

Extrapolating outward from warnings about false worship, Packer concludes that God communicates best through word, not symbols. We have already encountered his conclusion in this chapter with Noll, Wells, and Plantinga, who spoke of the need to avoid the entertainment culture in order to get back to reading and thinking. Again, word is seen as paramount over image.

Such rhetoric, typical of some Calvinists, is softened within other branches of Protestantism. Luther, for example, was not against the use of even such religious images as the crucifix so long as they were used not for worship but only as memorials. He wrote:

> It is possible for me to hear and bear in mind the story of the Passion of our Lord. But it is impossible for me to hear and bear it in mind without forming mental images of it in my heart. For whether I will or not when I hear of Christ, an image of a man hanging on a cross takes form in my heart just as the reflection of my face naturally appears in the water when I look into it. If it is not a sin, but good to have the image of Christ in my heart, why should it be a sin to have it in my eyes?[25]

Luther thus felt free to publish his New Testament in 1522 with twenty-two woodcuts as illustrations, though Luther's theology of images was still a cautious one. More in keeping with Augustine's thought perhaps, Luther believed images could "engage reason about revelation. They are icons for the mind, didactic proclamation. . . ."[26]

Turning to Protestant filmmakers, it is not surprising to discover that movies often remain icons of the mind, where the primary message is conveyed through words. In the works of two of the best—Ron Shelton, who grew up a Baptist and went to Westmont College, an evangelical school in Santa Barbara, and Paul Schrader, who went to Calvin College, a Dutch Reformed institution in Grand Rapids, Michigan—the movie's message often is communicated through voice-overs. Recall, for example, the opening of *Bull Durham* (1988), where Annie Savoy's monologue begins, "I believe in the church of baseball. . . ."

It is not to the Protestant traditions that we should turn if we are to see embodied a robust theology of the image, but to Roman Catholic filmmakers.[27] It is in the works of such directors as Martin Scorsese, Alfred Hitchcock, and Francis Ford Coppola that we see meaning conveyed through image. Such directors have both inherited an iconic culture and helped embody it. The fight scenes in *Raging Bull* (1980), the shower scene in *Psycho* (1960), and the baptism scene in *The Godfather* (1971) go beyond what words can express, giving viewers a visceral experience of evil's presence.

Taking its lead from Aquinas, Roman Catholicism has valued creation as well as salvation, the natural together with the supernatural. H. Richard Niebuhr, in summarizing this position, writes that Catholicism (what Niebuhr calls the "synthesist" view) expresses "a principle that no other Christian group seems to assert so well but which all need to share; namely, the principle that the Creator and the Saviour are one, or that whatever salvation means beyond creation it does not mean the destruction of the created."[28]

Recognizing the wisdom of having such a theology of natural life, the Lutheran theologian, Dietrich Bonhoeffer, argued that it was folly to consider, as many Protestants did, that "both the natural and the unnatural were equally damned. All this meant complete disruption in the domain of natural life." Did theology not have anything to say that was relevant to life's ambiguity and complexity? Was theology only to speak of the person and work of Jesus Christ (the ultimate) and ignore all that was penultimate? How could the church recover a christologically informed, but creationally based, understanding of the natural, one that would challenge the perennial heresy of gnosticism? Bonhoeffer concluded, "The concept of the natural must . . . be recovered."[29]

The Protestant suspicion of the image, its reverence for the rational word, and its concentration on redemption theology to the sometimes exclusion of creation theology have all combined to have a major dampening effect on this church's engagement with Hollywood. If a full-orbed conversation between theology and film is to go forward, it will be necessary for the Protestant church to recover a more adequate theology of image, one rooted in experience and grounded in creation itself. As David Harned colorfully expressed it, we must "prevent the reduction of the Genesis account to a sort of dubious archeological appendage to Christian faith."[30]

The biblical creation account shows more than God's omnipotence and humankind's fallenness. It also reveals God's gracious desire to enter into relationship with human beings and to bless them. Though Barth is certainly correct to stress the infinite qualitative distinction between humankind and God, this does not deny the goodness of God's creation of us, his creatures. We have, in fact, been created "in his image, in the image of God he created them; male and female he created them" (Gen. 1:27). The meaning of this reference to image is still debated by theologians, though it surely has something to do with the way we relate together. We are created male and female and called to live together in community with each other and with God. But God's image in us has also something to do with our participation in life, as the next verse in the Genesis text makes clear: "God blessed them, and God said to them, 'Be fruitful and multiply, and fill the earth and subdue it; and have dominion over the fish of the sea and over the birds of the air and over every living thing that moves upon the earth'" (Gen. 1:28). All that we do, we do in the power of the God who created us. This includes the making of images. Images are one means of responding to the divine call to fulfill life. The Image-maker has blessed us, his creation, with the freedom to be image-makers too.

Having said this, there is no single form of image making that is theologically more significant than others. An image doesn't have to be explicitly religious, for example, to be theologically helpful, though it might be. I have found the theology of Paul Tillich useful at this point. We have noted above how Tillich himself experienced divine revelation through his experience of seeing Botticelli's *Madonna and Child with Singing Angels* at the Kaiser Friedrich Museum in Berlin at the end of World War I. Images, thus, became for him a means to "penetrate to the level where an ultimate concern exercises its driving power."[31]

Tillich identified five types of images, each with their own possibilitity of expressing human beings' relationship to ultimate reality. The first is the *sacramental*, a numinous realism that "depicts ordinary things, ordinary persons, ordinary events . . . in a way which makes them strange, mysterious, laden with an ambiguous power." The second is the *mystical*, which reaches out for ultimacy without dependence on concrete things or persons, using "basic structural elements of reality like lines, cubes, planes, colors, as symbols for that which transcends all reality." The third type is *critical realism*, where "sober, objective, quasi-scientifically observed reality is a manifestation of ultimate reality, although it is lacking in directly numinous character. It is the humility of accepting the given which provides it with religious power." Fourth is *idealism*, which "sees in the present the anticipation of future perfection" and produces images either of remembrances of the lost or anticipations of the regained. Lastly, Tillich describes what he labels *expressionism*, which is realistic and at the same time mystical; it both criticizes and anticipates, disrupting the given appearance of things. There is in expressionism an element of depth which is conveyed in and through the encountered image.[32]

Tillich's typology of image was formulated with reference to paintings like Picasso's *Guernica,* and its particulars need not concern us here, other than to say that what is common to the above types of images is their ability to become mediators of ultimate reality. None need be what we have traditionally labeled "religious images," although religious images can be used. The key, instead, is the image's ability to transport the viewer to some more central place, to provide the viewer that experience of "Joy" of which C. S. Lewis speaks. It was just such an experience through the movie *Becket* that was transformative for me.

Theology's Narrative Shape

Biblical truth has a definite narrative shape. Jesus used parables, not treatises. Nathan spoke to David in stories. The Israelites used narrative to speak of the God of Abraham, Isaac, and Jacob and to recount the mighty acts of God in shaping their history. The sermons of Peter and Stephen, which are recalled in the opening chapters of the Book of Acts, recite these same stories of Israel and recall the Christ event. Even Paul's more systematic theology is far removed from the abstract reasoning that goes by that term today. His is a mission theology. His argument is never separated from the passion narrative, from his own life story, or from the particular context and stories of those he addresses. To the Corinthians he wrote,

> Now I would remind you, brothers and sisters, of the good news that I proclaimed to you, which you in turn received, in which also you stand, through which also you are being saved. . . .
> For I handed on to you as of first importance what I in turn had received: that Christ died for our sins in accordance with the scriptures, and that he was buried, and that he was raised on the third day in accordance with the scriptures, and that he appeared to Cephas, then to the twelve. Then he appeared to more than five hundred brothers and sisters at one time. . . . Last of all, as to one untimely born, he appeared also to me. For I am the least of the apostles, unfit to be called an apostle, because I persecuted the church of God. But by the grace of God I am what I am, and his grace toward me has not been in vain.

> 1 Corinthians 15:1–10

Christianity is, at core, not an abstract philosophy, but a story; not pure factual reportage, but a recounting of one life in order that other lives might be transformed. Christian theology is rooted in the testimony of what has been both seen and lived—what is both real in its own right and redemptive in those who experience the story and respond to it. When preachers testify to the death and resurrection of Jesus and its efficacy for the Christian, they are speaking of both past event and present reality. And story provides this bridge.

Theologians have not always recognized the importance of story—or, at least, have let it become submerged under a welter of abstract analysis. John Macquarrie, for example, defines systematic theology as "the intellectual discipline that seeks to express the content of a religious faith as a coherent body of propositions."[33] But systematic theology's analytical rigor is also its limitation. It "has difficulty in maintaining touch with the narrative nature of the faith upon which it seeks to reflect, and therefore with the object of its concern."[34] Noting this fact, Old Testament scholar John Goldingay wonders about the preeminence of systematic theology in some circles. Even if we are rational creatures, disciplined reflection need not take the form of systematic theology, he suggests. In Judaism, for example, reflection has for centuries taken the form of the retelling of biblical narrative so as to answer contemporary questions and clarify difficulties. We can think sharply and coherently on our faith using narrative as well.

In his introduction to the Hassidic stories, Martin Buber writes of the importance of the narrative form:

> The story is itself an event and has the quality of a sacred action. . . . It is more than a reflection—the sacred essence to which it bears witness continues to live in it. The wonder that is narrated becomes powerful once more. . . . A rabbi, whose grandfather had been a pupil of Baal Shem Tov, was once asked to tell a story. "A story ought to be told," he said, "so that it is itself a help," and his story was this. "My grandfather was paralyzed. Once he was asked to tell a story about his teacher and he told how the holy Baal Shem Tov used to jump and dance when he was praying. My grandfather stood up while he was telling the story and the story carried him away so much that he had to jump and dance to show how the master had done it. From that moment, he was healed. This is how stories ought to be told."[35]

Stories are performative; they give meaning to facts. In the process they help answer questions concerning who we are and point us to that larger truth which lies beyond our grasp. But what has this to do with theology and film? A growing number of persons are finding that movies as story provide their viewers a means of recapturing the meaning and power of our story-shaped gospel, something we have all too often abstracted. Robert Jewett, for example, entertains what he calls the "seemingly preposterous proposition" that "certain movies afford deeper access to the hidden heart of Paul's theology than mainstream theologians like myself have been able to penetrate."[36] He argues that Pauline scholarship in the West has centered in issues of guilt rather than shame, and has understood grace chiefly in terms of individual forgiveness. But he asks, could it be that shame is the deeper and more problematic dilemma that Paul deals with in his description of salvation? And are there not corporate as well as individual dimensions to the gospel? As Jewett, a New Testament scholar, has explored this interpretive possibility with regard to the Book of Romans, he has found contemporary film to provide greater insight into Paul's references to honor, shame, and grace than many of his colleagues' scholarly essays. Conversely, he is convinced that the New Testament can also shed light on the deeper dimensions of films like *Babe* (1995), *The Shawshank Redemption* (1994), and *Mr. Holland's Opus* (1995). The conversation is two-directional.

Jewett is not alone in believing that we need at times to reverse the hermeneutical flow between theology and film. Film's story can affect our understanding of the Christian story, not just the reverse. In two volumes published in the early nineties, Larry Kreitzer shows that the meaning modern people have attached to biblical incidents and concepts, as these are evident through film (and the novel), can suggest fresh interpretations of the original meaning of the biblical text.[37] Modern versions of biblical truth as they are enfleshed in film can send us back to the originals with new insight. A recent and popular example of this reversal of the typical hermeneutical flow between Scripture and film is Philip Yancey's *The Jesus I Never Knew* (1995).[38] Yancey narrates how it was through watching a dozen or so Jesus movies, which had come out of Hollywood over the years, that he discovered a new sense of Jesus' true humanity. Yancey had been so heavenly-minded that his Christology was of little earthly good until such movies as *Jesus Christ Superstar* (1973), *The Gospel according to Saint Matthew* (1966), *Jesus of Nazareth* (1977), and *The Last Temptation of Christ* (1988) showed him new ways of seeing the Messiah.

If the church has forgotten that the heart of its theology is story (God's story, which begins in Genesis, "Once upon a time," and ends in Revelation, "They live happily ever after"), if the church has concentrated too often on structure and ethics and dogma, then God's story will be heard in other venues, such as the movie theater. In 1999 alone, movies like *The Matrix*, *The End of the Affair*, *Dogma*, *The Third Miracle*, *The Green Mile*, *The Straight Story*, *The Iron Giant*, *The Hurricane*, and *American Beauty* all became the context for theology to be given narrative shape. Each invited a subsequent theological conversation.

A good example of film's potential through story to engender theological conversation was *The Spitfire Grill*, a film that came out in 1996. Made on a modest budget ($6+ million) by a Roman Catholic organization in Mississippi, it was the surprise hit at Robert Redford's Sundance Film Festival before playing to general release. The movie tells the story of Percy Talbott, who comes to Gilead, Maine, to find a job after finishing her prison term. Percy is given work by Hannah, the owner of a diner, the Spitfire Grill, and is befriended by Shelby, Hannah's niece by marriage. A rocky but genuine friendship ensues between the three women, and their relationship forms the center of the film. Early in the story, when Hannah falls and breaks her leg, Percy takes over the diner with the help of Shelby. Percy cannot cook(!), but she is willing to learn, and the two younger women keep the restaurant in business. One evening, as she rubs lotion on Hannah's tender leg, Percy asks: "You suppose if a wound goes so deep, the healing of it might hurt as bad as what caused it?"

Here in microcosm is the question of the film. For Gilead, too, is suffering from a wound. All of the citizens of this small hamlet have been deeply hurt. Their hopes have been shattered by the disappearance of Hannah's talented son, Eli, who represented their future. He has failed to "return" from Vietnam. Their "dis-ease" needs treatment, but the healing will prove painful. It is Percy who acts as a balm to bring spiritual healing and new possibility to Gilead. At first, Percy simply substitutes for Hannah in running the café and in providing food for a mysterious and needy recluse who lives in the hills. But the wound is deep. Healing can come only as it is pierced ("Perced") through sacrificial love. Reconciliation does take place and a son comes home; but it is not without its heavy price. Percy's death brings hope to Gilead.

When the movie's sponsorship became known, this film was criticized by some as "hidden propaganda," though they had trouble knowing what specifically to criticize. There is no explicit religiosity present. Not all people in the larger society were willing to accept the film's indirect spiritual gift, however, for it had come from a Christian organization. Yet most viewers were taken by the film's story. Perhaps we can understand the value of *The Spitfire Grill* by recalling the fiction of another indirect storyteller. Almost fifty years ago, C. S. Lewis sought to overcome the narrow secularity of our modern age, not by producing movies, but by writing children's stories. He was concerned that modern women and men were in danger of becoming little more than "trousered apes." It was not enough to have "just the facts," as Joe Friday wanted on *Dragnet*, a television series of the time. Lewis was convinced that we were being cut off from our roots and destiny. Story could help heal our malady.

The purpose of Lewis's *The Chronicles of Narnia* was, thus, to give a new generation of readers the taste and feel of truth—to baptize their imagination. In this way, Lewis hoped to assist others in getting beyond the tiny windowless universe they had mistaken for reality. A good story, thought Lewis, should do more than offer an engaging plot or produce excitement. In a good story, plot is important, but as a "net" to catch something else. The story should mediate something more, or other, than what we are conscious of in our day-to-day existence. In *The Chronicles of Narnia*, Aslan, the lion (the Christ-figure), explains to the children that he has brought them to Narnia so that, having experienced him there, they might be able to recognize him in another guise where they live. Here is a "theology" of story every bit as applicable to movies as to children's literature.

What Lewis did for his generation through children's fiction—the baptizing of our imaginations—others are attempting in our day through the use of film. A wonderful example of this is *The Spitfire Grill* (*The Green Mile* [1999] also comes to mind). Such films need not be created by Christians. In fact, the director of *The Spitfire Grill* was Jewish. It is enough that life be portrayed at some more central region. The shame that a town feels over the "loss" of its son needs healing. And Percy Talbott, unlikely Christ figure that she is, nonetheless comes with her balm to Gilead to make the wounded whole. Though she comes into the town from the outside, has a questionable reputation, and experiences rejection, Percy is able to expose the hurts of this small town and bring healing (salvation) both to a family and to a town.

Theology's Dialogical Character

Karl Barth once described the theologian as having a Bible in one hand and the newspaper in the other. That is, the theologian's task is a dialogical one. We can observe theology's interactive nature, for example, by reflecting on one expression of it, preaching. How do ministers develop a sermon for a worship service? They might rely on the lectionary which church tradition has provided. Or it might be Christmas or one of the other major holidays of the church year. They might seek to address a crisis in the congregation or in the wider society. They might choose to preach a series of sermons on a particular section of Scripture, perhaps one of its books. They might want to comment on a personal area of growth, meaningful to them, and which they hope will prove significant to others. All of these are valid and typical ways ministers begin sermon preparation. But unless the sermon is *both* rooted in the "Bible" (both directly and as mediated through tradition and the worshiping community) *and* sensitive to the congregation's personal and social context (the "newspaper"), it will remain stillborn.

The co-editor of the Engaging Culture series, William Dyrness, describes the theological task as seeking to bring together in reflective obedience the telling

Figure 4.1 The Nature of the Theological Task

of our stories and the hearing of God's story. Again, the basic dialogical nature of theology is evident. We can diagram the nature of theology's constructive task as in figure 4.1.

Theologians have often added components to this simple schematic for doing theology, altering its shape in the process. But theology's basic two-way conversation remains. For example, it can be helpful to distinguish some of the different ways in which we hear God's story, for theologians have recognized the unique authority of Scripture over tradition. Thus many theologians use a triangle (fig. 4.2 A) to diagram their theological sources.

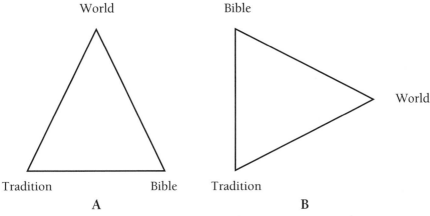

Figure 4.2 Threefold Source of Theology

If one sets this triangle on its side (fig. 4.2 B), we can again note the basic interactive nature of the theological task. The dialogue cannot be simply between Scripture and tradition; our position in the world is also significant for our theological reflection. At a minimum, the world (culture) must be seen as theology's setting (it is the form in which we think and learn) and application (theology rethinks God's thoughts in every generation).

Others have recognized the need not only to differentiate resources in hearing God's story, but also in telling our stories. John Wesley, for example, posited a quadrilateral of theological resources that in addition to Bible and tradition included reason (what within your culture you consider reasonable) and personal experience.

Personal experience matters theologically. Varied experiences, for example, sometimes cause women to read Scripture differently than men. If you have had a child die, you will read the Book of Job differently. What is thought reasonable also varies culturally. If you think about life from within the thought structures of Asian culture, you will view it differently than in the West. Latin

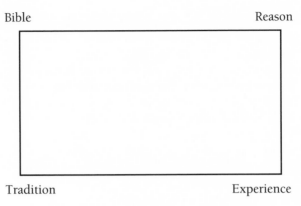

Bible   Reason

Tradition   Experience

Figure 4.3 Fourfold Source of Theology

America, which spent centuries under the yoke of the few, was particularly sensitive to biblical themes of liberation during the seventies when opportunity for new forms of government presented itself. Such variations in how people reason are significant for how they do theology. Both reason and experience help give shape to our theological reflections. But Wesley's quadrilateral (fig. 4.3) can also be understood as simply a variation of our twofold conversational paradigm. We hear God's story through Bible and tradition. We tell our stories through reason and experience.

My own model for doing constructive theology (fig. 4.4) has five components:

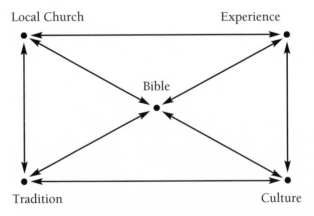

Local Church   Experience

Bible

Tradition   Culture

Figure 4.4 Fivefold Source of Theology

Hearing God's Story now has three components (one's particular worshiping community; the larger Christian community of witnesses, past and present; and the Bible). Our interaction in the world includes both our individual experience and our participation in a larger culture, a shared meaning system. In observing the diagram (fig. 4.4), one will note that our knowledge from Scripture is always a mediated knowledge. The interpreter, that is, has no access to the Bible except as he or she comes to it from one of theology's other resources. The Bible is at the center of the scheme, in part to emphasize its primacy of place; the Bible is theology's authority for faith and practice. But it is also located in the center because our access to biblical truth is always mediated through one or more of the other sources. We read the authoritative biblical text from out of a worshiping community, in light of centuries of Christian thought and practice, as people embedded in a particular culture, who have a unique set of experiences. Here is the theological process.

Seen in this light, cultural expressions (including movies) function as important resources for theological reflection. Movies need not be explicitly "Christian" in their theme to be theologically significant. As a means of telling our stories (and even hearing God's story pseudonymously), movies have the potential of helping us to hear God as God's story and our stories intersect. God is present in all of life and communicates with us through all of these theological resources. Film, as an expression of the broader culture and as the occasion for our own personal experiences and growth, can serve as a theological resource, providing both insight and conviction to its viewers. For when the dialogue comes together between a viewer and a film, one may glimpse something hidden, either in one's self, another, or even the Other.

An example from my own experience of the theological importance of film might add clarity. I remember seeing *The Elephant Man* (1980), a movie based loosely on the true story of John Merrick, a grotesquely deformed young man who lived during the last part of the nineteenth century in England. Reduced to making a living in the sideshow of the circus, Merrick was thought incapable of either feeling or speech. That is, until he was rescued by Sir Frederick Treves of the London Hospital. Treves had wanted a "specimen" to analyze as he gave his anatomy lectures; but his compassion for John grew daily. Hiding him in an isolated ward of the hospital, Treves sought to give John a life. But hospital policy did not allow "incurables" to permanently take up scarce beds, so the chief administrator asked Treves to show him John in order that he might assess whether Merrick might be helped. Central to the decision of whether John Merrick would be forced onto the streets again was whether he was capable of thought and speech.

In the movie, Treves thus pleads with John to show the administrator that he can speak. "I can't help you unless you help me. I believe that there is something you want to say to me. . . . We must show them that you're not a wall." And John responds; he tentatively tries to speak. Excited, Treves tries to prepare him for the impending interview by having him repeat the first verses of the Twenty-third Psalm. These would be his elocution lessons. But when Carr

Gomm, the hospital administrator, comes the next afternoon, John is too frightened to say anything other than a few words that seem almost rote. Frustrated, Gomm asks John cynically, "How long did you and Mr. Treves prepare for this interview?" John has failed, and the two doctors leave him.

As they stand outside John's room discussing the case quietly, the doctors hear John speak again. He is again quoting the Twenty-third Psalm. This time, however, he is reciting not only the first three verses, but the remaining ones as well: "Yea though I walk through the valley of the shadow of death, I will fear no evil; for Thou art with me." Hearing John articulate as his own this radical affirmation of trust in God, Treves realizes that he has not taught that part of the psalm to Merrick. The doctors return to John's room, where they learn from him (he is now relaxed enough to speak) that his mother had taught him the psalm when he was a child. John is spared, and he becomes a model to all who later meet him of what true humanity is.

As I saw *The Elephant Man*, I understood one of the most frequently quoted texts in the Bible in a new light. This psalm was not simply a general affirmation of faith by someone reflecting on life. It is not a psalm written when all is well. Rather here is a cry of one in crisis; though all else fail, God's extravagant care will provide. No wonder the psalm is used in hospital settings and at funerals worldwide. But that night at the theater, I experienced more. My theology was enlarged as I understood better what it was to be a human. I experienced this both as I watched the contrast between Carr Gomm's legalism and Frederick Treves's grace, and as John's compelling personage filled the screen with life. My Christian understanding of what it is to be human took on a new depth it had previously not had. I would not only read Psalm 23 differently, but also Psalm 8:

> what are human beings that you are mindful of them,
>   mortals that you care for them?
> Yet you have made them a little lower than God,
>   and crowned them with glory and honor.
>
> Psalm 8:4–5

My conversation between God's story and our stories took on a new richness and depth that night. John Merrick had taught me about theology.

God can be experienced through film's stories and images in a myriad of ways, and these experiences both invite theological dialogue and feed into our constructive theology. But in order to make use of the resources that movies provide the Christian believer, in order to hear God speak pseudonymously as spirit encounters Spirit, it is helpful to know better how to view movies on their own terms. It is to this we now turn.

5

are movies art?

Movies are often not viewed as legitimate art. Many reasons are given for this common perception, but chief among them perhaps is film's commercialism. Consider the viewpoint of Max Horkheimer and Theodor W. Adorno, philosophers and social critics, who expressed the following in 1947: "Movies and radio need no longer pretend to be art. The truth that they are just business is made into an ideology in order to justify the rubbish they deliberately produce."[1] All too frequently, movies are controlled by crass commercial interests. They merely provide escape or indulge our prejudices and fantasies, oversimplifying life in the process. Movies are geared to the masses through their marketing techniques and star system. Hollywood seems fixed on the lucrative subjects of sex and violence and is prone to create spectacular special effects in order to generate a crowd rather than to portray the nuances of everyday life.[2] Where is the art in this?

Criticism of Hollywood's commercialism must be taken seriously. Too much in Hollywood is formulaic and indulgent. But the basic presupposition that art and business cannot mix is erroneous. Film has the power to disturb and enlighten, to make us more aware of both who we are and what our relationships with others could be. It can even usher us into the presence of the holy. Michelangelo painted the Sistine Chapel's ceiling on commission; Charles Eames designed for the Herman Miller Corporation his award-winning chairs, which are now shown in leading museums around the world.[3] We might not typically speak of the opera business or the symphony business, but these too are highly sophisticated enterprises. When Esa-Pekka Salonen, the music director and conductor of the Los Angeles Philharmonic, plays Brahms and Beethoven for the sake of pleasing his audience, instead of a steady diet of the twentieth-century composers which he favors, this does not result in the dismissal of these past masters. The Philharmonic's music is often glorious despite its commercial intention. How many ballet companies perform *The Nutcracker Suite* at Christmas time in order to help finance the rest of the year's activity? Yet how many audiences are captivated by the magic of that story in dance? When the Los Angeles County Museum of Art mounted its exhibit on Van Gogh in the winter of 1999, it was for the express purpose of drawing large crowds to buy high-priced tickets. That did not prevent thousands from being transfixed by the paintings they saw. Marketing need not negate art.

Others condemn Hollywood for producing mere entertainment. It took European film critics in the fifties and sixties to discover the value of American Westerns or of a Hitchcock thriller. Americans who had seen them earlier thought these movies to be simply escapist fare, the equivalent of pulp fiction. More recently, when Horton Foote, the Academy Award winning screenwriter (*To Kill a Mockingbird*, 1962; *Tender Mercies*, 1983; *The Trip to Bountiful*, nominated, 1985), was asked for his opinion of the American film industry today, he said,

> Oh I don't like to knock things. . . . You know, I'm sure there's a lot of sincere, wonderful work out there, but a lot of it just doesn't appeal to me. . . . I just feel that whatever it is, whatever's driving films right now, I feel they're just trying to "out-sensationalize" each other. I think it's superficial and I think it's gotten to be dominated by an MTV mentality. A lot of the photography looks like advertisements.[4]

But for every distortion, one can also recall a *Dead Man Walking* (1995), a *Forrest Gump* (1994), or a *Shine* (1996). Popular movies need not be trivial or tabloid in their storytelling. They need not be—in fact, often are not—mindless entertainment. It is perhaps helpful to recall that much of what we might now consider high art began as more popular ventures. Consider Shakespeare, for example, or Dickens.

A matrix can be used to help us understand the range of cinema:

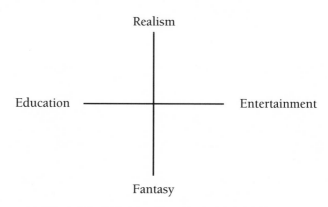

Figure 5.1 Cinema's Communication Matrix

————reel spirituality

Film is a hybrid, along with other creative and performing arts. Each movie can be placed at a particular location on this matrix whose one axis runs from realism to fantasy, and whose other matrix is a continuum between education and entertainment.

Historically, some critical approaches to film have considered movies to be a "window to reality."[5] They have prized realistic costumes, nonprofessional actors, and themes and stories taken from everyday life. A film like Robert Duvall's *The Apostle* (1997) would fit near the realistic end of the fantasy/realism continuum, as would Thomas Vinterberg's *The Celebration* (1998). The latter was the first to use the precepts laid down by the *Dogme 95* manifesto. Purposely alluding to Luther's ninety-five theses, the dictum was signed by a group of Danish filmmakers who pledged to shoot only on location without props, to produce sound and images together rather than rely on later dubbing, to have a handheld camera and use color film without filters, to center the story in the here and now, to reject genre movies, to not credit the director, and so on. As Richard Corliss commented in *Time* magazine, "*Dogme* is a call to disarm, to strip away the veneer, to walk without crutches supplied by Industrial Light and Magic."[6]

Other moviemakers and critics, sometimes called formalists, have emphasized the ability of film's formal techniques, such as editing and camera position, to transform reality into a fantastic universe.[7] *Thelma & Louise* (1991) is meant to be seen as a fable, a fictional universe created to communicate meaning. How else are we to understand the backlit mountains, the dust-free trucks, or the stop-action ending? Some movies are more realistic in their perspective; others, more fanciful. But most are a combination of reality and fantasy.

Similarly, while some movies might best be classified as mere entertainment—one thinks of *Ace Ventura: Pet Detective* (1994)—the majority are a combination of education and entertainment. Consider another of Tom Shadyac's movies, *Liar, Liar* (1997). To the degree that a movie appeals to popular culture, it is entertaining. To the degree that it seeks to portray some aspect of truth, beauty, and/or goodness, it is educating. Again, the vast majority of movies can be located somewhere between the extremes of the education/entertainment axis.

Using this matrix, it is possible to locate individual films within particular quadrants. A James Bond thriller will be located in the entertainment/fantasy quadrant, *Saving Private Ryan* (1998) in the realism/education quadrant. But neither is pure entertainment nor pure art; nor was it meant to be. Good art is entertaining and educational. Some people criticized the Academy Award winning film *Life Is Beautiful* (1998) for "joking about the Holocaust," not realizing that the movie is a fable, as the film itself states at the beginning, and should be put in the fantasy/education quadrant. Though here too, the film is not pure fantasy, the Holocaust being all too frighteningly real.

To the degree that a film is simply escapist entertainment, it should be viewed as such, and there will be little, if any, need for theological dialogue with it. Here is the equivalent of pulp fiction—fare created simply to divert attention from life's ongoingness. Other movies offer little for the theological critic because of the smallness of their vision and/or the confusion of their craft. Since movies are experienced differently by various viewers, what is engaging for one will be mindless entertainment for another. But to the degree that a film, whether through fantasy or realism, and even when primarily entertainment, succeeds artistically in depicting life, it engages our lives. As it does, it educates, inviting our response as whole persons, including our religious convictions.

The truth is, art cannot be easily dismissed, even when it is commercialized or created for mass entertainment. We must not confuse film's technology for its technique of storytelling, nor its marketing with the portrayal of life that it offers. In his "Nobel Lecture on Literature," Aleksandr Solzhenitsyn expressed the possibility of all art transcending its limitations, whether those be commercialism or amusement or politics:

> So we also, holding Art in our hands, confidently deem ourselves its masters; we boldly give it direction, bring it up to date, reform it, proclaim it, sell it for money, use it to please the powerful, divert it for amusement—all the way down to vaudeville songs and nightclub acts—or else adapt it (with a muzzle or stick, whatever is handy) toward transient political or limited social needs. But art remains undefiled by our endeavors and the stamp of its origin remains unaffected: each time and in every usage it bestows upon us a portion of its mysterious inner light.[8]

Here is the power of movies.

Film as the American Art Form

Movies are perhaps singular in their ability to reveal American culture. We might study Greek tragedies and epics to know ancient Greek culture, the theater to understand Elizabethan England, and the novel to discover the core of the Victorian period. "Similarly," writes Richard Blake, "if one wants to gather some sensitivity to the United States in the twentieth century, then go to the movies."[9] Robert Sklar, in his book *Movie-Made America*, writes, "Are we not all members or offspring of that first rising generation of movie-made children whose critical emotional and cognitive experience did in fact occur in movie theatres?"[10] It is film, just as it once was the epic, or the theater or the novel, which now dominates and best expresses our particular historical moment. Problems notwithstanding, Hollywood continues to do what film as an art form does best—tell our stories. The American movie industry has become internationally the single most dominant cultural force of our century. Through movies, the hopes and fears of our contemporary age find expression.

Film as Probing Life

Over the centuries, the characterizing elements of art have changed, but its center continues to be its exploration of the meaning of life. Art seeks to initiate a dialogue as it shares the vision of its creator with its audience. It is through this sharing that life takes on added meaning and wholeness. For as Kierkegaard suggests, art recreates experience and awakens it to life.[11] Filmmakers use images and story to probe hypothetically life's possibilities. In a movie, every camera angle has a meaning, every costume a significance. After all, filmmakers have only two hours, more or less, to tell their stories convincingly. A movie implicitly says to us, If you will just suspend judgment and enter into my world for the duration of this film—if you will grant me my initial sketch of life's conditions—then such and such would, or at least might, follow.[12]

In making a similar case for the work of literature, Giles Gunn quotes approvingly Roy Harvey Pearce, who argues that a work of art is not literally "true," but

> consists instead of a series of hypothetical situations, imaged and motivated in such a way that, within their confines, we can accept as necessary the actions and responses into which the situations—and the imagined human beings in them—are made to issue. What primarily interests us in "created" situations of this sort is, of course, not their inevitable relevance to factuality, but their possibility: their resonance with our deepest sense of ourselves.[13]

Like the novel, film reveals life at a more central region than we are often aware of otherwise. In the everyday or the fantastic, it sees hidden possibilities, which if not "natural" in a literal sense, are nonetheless compelling to our deeper sense of reality. Movies show us what our unaided eye doesn't see.

Movies, like all art, prove self-authenticating. If they are artificial or forced in their portrayal of the human situation, they are judged harshly. If their images, whether real or fantasy, are beyond the viewer's plausibility, they will remain inert and unconvincing. As Aleksandr Solzhenitsyn said of all true art: "[W]orks which have drawn on the truth and which have presented it to us in concentrated and vibrant form seize us, attract us to themselves powerfully, and no one ever—even centuries later—will step forth to deny them."[14]

Recently I saw two silent film classics for the first time, Victor Sjöström's *The Wind* (1928) and Carl Dreyer's *La Passion de Jeanne d'Arc* (*The Passion of Joan of Arc*, 1928). Their ability to evoke empathy and provide insight remains undiminished over time, for their probings of the human situation reveal themselves to be based in life at its deepest level. *The Wind* has influenced countless film-makers, not the least of whom was the fellow Swede Ingmar Bergman. It stars Lillian Gish as Letty, an innocent girl from Virginia who after moving to the Wild West is forced into a loveless marriage in order to survive. The brutality and isolation of the West in the nineteenth century is portrayed symbolically by the ever-present wind that stirs up dirt and dust, both literally and metaphorically. And it is this wind that eventually causes Letty to go crazy.

When Wirt Roddy, a traveling salesman, forces himself on Letty during a period of isolation caused by a fierce windstorm (a "Norther"), the now-crazed woman is able in one final act of courage to shoot him as the wind and dust blow unmercifully. When her husband Lige returns, he sees her really for the first time. As a result, Letty's head clears, and there is finally a recognition of each other's humanity. For both of them, a future now seems possible. Hollywood forced Sjöström to adapt the story in such a way as to have this "happy" ending. Perhaps the movie, therefore, is not "natural" in a literal sense (after all, Letty had become deranged); but its "resonance with our deepest sense of ourselves" is profound. The audience can feel her pain and is rooting for some sense of basic justice, not to mention compassion. It gets both.

La Passion de Jeanne d'Arc tells a parallel story of a woman's fight to remain true to herself despite all odds. The story centers on the historical trial of Joan for heresy. In one of the most riveting performances in cinematic history, Maria Falconetti plays an illiterate nineteen-year-old girl who is pitted against a committee of stern male theologians and lawyers. Her vulnerability before her accusers arouses empathy as it forces upon the viewers issues of power and gender, and ultimately of what it means to be human. Though her fate seems sealed from the beginning, having heard God's inner voice, Joan proves the match of officialdom, even through her martyrdom. As the movie title suggests, it is Joan's passion that is the film's center, and she remains true to herself.

In framing the movie, there is little shown of the wider landscape. Repeatedly, the camera moves from close-up to close-up, first to Joan's face and then to the judges. The contrast between innocence and craftiness, sincerity and hypocrisy is riveting. Sometimes we are almost too close to the characters for comfort. The chief inquisitor's moles and nose hair seem sinister, just as Joan's shaven head seems saintly. Joan is a sacrificial lamb. As she is led to her death at the stake, the camera moves from a flock of birds soaring away, to a priest holding a cross, to the bonfire itself, to the villagers' passive faces and, of course, to Joan herself. We as viewers are given the choice of how we will respond to Joan's martyrdom—as the evil establishment, the uncommitted townspeople or perhaps in terms of the symbol of the soaring birds. The closing images are left open-ended, an invitation to further reflection.

Screenwriter and director Paul Schrader begins his study of the transcendental style of three filmmakers (including Dreyer) by using as an epigraph a quote from Gerardus van der Leeuw: "Religion and art are parallel lines which intersect only at infinity, and meet in God."[15] Schrader would have us understand that film has its own integrity as it probes life in its fullness. It is not a replacement for religion and cannot be conflated with it. But because art (in this case film) images forth life, its parallels with religion invite reflection and dialogue.

Martin Scorsese, who has used Schrader as his screenwriter in such movies as *Taxi Driver* (1976) and *The Last Temptation of Christ* (1988), has a complementary perspective as he reflects on his experience as a film director vis-à-vis the church. He comments that when he was younger, he wanted to be a priest. However, he says, "I soon realized that my real vocation, my real calling, was the movies." But rather than portraying these as in conflict, Scorsese goes on to remark much like Schrader on the formal and material similarities between these two callings.

> I don't really see a conflict between the church and the movies, the sacred and the profane. Obviously, there are major differences. But I can also see great similarities between a church and a movie-house. Both are places for people to come together and share a common experience. . . . And I believe there's a spirituality in films, even if it's not one which can supplant faith. . . . It's as if movies answer an ancient quest for the common unconscious.[16]

In their concreteness, movies nevertheless have the capacity to grasp something general, something universal, about life and to portray that convincingly to their viewers. Movies might not portray reality in a superficial sense, but they have the capacity to reveal life at a more central region—to show us our deepest selves. In his Nobel speech, Solzhenitsyn recognized that

> Not everything can be named. Some things draw us beyond words. Art can warm even a chilled and sunless soul to an exalted spiritual experience. Through art we occasionally receive—indistinctly, briefly—revelations the likes of which cannot be achieved by rational thought.
>
> It is like that small mirror of legend: you look into it but instead of yourself you glimpse for a moment the Inaccessible, a realm forever beyond reach. And your soul begins to ache.[17]

For some this transcendent experience will be a glimpse of what it is to be truly human, even in our fractured and fallen world. I sometimes tell my students that it is seeing Humpty-Dumpty put back together again, if only for a moment, that is revelatory. For others it will be an encounter with the holy, with that which lies outside the human but which nevertheless invests the human with meaning and dignity. But whether a this-worldly or otherworldly transcendence, this experience through film awakens us to life.

Film as Communicative

It is popular today to define art almost solely in terms of the artist's self-expression and to minimize the communicative aspects of art, as if the artistic act had no intended audience. But while this might seem a plausible, if limited, explanation for a poet such as Emily Dickinson who wrote much of her poetry in private (though it flies in the face of centuries of art criticism), such solipsism is surely foreign to Hollywood.

While a poem can remain unread, a movie, like drama, is a performance piece. A movie is not simply for itself. Moviemakers are seeking to make contact with others through their work. Movies thus help us to learn from the experiences and imaginative insight of others. In the words of the early filmmaker D. W. Griffith, "The task I'm trying to achieve is above all to make you see."[18]

Film has a power to grip the viewer's emotion, even while it engages the mind. It is not only an appearance—that is, *something* to be seen, but also an experience—something to be *seen*. Movies are not just "discursive," providing information to be digested, but also "presentational," says James Wall.[19] We do not just focus voyeuristically on the material before us in an audiovisual sense, allowing the movie perhaps to show us a slice of life or inform us about a "truth." We also focus on the vision of the movie and become vicariously engaged with it (or not) depending on whether we as its viewer can relate the film's understanding of life to/with our own. A film dealing only discursively with the sex act, for example, might be used clinically (or perhaps pornographically). But there is a detachment in the viewer. We are seeing something happening out there. A similar action, however, when presented in an engaging narrative, captures our imagination by illuminating the film's vision, drawing us into the event, even if it is a perspective we do not share. It is not enough for a movie to illustrate; it must also involve.

The filmmaker seeks to make contact with the audience through a complex art form that includes both images and words, both sight and sound. Critics have at times debated this point. Wanting rightly to understand movies as primarily about images—as visual—and reacting against interpreted, second-order experience that has sought to dismiss imagistic thinking as less profound than abstract thought, some have swung the pendulum too far. They have wanted to reduce film solely to its images. With the internationalization of movies and the difficulty of adequate translation of text, the minimization of dialogue has also been encouraged by some studios for economic reasons. But movies are interpreted act that includes not only editing, camera angle, and the like, but words.

Having said this, movies, like all art—even literature—is about images. Art is not simply imitation, but the creation of images, the incarnation of creative insight and/or ideas that outpace even the artist's awareness or ability to articulate. A film is not a mere copy or representation of something else, certainly not of an idea. It is something new. In the process of its creation, something will be re-presented, but that is not what makes it a good film. As Dorothy Sayers wrote concerning Aeschylus's play *Agamemnon*, its images present "something bigger and more real than itself. It is bigger and more real than the real-life action it represents. . . . When it is shown to us like this, by a great poet, it is as though we went behind the triviality of the actual event to the cosmic significance behind it. . . . [H]is art was that point of truth in him which was true to the eternal truth, and only to be interpreted in terms of eternal truth."[20] So, too, for the moviemaker.

But more needs to be said about images. It is not enough to compare film to literature, or even drama. For while both literature and film are narrative arts, they portray their stories through different means. A drama, for example, can be heard on tape with little of the meaning lost. Not so a movie. Literature uses words to penetrate beneath surface phenomena and to connect the reader with a larger reality—a law to be learned or an essence to be understood. Movies use images.

As we enter the twenty-first century, we are at the beginning of what many think will be a communication revolution. Just as in earlier centuries we made the transition from an oral to a written culture, and again from a writing to a print culture, so we are now moving "from a culture dominated by the printed word to one dominated by moving images." We are just at the beginning of this shift, argues Mitchell Stephens, but a new set of intellectual and artistic tools are being forged. Moving images use our senses more effectively—there is more to see and hear:

> Moving images can cut in, cut away, dance around, superimpose, switch tone or otherwise change perspective, without losing their audience's attention; they can encompass computerized graphics, even words. Seeing, consequently, can become a more complex activity; we might see from more perspectives. For when video is cut fast, it allows the interchanging and juxtaposition not just of actions within a scene, not just of angles upon a scene, but of entire scenes themselves—dozens of them. Printed words risk their believability and entertainment value when they attempt such maneuvers.[21]

Moving images can help us gain a new slant on the world. They can capture the chaos and ambiguity of life; they can step back and cut in as never before.

In showing you what an unaided eye would not see, movies use a variety of artistic media to communicate with their public—music, words, dance, drama, pictures, architecture, and more. In his discussion of *The Passion of Joan of Arc* (1928), for example, Paul Schrader refers to the architectural setting as adding to the horror of Joan's situation:

> The receding arches, each with its separate shadow, give the corridors an emotional weight of their own, and as Joan moves unwillingly through them she acquires that

weight. The architecture of Joan's world literally conspires against her; like the faces of her inquisitors, the halls, doorways, furniture are on the offensive, striking, swooping at her with oblique angles, attacking her with hard-edged chunks of black and white.[22]

Architecture has largely replaced landscape as background for the film, and this environment adds to the sense of foreboding. And lest we miss its meaning, Dreyer often lets the camera remain focused on a space even after the action has passed. When, for example, Joan walks through a door and it closes behind her, the camera remains focused on the door. And the doom increases.

What Schrader observes with architecture is equally true of music in other movies. The right music can guide viewers to perceive a situation in ways they otherwise would not be able. It can provide comic relief, create tension or a sense of resolution, interpret dialogue, or foreshadow a scene. When studio musicians for Warner Brothers were kept on after the advent of "talkies," they suggested that they play music to interpret the dialogue and action on the screen. The idea was greeted lukewarmly, some believing it would be intrusive. But given their contracts, the musicians had to be used in some way, and so the revolution began. Think of the difference music makes. *Schindler's List* (1993) would not be the same movie without Itzhak Perlman's violin solos. *Life Is Beautiful* (1998) is able to portray the fragility and wonder of life and love through its haunting score. The music, in both cases, enhances the narrative of the story, communicating a sense of its meaning.

Sometimes music can be so central that it actually dictates the structure and shape of the plot. Martin Scorsese's *Kundun* (1997), a film about the Dalai Lama, uses a score by Philip Glass. The music is not narrative in shape with conflict and resolution, that is, with the structural logic of the West. Rather, the music is repetitious and has continuous flow and development. In the words of music critic Mark Swed, "It is expansive, ongoing. It doesn't cadence, because, not going anywhere, it doesn't need to. It is more like the mandala itself, patterned and cyclical, infinite. We feel, as we listen to it, that it could simply go on and on, the way the universe does."[23] Scorsese takes this electronic music and actually builds his film around it. Just as with the music, the movie lacks a clear narrative with a beginning and ending. The movie was, in fact, criticized for ending so abruptly, but that is to miss its intention. The film and its music, like the message of the Dalai Lama himself, is more attuned to the cadences of nature's ongoingness than to the need for a sense of an ending.[24] It is Eastern, not Western, in its perspective.

Film is a complex art form capable of producing an all-encompassing environment. It has a unique ability to interpret this total experience, for it can include in its form a variety of artistic expressions, expressing itself comprehensively through the use of sounds and shapes, words and images.

Film as Art and Theology

The theological implications of drama, architecture, music, literature, and painting have long been recognized. Michelangelo's *David* is inspired art. Theater had its origins in religious ceremony and still has the power to make the spirit soar. Gorecki's Symphony no. 3 was composed in 1976 for a performance at St. Magnus Church near Auschwitz. Its haunting laments carry the listener beyond sorrow into an experience of hope. We have little trouble making such connections. Such is the nature of art. But few believe the filmmaker to be a sacrament maker of the same caliber. In this book, I am arguing otherwise. Film has unique possibilities for conveying theological truth.

Andrew Greeley argues that God's self-disclosure happens through objects, events and people. There is, he suggests, a "sacramentality of ordinary folk, their hopes, their fears, their loves, their aspirations."[25] This is what movies can capture and create. In the experiences, images, and stories of life, God can be heard. In his typical sarcastic style, Greeley says it is perhaps asking too much to expect the church's hierarchy to "be as sensitive to sacramentality in films as the laity." He mentions six films—*Places in the Heart* (1984), *The Purple Rose of Cairo* (1985), *A Sunday in the Country* (1984), *Ladyhawke* (1985), *The Breakfast Club* (1985), and *The Gods Must Be Crazy* (1980)—as movies he has recently seen that provided "hints that are obvious and even easy to comprehend of the Being who lurks in beings." He continues, "If the rich sacramental power of films that are currently being made is not being disclosed reflectively and explicitly to the Sunday congregations, the reason is that those who preach to those congregations have not themselves been sensitized to the enormous sacramental power of film."[26]

If theology is boring to many (and that seems hardly controvertible), if one of the church's primary tasks is to somehow reconnect the church and contemporary life (one thinks of Schleiermacher's *On Religion: Speeches to Its Cultured Despisers*), if theology is wrongly absent from too much of public discourse—then movies might provide a means of reconnection.

6

in film, story reigns supreme

Our modern art form is the movie. Like all art, it is rooted in dialogue. Movies address a public and invite a response. They do so, in large part, because the nature of film is story. Storytellers are always aware of their audience, and film-makers are no different. Moviegoers are also aware that they are seeing a story, and they respond accordingly; they actively engage the film at many levels, some of which they are scarcely aware. We have been watching movies and television for so long that our brain takes in and translates the visual and auditory stimuli as easily as the air we breathe. We respond naturally to spatial, vocal, musical, and photographic codes, or "languages." But as Louis Giannetti states, "[I]n the American cinema especially, the story reigns supreme. All the other language systems are subordinated to the plot, the structural spine of virtually all American fiction films, and most foreign movies as well."[1] Both the filmmaker and the filmviewer are in the storytelling business.

At its best, Hollywood tells memorable stories, for that is what this art medium is set up to do. We go to movies to see stories. We go to experience compelling plots and interesting settings and to respond to memorable characters and themes. We also go to find ourselves in the stories. As Frederick Buechner has written, "My assumption is that the story of any one of us is in some measure the story of us all. . . . I suppose, it is like looking through someone else's photograph album. What holds you, if nothing else, is the possibility that somewhere among all those shots of people you never knew and places you never saw, you may come across something or someone you recognize."[2] To be sure, Hollywood has its own unique style of storytelling—framing, editing, sound, photography, light, and the like. Its character development is largely through action, for movies find it difficult to probe the inner workings of the mind in the same way a novel can. And a movie's plot has a typical shape to it, as we will discuss below. But story

99

is story. Film stories can be told with grandeur, as with James Cameron's epic *Titanic* (1997). Or they can be more intimate, as in the Japanese film *Shall We Dance?* (1996). They can be fast paced, as in *The Fugitive* (1993), or move at a slower speed, as with *Ulee's Gold* (1997), starring Peter Fonda. But basic to all else, both for the creator and the viewer, is the story.

Film's Story

Garrison Keillor once remarked: "If you can't go to church and, for at least a moment, be given transcendence; if you can't go to church and pass briefly from this life into the next; then I can't see why anyone should go. Just a brief moment of transcendence causes you to come out of church a changed person."[3] Commenting on this observation, Ken Gire writes, "I have experienced what Garrison Keillor described more in movie theaters than I have in churches. Why? I can't say for sure. . . . movies don't always tell the truth, don't always enlighten, don't always inspire. What they do on a fairly consistent basis is give you an experience of transcendence. They let you lose yourself in somebody else's story."[4] What many churches have forgotten and preachers ignore, the movie theater recognizes: "story reigns supreme."

There are multiple ways to consider film's story. Some commentators concentrate on its plot, recognizing the importance of pace, and note that particularly in the American context, things must keep happening—the plot must keep moving along. This is as true for Disney's *Tarzan* (1999) as for *Run Lola Run* (1998), a Sundance Film Festival winner that provides three possible endings to the story of a young woman who has twenty minutes to get her hands on one hundred thousand deutsche marks in order to save her boyfriend's life. The pace is frenetic as Lola literally runs through the streets racing the clock. But just as interesting is the way the filmmakers have shortened the story as they tell the second and third alternate endings so as to keep the plot lively and engaging.

A film story's style might be realistic, so that the storyteller is almost invisible as the plot unfolds. It can be classical in its structure, combining both "showing" and "telling" as editing shapes the action so that the viewer can be brought forward to the intended resolution of the story. Or again, the story can be formalistic, the filmmakers telling their story by overtly restructuring the plot or emphasizing events in order better to present a theme. Stories can be told in a variety of ways. Here is part of their interest.

Movies are criticized by some today for neglecting story for action. In too many current Hollywood movies, the plot is thought to be both confused and confusing. The story for *Independence Day* (1996) was written in one month, and it shows. Benjamin Svetkey, in a popular article in *Entertainment Weekly*, castigates *Mission: Impossible* (1996), the Tom Cruise blockbuster, for "such a tangled mess of mixed-up plot points you'd need a machete and pith helmet to hack your way to the third act."[5] Though it was rewritten by various screenwriters (and that might be part of the problem), the plot still remains incoherent. Moviegoers flocked to see the film (it grossed close to $200 million), but it was for the action and the star, not the story line. Svetkey acerbically comments: "The fact is, pretty much *all* of the big commercial films being released by major studios these days have a certain written-by-chimps-locked-in-a-room-with-a-laptop quality. Story lines veer in nonsensical directions, dialogue is dim or dopey, characters have the heft of balsa wood."[6] The studios are partly to blame, he thinks, given their unwillingness to take chances with a product that costs so much. But actors and even screenwriters themselves share in the problem. Every script must have a script doctor, and stars often demand the privilege of rewriting their lines. The result is that cohesive stories become little more than a collection of choppy scenes. Of course, there are exceptions. But many critics believe that the story is under attack in Hollywood—spectacle seems to be supplanting drama based in storytelling.

Or is it? Sure, there are action movies that demand little of the viewer. There are also romances and dime-store mysteries, but these do not negate the power of fiction. Recall the story of a recent movie you have seen. When you discuss movies with friends over coffee, along with the actors and perhaps the special effects, is not the story with its plot and characters, its situation and point of view, a focus of your conversation? Each year in Hollywood, scores of good stories are produced. My wife, Catherine Barsotti, and I write film reviews for *The Covenant Companion*, a periodical of the Evangelical Covenant Church. Here are two of our reviews, one of a children's fable and the other of an adult drama.[7] Both are typical Hollywood fare. And for both, story is central—central for the filmmakers and for their audience. There is no other way to discuss the films adequately.

Two Examples

Fly Away Home (1996)

C. S. Lewis, in writing about children's stories, commented that any story worth reading as a child should be worth rereading as an adult. The same is true of film. Unfortunately, anyone with children knows that such a standard is rarely realized. Now out on video, *Fly Away Home* is one of those wonderful exceptions—a children's movie the whole family will enjoy.

Fly Away Home is "about" parenting. Amy, a thirteen-year-old New Zealander played by Oscar winner Anna Paquin, loses her mother in a car crash as the film opens (the scene is not gruesome) and must go to live with her father on a small farm in Ontario. Thomas Alden, an eccentric artist and inventor who creates strange metal sculptures and constantly tinkers with the latest glider or ultralight plane, largely ignores his daughter out of guilt for the divorce and because of his preoccupation as an artist. For her part, Amy disengages from life at her new home out of pain and confusion. Does he care? Can I trust him?

Amy's isolation and her father's bewilderment begin to change only when Amy finds sixteen goose eggs, their mother a victim of a land developer's bulldozer. Amy rescues the eggs and helps them hatch in a drawer of her mother's old scarves. These goslings literally become her new family. The chicks begin to follow Amy, now their mother, anywhere and everywhere. As the new family develops, so too a bond begins to form between father and daughter. We follow them as they first teach the young geese to fly and then to migrate south for the winter, their only hope of survival. The unwavering trust of the geese in Amy becomes mirrored in the growing trust between Amy and Thomas. Father and daughter soar in their ultralight planes with the geese in formation behind their "mother." And the movie soars, too. Even a contrived deadline set by evil real-estate developers in North Carolina cannot derail the movie. The message of "garden over machine" is too simplistic for real life, but in this fable, it works. You will cheer for Amy and her geese.

The movie is based very loosely on the experiments of Bill Lishman. During the mid-eighties, he showed that newly hatched geese identified with humans and followed them in flight as they guided the geese southward using small planes. But this film is not meant to be a biography; it is a fable to inspire. Stunningly photographed by Caleb Deschanel and lyrically directed by Carroll Ballard, *Fly Away Home* was made by the same team who created the children's classic *The Black Stallion* (1979).

There are some magical moments, as when Amy and a newly hatched gosling just look each other in the eye, or when Amy and her father emerge from the fog to find themselves among the skyscrapers of Baltimore. But equally awe-inspiring is the growth of a new love between father and daughter. When Amy asks her dad why he never came to see her, Thomas answers, "New Zealand's really far away." To which Amy replies, "That's a really lame excuse, Dad." And Thomas is able finally to say, "I was afraid, Amy. Angry. I'm really sorry." Not only have the geese found their way to a new home in North Carolina, but Amy and Thomas have come home too.

There are several themes in this film worth discussing with family or friends: the sanctity of life, all life; the rewards of perseverance; the wonder of human inventiveness; and the importance of keeping promises. But first and foremost, the film portrays the rebirth of a family—families can have second chances, too.

Cinque (Djimon Hounsou) cries out in the courtroom, "Give us free!" *Amistad* (d. Spielberg, 1997). Photo by Andrew Cooper. ©1997 DreamWorks LLC. All rights reserved.

Amistad (1997)

Steven Spielberg is known for such blockbuster movies as *E.T.* (1982) and *Jurassic Park* (1993). He has been most honored, however, for *Schindler's List* (1993), his retelling of the story of one man's resistance to the Holocaust. Now with *Amistad*, Spielberg has again dramatized an historical event of resistance to corporate evil. The film has such symbolic importance for another minority group—African-Americans—that some have questioned Spielberg's right to tell their story. After all, isn't he Jewish? But tell it he does, and the film has moral implications for us all.

The movie dramatizes the story of a group of Africans who rise up against their slave-trading captors and are, as a result, brought to trial in a New England court. But that is only one of the stories that this film tells so well. There is the story of slavery, the story of an African named Cinque, the story of Christian abolitionists, the story of two presidents and their own struggles with a nation divided, and even the gospel story. The importance of the historical event may have been the initial reason the movie was made, but the interplay of its various stories is the reason you should see it.

Let's take one story at a time. In 1839, fifty-three Africans threw off their chains on board the Spanish slave ship *Amistad*, killed most of the crew, and tried forcing two of the survivors to sail them home to Africa. Eventually captured by the U.S. Navy because their guides had instead sailed them along America's eastern seaboard, the Africans and their charismatic leader, Cinque, were forced to go through a series of complicated legal proceedings as their fate became a focal point for the antislavery movement. Former President John Quincy Adams ultimately pleaded the case for their freedom before the U.S. Supreme Court. Yes, Spielberg has certainly brought the skill (and glitz!) of Hollywood to this historical recreation, and critics may argue minor detail (Morgan Freeman's abolitionist character is fictitious; Adams's speech is not the original words). But the power of this story to name our national sin is evident to all who have eyes to see.

While this story based on history shows the inhumanity of humankind (as the Africans are treated as mere property) and the degradation of slavery for both slave and slave owner, it is only when the human story of Cinque unfolds that the movie becomes compelling. John Quincy Adams, when pressed by the black abolitionist to take the case, asks, "But what is their story, Mr. Joadson?" Though the trial is at one level about laws and property, it is in reality about people—Africans who have suffered unjustly. Their story needs telling. The abolitionist and the young lawyer defending the Africans press Cinque to tell his story. And tell it he does. We see Cinque's family in Africa. We see his kidnapping and sale into slavery. We see the horrifying voyage to Cuba and the atrocities inflicted on the prisoners (note: the violence is too graphic for young children). We see the dignity, intellect, passion, and grief of a fellow human being. And then we weep for the shame of slavery; our shame and our country's shame. The power of this human story is the power to convict and to call out for repentance.

Yet a third story is present in the movie—the *gospel* story. Some reviewers have questioned this insertion, but the Christian presence in opposing slavery is historically accurate. We see the Christian abolitionists being portrayed at times humorously, at other times cynically, at still other times kindly. And never has film recorded a more beautiful telling of the gospel story than when one of the Africans tells the story to Cinque using only the illustrations from the Bible an abolitionist had given him. From the slave of Egypt crying out to the God of salvation, to the baby Jesus' birth, to his teaching and healing, to the cross and then the resurrection, we hear the good news in all its simplicity and power. Although the African storyteller is fearful that they will be killed, he can point to Christ rising into the heavens and believe that "where we'll go if we die doesn't look so bad." The power of the story brings hope and freedom.

Like *Schindler's List, Amistad* does not simply portray the dehumanization caused by racial bigotry; it also reveals human goodness even within evil systems, hope within horror. How is such hope possible? Partly, it rises up from out of the indomitable human spirit. At his trial, Cinque cries out for us all, "Give us free!" But Spielberg hints at something more. There is also God's Spirit at work in and through us.

These two examples of the centrality of story are not the exception in film, but the rule. We go to movies to see such stories. And even when a movie has a confused or confusing story, that too is noteworthy. We complain about its incoherence or lack of plausibility to our friends, just as Benjamin Svetkey did in his critique of *Mission: Impossible* (1996). The heart of film is story.

Film's Three-Part Structure

Every story, regardless of the medium, will have a beginning, middle, and end. ("Once upon a time. . . . And they lived happily ever after.") This is equally true for a movie. Screenwriters often speak of a movie script's three-part structure. In the words of screenwriter Craig Detweiler, a movie shows (1) someone climbing up a tree; (2) then being shot at; and finally (3) climbing down a hero. That is, a need or a desire must first be established for the hero or heroine. (The storyteller must get them "up the tree.") After the possibility of achieving what they want briefly appears, opposition arises and a test or battle ensues. This struggle is not only external, but also internal in the life of the hero or heroine. (That is, "shots are fired.") Finally, after all seems lost, the hero or heroine does something new and things turn around, the heroic act bringing self-revelation or new equilibrium. (The character "climbs down a hero.") Or, in the anti-heroic movie, the leading character fails to act and there is no redemption.

Paul Woolf, who teaches screenwriting at the University of Southern California's Cinema-TV School, explains how he discusses this pattern in the classroom:

> So I say to my students, take my word that this pattern exists. If you look, you'll find it. Why do you think it exists? Because some screenplay writer invented it? Is it a formula? Finally, someone in my class thinks about it, and says, "It's there . . . because it is life." Movies are life. That's why we go. We're hoping the characters will do *teshuvah* [i.e., come back to something you once were, return to God, journey homewards] because we want to know it is possible.[8]

Typically, the first and third acts of a movie are twenty-five to thirty minutes in length. Their transitions are signaled by an event that changes the course of the action. The middle act is approximately an hour in length. There are, of course, exceptions to this pattern, for it is not a rote formula. Robert Altman's *Nashville* (1975) and *Short Cuts* (1993) and Paul Thomas Anderson's *Magnolia* (1999) are good examples of an alternate pattern that is more like beads strung on a necklace. Some recent films are also purposely adopting a nonlinear storytelling approach, juggling time in the hopes of keeping their audiences involved. In the hands of a master filmmaker this works, as with Quentin Tarantino in *Pulp Fiction* (1994). But in the hands of less competent directors, such techniques are mere gimmickry. Moreover, these exceptions only reinforce the existence of the norm by their rarity. And we notice their differences easily, because we are used to the pattern.

Story's General Characteristics

Such descriptions of a movie's script, while central to screenwriting and standard for the movie industry, do not exhaust the way we can speak about film's stories. As with storytelling in general, film stories have certain characteristics that help convey their meaning and significance. Wesley Kort, a professor of religion and literature at Duke University, argues that the power and meaning of a story (as well as its relationship to religion) can best be understood by analyzing the story in terms of its constitutive parts: character, plot, atmosphere, and tone (what I will call "point of view").[9] Some stories are more like parables and others like myths, but all share certain structural properties. Moreover, in any given telling of a story, one or another of these four aspects of the narrative will be emphasized, or given precedence. It is by reflecting on a story's makeup that the audience can find a key to the heart of the story.

Stories that emphasize character portray issues of human need or potential. They deal with the question of human nature by offering paradigms of possibility. What is it to be human? Here, in a given film, is portrayed one option. In the movie *Shine* (1996), for example, we are told the story of an obscure Australian pianist who suffers a breakdown while trying to capture through his fingers the emotion of Rachmaninoff's Piano Concerto no. 3. *Shine* portrays the struggle of David Helfgott's fragile life, but it does more. Despite obstacles, Helfgott is finally able, through the compassion offered by another, to again sound forth glorious melodies, and viewers everywhere have found their spirits quickened by his example. The film's story has the power to inspire as it portrays the triumph of the human spirit against overwhelming adversity. *Shine* gives its viewers hope concerning the possibilities for their own—perhaps less-fractured, but nevertheless fragmented—lives. It matters not that Helfgott is not quite in real life the virtuoso pianist the movie claims. In fact, audiences flocked to sell-out concerts by the real-life Helfgott once the movie came out in 1997, despite music critics panning the music in advance. As one concertgoer said at a concert in Pasadena, "I love the music; I love the story; he's a fascinating man." The ascending order of her comments is significant. It is not so much the music as the story that attracts, and the story is compelling for it is about a fascinating character.

There are also movie stories that are plot-driven. The playwright Lillian Hellman has described the difference between plot and story in this way: "Story is what the characters want to do and plot is what the writer wants the characters to do."[10] Plot is the way the movie constructs and conveys the unfolding of action over time. Movies that portray how our existence in time might be thought significant, how our lives reveal patterns that can take on meaningful shape, have plot as their center. Do you remember the movie *Sister Act* (1992)? It tells the story of Deloris, a Nevada lounge singer whose life is threatened by mobsters and who must hide out as a "penguin" in a convent attached to a dying urban church. Assigned to direct the off-key and unsuspecting choir, she leads her sisters in a new type of sacred music. Their Sunday choral pieces now include "My God" ("My Guy") and "I Will Follow Him."

Sister Mary Clarence (Deloris) does more than lead the choir, however. She also leads her colleagues out into the neighborhood to a biker's bar, to painting projects and car repair in the neighborhood, to jumping rope and dancing with the youth. There is opposition from the establishment of course, but the result is the revival of a dead church, which is packed to overflowing once again. Even the pope comes to celebrate the renewal of this parish! This is not a complicated plot, but church leaders can nonetheless learn from this movie. Vital worship and ministry in the neighborhood are basic ingredients for the renewal of any church. Here from the antics of Whoopi Goldberg and her colleagues we learn good theology, a pattern for the life of the church in other times and places.

Third, movies can find their center of power and meaning in the story's atmosphere, the unalterable given(s) against which the story is told and the characters developed. Atmosphere is more than just the prevailing mood, or emotional element, of a story. It is the unchanging backdrop against which the story is played out. *Jurassic Park* (1993) is not just a dinosaur movie, but a story about the existence of lost worlds. In the movie *The Wizard of Oz* (1939), as in *E.T.* (1982), the story is shaped around the notion of "homecoming." In both movies, we are not simply dealing with interesting characters on the road. Without that yearning to come home that all of us experience, the story in both these movies is simply another story.

There is a basic given that characterizes an atmosphere's presence. It is that which is beyond the story's ability to control. In *Schindler's List* (1993), for example, the story is dominated by the specter of anti-Semitism. Its presence is not up for debate—only how characters will respond, given its ghastly reality. We see the commandant force a young Jewish woman into sexual slavery. We see Jews stripped naked and, heads shaved, being led to the "showers." We see fear in the eyes of Jewish people as they are herded into railcars. As Oskar Schindler comes to care for his Jewish workers over the course of the film, we witness his growth as a human being. But what is going on is bigger than just Schindler. What is at stake is the very sanctity of human life itself. When his workers give him a gold ring made from the fillings of their teeth on which is engraved "Whoever saves one life, saves the world in time," we sense that Schindler's resistance to Nazi anti-Semitism has larger meaning than even he knows. And to emphasize this fact, the movie ends with streams of people, some actors in the movie and some the Jews Schindler rescued, together with their descendants, walking by his grave. Anti-Semitism will not have the final word. Humankind's very survival depends on our resistance to such tyranny. We must oppose the given of this film.

Lastly, stories are told with a certain point of view, the implied narrator's attitude toward the story's subject and audience. Achieved at times by voice-overs or by monologues, it can also be conveyed through the movie's language—its editing, photography, composition, music, pace, and lighting (we will discuss the formal aspects of movie's tone below). A movie's point of view is the way a story is given value. There is a narrator to each story, even if his or her presence is only implied or submerged in the storytelling process itself.

With movies, the concept of a coherent point of view is complicated because most movie stories are often created not by a single storyteller but by multiple scriptwriters. Producers, directors, stars, editors—all have their influence on the final product. But if we deal with film as story, then we can locate a storyteller's perspective within the movie itself. Its creation and creators have relevance. But there is also an author's point of view inherent in the movie itself, and at times this can be the dominant means of conveying a story's power and meaning.

In Woody Allen's movies, point of view is often central. *Broadway Danny Rose* (1984), for example, tells the story of Danny Rose, another of Allen's perennial losers. Danny, played by Allen himself, is a down-on-his-luck Broadway talent agent, who invariably loses any acts worth having just when they start to make it big. His clients include a one-legged tap dancer, a skating penguin, and a blind xylophone player, as well as Lou Canova, a washed-up lounge singer with a drinking problem and a wandering eye. It is not character or plot that is most important to the story, however. What makes this story interesting is how it is narrated. A group of retired stand-up comics (playing themselves) from the 1950s and 1960s tell the story as they sit around a table at New York's Carnegie Delicatessen recalling the old days. There is thus a "shaggy dog" quality to their tale, exaggerated and loosely constructed. For these real-life comics, Danny is a "*schlemiel* become saint*.*" These retired comics would make losers into winners, we suspect, if only for personal reasons. As they tell the story, fast-talking, bighearted Danny gets involved with Lou's hard-as-nails girlfriend, Tina Vitale, and eventually creates a lifestyle of "acceptance, forgiveness, and love" so that she becomes a new person. We do not know where reality leaves off and nostalgia begins, but it doesn't matter. As told by these comics, the story gives moviegoers a lesson in hope. We are to celebrate the transformational power of a generous spirit.

To talk of a movie in terms of its characters, plot, atmosphere, and point of view is of course artificial. It is to risk making abstract the film's concrete story. We don't go to a movie to see a plot or to sense an atmosphere, but to experience a story. Moreover, many movie stories are complex, with character, plot, atmosphere, and point of view all exhibiting a power. It can be artificial and self-defeating to argue over which narrative element is most important in a given movie story. While stories tend to concentrate their center of meaning and power in one or another of these narrative elements, they can also invite internal dialogue between the various components of a story as the viewer responds, for example, by playing character off atmosphere (as in *Schindler's List*), or point of view off plot (as in *Broadway Danny Rose*). Having said this, however, story assumes an audience and invites a response. Using the above critical apparatus, the movie viewer is often able to focus attention where it belongs—on the film itself—and to respond to the movie from its own center. All four of these aspects of a movie story are simply analytical constructs, but as such they can be useful as we seek to appreciate film on its own terms.

Film's Uniqueness as Story

Using a literary model for understanding *film's* story has limitations. It is easy to ignore the unique form of the movie—that is, how the *movie* story is told. For example, movie stories do not have time to explore a given idea or emotion as do novels. The plot must keep moving forward, for there is only a couple of hours to tell the tale. Thus, a story's plot has special demands placed on it by the motion picture medium. Again, audience studies suggest that it is a movie's characters who are most easily and forcefully remembered by those coming out of the theater. Yet, characterization must largely be accomplished through action, for movies do not have the means of a novel to uncover self-consciousness. The means of characterization available to the filmmaker has implications for how movie stories are shaped, and thus for any understanding of film as story.

Even more fundamental to a movie than the unique features of plot and character, however, are the formal aspects of point of view that the movie storyteller uses. For the meaning of a movie is not simply communicated by the story's explicit narrators (as in *Broadway Danny Rose*), whether present or implied. It is also imbedded in the very techniques the filmmaker uses to bring the story to the screen. Film has its own idiom. The artistic creators of a film (writers, director, cameramen, editors, producer) shape a picture every bit as much as painters or writers shape their canvas or novel.

The first movies were brief, straightforward depictions with little if any story—a train coming down the track toward the viewer, or perhaps a fistfight. Soon, however, film developed a language of its own. E. S. Porter was one of the early pioneers who discovered that by editing the film, a point of view could be given and a story told. Cameras could be moved so that there could be close-ups and long shots. In *The Great Train Robbery* (1903), Porter took his cameras offstage to film in the great outdoors and then edited the footage to contrast scenes of the robbers escaping with those of the good guys in pursuit. When D. W. Griffith filmed *The Birth of a Nation* (1915), he used a split screen and included a musical score for full orchestra that was meant to be played as an accompaniment. The movie lasted three hours, an unheard-of length in that day. The art of filmmaking was born.

Lynn Ross-Bryant has written, "One way of defining art is, of course, just this: it is a process of selection and interpretation that gives a work of art a coherence and completeness not found in life."[11] Filmmakers shape their works through a number of means. But in particular, it is helpful to be aware of the role that editing (montage), framing (*mise-en-scene*), and sound and special effects can have on how a story is heard and understood. A technical study of the language of film is beyond the focus of this book. But those interested in the relationship between theology and film must also be concerned with how the story is told, for technique shapes meaning by providing a point of view.

Editing

Jon Boorstin tells of a famous experiment by Lev Kuleshov, an early Russian filmmaker who showed on the screen an actor with an expressive but neutral look. He repeatedly used the same footage of him, but placed him in different situations so as to trigger different emotions in the audience. Spliced between identical images of Mosjukine, the well-known actor, were scenes of a crying baby, a coffin, and even a bowl of soup. Not knowing that the shots of Mosjukine were identical footage, the audience praised the actor for his performance, noting how well he displayed a father's love, a man who was hungry, and again a person in mourning! What had happened was that through editing, the same expressive face had taken on appropriate connotations to match the context. Members of the audience read into the actor's face what they would have felt if they had been in his place.[12]

Sergei Eisenstein, another famous Russian filmmaker, called such juxtaposition of film images "montage." He wrote that "two film pieces of any kind, placed together, inevitably combine into a new concept, a new quality, arising out of that juxtaposition."[13] Europeans still call this process "montage," the art of constructing, or putting together, a sequence. Americans call the same process "editing," the art of cutting. But whether we speak of removing images or building up images, the goal is the same, the construction of narrative meaning in a movie.

There are few better examples of the power of editing than the shower scene in Alfred Hitchcock's *Psycho* (1960). Although we never see the knife cut Janet Leigh's flesh, the seventy separate pictures that are spliced together in less than a minute tell the story as slashing knife and screaming face are juxtaposed to create a sense of fear in us. (The repeated screech of violins adds to the sense of horror, as well.) Or again, in Francis Ford Coppola's *The Godfather* (1972), a film that uses the Mafia as a metaphor for America itself, the church is portrayed as oblivious to the seared consciences of the Corleones. As the film ends, we see a high church baptism going on with all its pomp and formality. Then Michael Corleone is asked by the priest on behalf of his godson, "Do you renounce Satan?" And Michael responds strongly, "I do renounce him," just as the movie cuts to show the first of a number of gangland executions, brutal and effective in establishing Corleone as the new Godfather. (One victim is caught inside a revolving door that is jammed; another in a barbershop as he is being shaved; still another as he is being massaged in a steam room.) The baptism is notable for its ritual formality; the slayings, for their gruesome reality. The killings are all the more shocking because of the constant splicing. In between these murders, we watch the priest repeatedly ask Michael the baptismal questions: "And all his works?" "I do renounce them." "And all his pomps?" "I do renounce them." The hypocrisy of the scene—the immorality of Michael's orchestrated violence juxtaposed with the impotent ritual of the church—leaves viewers speechless as they exit the theater.

Framing

Editing is one means of giving the story coherence and perspective. So too is framing. If editing, or montage, has to do with modifying the sequence, or time, of the story, then framing, or *mise-en-scene* (literally, "the world within the frame"), has to do with how the filmmakers shape, or modify, the space. Are the scenes shot on location, or on a sound stage? How does the camera isolate and frame? Does the camera show us a scene so that we remain objective viewers from afar, or do we see the world of the film through the eyes of a character in the film? Horror films, for example, often take this latter approach. Those interested in the image of woman in contemporary movies have often noted that a film's story is usually shown in terms of the male gaze. That is, a young-adult, male viewer is projected as the typical moviegoer, and the story is purposely told and shot in terms of what he would choose to see.[14] Proximity and proportion, lighting, color and black-and-white, texture, open framing (where the viewer is subliminally aware of the area outside the frame) and closed frames, close-ups and moving cameras, slow motion and freeze frames—the tool box available to the modern filmmaker is immense. Through the interplay of photography, lighting, and composition, film can make unlimited editorial comment on the story at hand by framing the scene.

To give an example, the movie *Thelma & Louise* (1991) is a fable concerning women's freedom from male oppression. The movie tells the story of two women finding their freedom as they light out for the territory in the West (a female variation of the American myth, "Go west, young man"; cf. *Huckleberry Finn*). Some viewers think this road movie to be anti-feminist, for it ends with the car driving off the edge of the Grand Canyon rather than the women submitting to the law with its male authority. But this is to misunderstand the symbolic intention of the movie. The movie is not meant as a realistic cultural depiction, but as a dreamwork, an adult fairy tale.

As is often the case in a movie, the opening credits help us determine the tone of *Thelma & Louise*. The mythic trajectory of the movie is foreshadowed during the credits as the landscape changes from black-and-white to bright color. We are going to see a story of awakenings. As the movie ends, the dream-like intention of the movie is reinforced. The car does not crash; the frame is frozen with the car flying off into the sunset. The final image is that of freedom, not disaster.[15] Moreover, to give a sense of immensity and grandeur to this tale, a deep-focused camera was used to follow the two women as they were escaping in their convertible along the highways in the Southwest. There is no "realistic" dust on their car, nor on the phallic stainless steel gasoline tanker that the women blow up. Rather, the scene has an intended surreal quality. The audience is ushered into the mythic vastness of the American frontier. The brightness of the sunlight by day and the lighting that illumines the underside of their car at night(!) only reinforce the mythical quality of the scene, as does the flood-lit brightness of the mountains even in the evening glow. The use of such techniques in the filming of *Thelma & Louise* provides interpretive clues about how to view its story. This is not a realistic story of two women escaping abusive contexts. It is instead a supra-natural fable of liberation, of two women finding themselves as they "go West."

Sound and Special Effects

The explosion of technology's capacity has increased the story-shaping possibilities of the filmmaker. Advances in special effects and in sound have made audiences flock to some movies just to see and hear the thrill. When used effectively as part of the language of the film's story, such technological wizardry increases the power and meaning of the story. George Lucas's *Star Wars* (1977) created not only a marketing revolution in Hollywood, but also an artistic one. Aljean Harmetz, writing in the *New York Times*, looked back on the impact of the film ten years later:

> The unprecedented success of a movie set in a galaxy long ago and far away turned Hollywood's attitudes toward science fiction upside down, changed the industry's definition of summer, re-established symphonic music in films, exploded the boundaries of special effects, helped unleash eight years of movies aimed at teen-agers, gave new importance to sound, created a pop mythology, and made merchandising the characters from a movie as important as the movie itself.[16]

The studios of George Lucas in northern California still represent state-of- the-art technology, and their advanced editing equipment, computer-generated special effects, and new sound systems have enhanced scores of movies and theaters. Nonetheless, it is important to hear Lucas himself reflect on his craft: "Technology enhances the tools you have available and expands your vocabulary. But they don't make a picture successful. A film is not about technique. It's about ideas."[17]

Turning from technology to consider the music itself, there are few better at the use of a score than the director Stanley Kubrick. As he struggled time and again with depictions of the emptiness of the human spirit, or with the ambiguity and contingency of life, it was music that helped interpret the surrealistic and satiric underbelly of life, despite its surface realism. One thinks of the final scene in *Dr. Strangelove* (1964) where Vera Lynn sings the original World War II recording of "We'll Meet Again"—a song originally recorded as a morale booster for the troops. But on screen, we see the mushroom cloud of the detonating hydrogen bomb. In *2001: A Space Odyssey* (1968), Kubrick uses Richard Strauss's *Thus Spoke Zarathustra* to bring home the mysteries of the universe. But he also later juxtaposed "The Battle of New Orleans."

In *A Clockwork Orange* (1971), classical music is again used for point and counterpoint, but this time it is often played on a Moog synthesizer, giving it an ethereal and even sinister quality. In the first scene the movie's violent action is organized around Rossini's score, the violence becoming almost like a dance. We also hear Beethoven's Ninth played while Nazis goosestep and Purcell's "Music for the Funeral of Queen Mary" while Alex is beaten and tortured. Handel's "Sarabande Duel" plays to highlight the actual duels on screen in *Barry Lyndon* (1975), squeezing a mythlike quality out of these otherwise realistic scenes. Similarly, at the beginning of *The Shining* (1980), the theme music has an unearthly quality. It sounds like a requiem mass, all the while the camera is soaring like a bird as it roams over mountain and water. The viewer is led to ask, Are we trapped in an endgame, or are we allowed to wander? For Kubrick, the answer is open-ended. Life is both ethereal and menacing. In his last film, *Eyes Wide Shut* (1999), Kubrick again turns to music in order to provide an interpretive language for the story. He has a single piano note pound harshly with little thought to melody, as much of the wordless action goes on. Life's menacing presence is palpable.[18]

Filmmakers craft a movie, telling a story for their viewers from a particular point of view. Meaning is conveyed through skillful editing and framing, as well as through the use of special effects and sound. While a movie might also have within the story an explicit narrator to interpret the action, these implicit "narrative" guides also direct the viewer's interpretation of the tale. When done well, when the storytelling is so seamless that viewers are unaware of editing and framing, special effects, and even the music, the movie works. If such technologies simply become a source of marvel, or a substitute for a good plot or engaging dialogue, the movie fails, and the story proves inert.

Some think that *Star Wars: Episode I—The Phantom Menace* (1999) failed because the story never engaged the viewer beyond its technology. Perhaps *Eyes Wide Shut* (1999) is similar, being more about the director Stanley Kubrick and his skill as a filmmaker, and less about the story itself. But this is less clear, as Kubrick shows one more expression of society out of control, whether through violence (*A Clockwork Orange*), technology (*2001: A Space Odyssey*), or, in this case, sexuality. When the filmmaker's craft is effectively brought into the service of the story itself, then the power and meaning of the movie is enhanced as a point of view has provided the viewer a way to receive it.

Film's Critical Circle

Story implies both a storyteller and an audience as it embodies a particular vision of reality. In the words of literary critic Northrop Frye, "There can hardly be a work of literature [a story] without some kind of relation, implied or expressed, between its creator and auditors."[19] To speak in this way is to recognize that, as with art more generally, there is in the telling of a story an impulse toward communion.[20] I use the word "communion" rather than "communication," for the latter is reductive as a word to describe the artistic process. When artists create, they are in constant dialogue, imagining an audience, even if that audience is only the artists themselves. In the words of T. S. Eliot, "The author of a work of imagination is trying to affect us [the audience] wholly, as human beings, whether he knows it or not; and we are affected by it [the work of art],

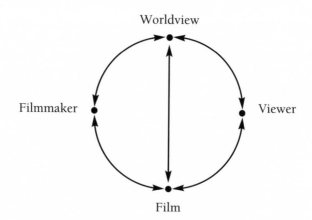

Figure 6.1 Story's Critical Circle

as human beings, whether we intend to be or not."[21] Walter Ong, borrowing the explicitly religious language of Martin Buber, speaks similarly, suggesting that a "literary work can never get itself entirely dissociated from this I-Thou situation and the personal involvement which it implies."[22]

In a movie, similarly, meaning is found not only in the story itself and its envisioning of reality, but also in the storyteller and the community of viewers. This relationship can be sketched as in figure 6.1.

An adequate critical theory of film will take into account not only (1) the movie itself, but also (2) the filmmakers lying behind and expressed through it, (3) the viewers with their own life stories that help interpret it, and (4) the larger universe, or worldview, that shapes the story's presentation.

All four of these critical moments add perspective and meaning to the artistic event. In chapter 7 we will take up the task of film criticism, looking at how "auteur" criticism (focusing on the filmmakers), genre criticism (focusing on the film's larger worldview), cultural criticism (focusing on the context of the viewers), and thematic criticism (focusing on the internal development of the film's theme) can all assist in helping the Christian viewer understand a film.

Occasionally a critic has tried to eliminate from view one of these four moments, or critical perspectives, whether for ideological or practical reasons; but there are dangers in doing this. A critic can focus on the filmmaker at the expense of the film, for example. A focus on the internal structure of the movie can produce a new aestheticism that refuses to relate film to meaning. Cultural criticism can lose the movie in a welter of sociological, political, and economic facts. And genre criticism can reduce a film to formula. What is wanted is a well-rounded approach to film; only then can communion with a story be both useful and honest to the artistic process. Let us see how each of these approaches works to affect our critical judgment of film as story.

The Filmmakers

When we view a movie, although we are removed from the filmmakers, we are still participating in dialogue. The movie is not self-contained but exists only as a conversation between artist and audience. The filmmakers present the story from their perspective; it grows out of who they are, what they've experienced, and how they perceive the world. Though this is the case, the usefulness of this observation is complex, since a film's creators are multiple, and their various influences not clearly differentiated.

There are, however, a few almost pure "auteurs" in the motion picture business who control script, direction, editing, and producing. John Sayles comes to mind, as does Federico Fellini and Woody Allen. *The Apostle* (1997), written, produced, directed, acted-in, and bankrolled by Robert Duvall, has the stamp of its creator from beginning to end. It thus portrays for its viewers something of Duvall himself, and the axiological convictions he holds. The movie brings to the screen a story of a flawed Southern Pentecostal evangelist who flees from the law, only to baptize himself "the apostle E. F.," start a new multiracial church, and in the process of ministry live into that baptism. Duvall had worked on this story for many years. Told with power and acted with aplomb, the movie garnered a 1998 Spirit Award (independent films) for Best Film, and Best Actor Award for Duvall from the Screen Actors Guild, as well as his nomination for an Oscar. But even here, the film as we see it is not totally the one Duvall envisioned. Just prior to release, the studio asked for a final cut, and thirty minutes were removed. Duvall related in an interview:

> The cuts stung me. We lost ethnic points, the religious differences. Previously, things had added up and it's so easy to mess them up. So it was a tough time for me. I had painted myself into a corner: the shorter the film the more showings you can get and the more money it would make. But some things I didn't want to lose.
>
> So I sat down and addressed sixty things I didn't like about the cuts, explaining them, and so on. Then the final version went to about two hours and fourteen minutes and it was, to my eye, like a trimming process rather than a degutting. . . . But the thing about it, which is really nice, is that people understood the film.[23]

That is, Duvall's point of view was not lost.

A movie's creation is often a corporate affair (sometimes almost literally, as the studio executives have the final say as to what should be added or deleted). A producer friend finished shooting a family movie for Disney in which the studio heads had said there should be enough action to hold the attention of teenagers. But after the writers, director, editors, and producers had finished their first cut, their studio bosses had them go back to the drawing board to tone down the movie (at the additional cost of several million dollars!). The result was so tame that reviewers generally said it was a pleasing story but lacked punch. And family box-office results were disappointing. But though, in this case, we must speak of a collective "auteur" who creates the movie we see in the theater, we still recognize the presence of a storyteller. There is a certain expectation concerning a Disney film, for instance. Executives believed that a too grown-up story would confuse the Disney storytelling persona, but the result was a movie that failed to capture the viewer's attention.

In cases where one individual (usually the director) is able to exercise sufficient control over the finished product, we can speak of a film's "auteur," even if others are involved in the process. We can bring into dialogue with the film our understanding of the director's typical film language—how he/she uses editing, framing, lights, symbols, and so on—as well as the director's informing vision and root convictions as portrayed in other of his/her movies. (We will do this in chapter 7.)

We might say that there is a moviemaker's version of a movie and a viewer's version of the same movie. That is, the meaning of a film is not found solely within the celluloid frames (though it initiates there and must find there its ultimate reference point), but also in the collective viewers' response to it. Norwood Russell Hanson provides an example that illustrates this simple point about the importance of the viewer's perspective in the interpretive process:

> Let us consider Johannes Kepler: imagine him on a hill watching the dawn. With him is Tycho Brahe. Kepler regarded the sun as fixed: it was the earth that moved. But Tycho followed Ptolemy and Aristotle in this much at least: the earth was fixed and all other celestial bodies moved around it. Do Kepler and Tycho see the same thing in the east at dawn?[24]

Given the presence of different life experiences and perspectives, moviegoers will see stories on the screen differently, just as Kepler and Tycho saw different universes. What we bring to the film experience is crucial. What Paul Woolf saw in *Spartacus* that day in downtown New York or what Catherine Sittser discovered in *Beauty and the Beast* was dependent not only on the story in these films but on what these two viewers brought with them when they watched the movies. There is a dialectic present between filmmakers' intentions and viewers' engagement, between viewers' immediate stories and the story flashed before them on the screen. And insight is achieved in the tension between these two stories.

Stories ask their audience to grant their initial premises or sets of conditions. People cannot come to the theater with a "hermeneutic of suspicion" and expect to receive from the film's story something of value. Though the created story need not seem altogether natural or inevitable, it must be judged "at least plausible and compelling to 'our deepest sense of ourselves.'"[25] Otherwise, the story simply fails its viewers.

In his introduction to the art of filmmaking, Jon Boorstin distinguishes three different ways in which an audience watches movies.[26] With each, viewers must give to the movie their "as-if" assent if the film is to work its charm successfully. Audiences watch some movies, Boorstin first notes, with a voyeur's eye, asking with their mind if what they observe is plausible. There is pleasure in simply watching a movie like *Star Wars* (1977), in looking for its own sake. Many of the Merchant and Ivory films provide similar pleasure, as did *The English Patient* (1996), with its vast panoramas and desert scenery. Second, audiences watch with a vicarious eye and are asked by the film to give their hearts over to the story. We, as viewers, do not feel our own emotions, for example, when we get involved with Jack Nicholson's character in *One Flew over the Cuckoo's Nest*

(1975), but someone else's on the screen. If we conclude that his character wouldn't have done that to Big Nurse, the film has failed. The same can be said for the movie *Titanic* (1997). We must both find Rose a believable storyteller and her story a plausible one, or the movie simply doesn't work. Do we believe her claim that her encounter with Jack was transformative?

Third, audiences see with a visceral eye. The point here is not to feel someone else's emotion, but to sense our own as a viewer. I went to see *Life Is Beautiful* (1998) a second time chiefly because I wanted to again identify with the father in the film. Roberto Benigni's character goes to extraordinary lengths to support and protect his son, even after he and his boy are arrested and put into a concentration camp because they are Jewish. The games he plays for the sake of his young son are deadly serious, and we as viewers do not know whether to laugh or cry. But what is abundantly clear is that he knew what it was to love with a father's heart. Having two daughters myself, I wanted to feel that experience again. His extravagant love knew no bounds. Here is what I wished for my relationship with my daughters as well. With some movies, we want the character to be us. Love stories, horror films, detective stories—lacking a visceral eye, they fall flat.

Three other comments are relevant here. First, movies encourage audience engagement as perhaps no other artistic expression can. The context of the presentation, the darkened theater with wraparound sound and high resolution photography, helps capture our attention. The full toolbox of storytelling technique allows filmmakers to direct our attention to the meaning of the story, as they would have us understand it. Second, the community of a quiet audience helps us respond empathetically to the movie. To see a movie on video is convenient, but it is a poor substitute for the darkened theater. I remember seeing the movie *Das Boot* (1981) in a packed theater in downtown Skokie, Illinois. The film is a sympathetic portrayal of the horror of war for young teenagers who were conscripted for submarine duty by the Germans near the end of World War II when manpower was short. The audience—98 percent Jewish, with many in attendance having been directly affected by the Holocaust—was asked by the movie to empathize with these German teenagers as their submarine was trapped beneath the ocean. The conflict in the audience between anger and pathos was palpable. I learned that evening the terrible price that forgiveness can demand. As a moviegoer, I not only experienced vicariously the story on film, but also an audience's visceral reaction to it. And it was the community's response that made the more lasting impression.

Last, with movies, a variety of "seeings" are possible, both by the individual viewer and by an audience. Not every opinion is supportable by the film's story; but multiple perspectives on a movie's story are the norm, not the exception. The pleasure of listening to Siskel and Ebert over the years as they reviewed movies on television was in part watching their disagreements. Even these best of critics often had differing perspectives. It is the universal experience of movie-goers to find others who liked a movie we didn't, and vice versa. "Did we see the same movie?" we ask. And the answer, as we know, is both yes and no.

Much is missed on a first viewing and a "re-seeing" of a movie allows for new insight and perhaps a refocusing of one's interpretive intention. The growth of video rentals and retailing has allowed viewers this luxury and has forever changed the nature of film criticism. (In 1998, Americans spent $8.1 billion on movie rentals.) Where earlier viewers were beholden to their memories and to reviews by others, now we can confirm perspective and challenge erroneous viewing by renting the film.

In *St. Paul at the Movies*, Robert Jewett discusses the film *Amadeus* (1984) and concludes that the movie is about sin.[27] There certainly is sin present for all to see, and to speak of the movie in this light is not mistaken. But a "re-seeing" might show another focus, perhaps one more primary to the filmmaker's intention. "Amadeus" means "loved by God," and Mozart is just that. It matters not a wit that Mozart is crude and childish in the film. He can write heavenly music. How odd of God to choose Mozart. Yet he does, with the result that Salieri ultimately goes mad from jealousy. For many viewers, the movie's theme is vocation, not sin.

Similarly, *The Shawshank Redemption* (1994) can be seen as a movie about hope, and there is much in the structure of the story itself to suggest such a primary reading. But other "seeings" might bring into the foreground the centrality of friendship, the importance of freedom, the fragility of humanity amid inhuman circumstance, or even the evil of the justice system. Because movies are viewer sensitive, even when the movie's own witness seems clear, the pluralistic nature of the audience means multiple interpretations will prevail.

Film's Worldview

Last, in understanding film as existing within a critical circulation between creator, work, viewer, and worldview, we need to consider the way a movie looks at the world. Any film, as a product of human creativity, contains hints of the worldview of the moviemaker. A movie story when "told" has an informing vision, or axiological perspective. There is a frame of reference imbedded in the film that invites our interpretation. In fact, no story can develop without some more-or-less coherent perception of reality, some fundamental opinion about life.

Stories offer meaning to the "facts" of life, even if they are presented as fantasy. Movie stories offer a pattern; they make a claim; they challenge or proclaim; they seek to make a difference in their viewers. In the words of Lillian Hellman, a story is given a plot.

There are surely movies made without such an informing vision. They are presented merely to showcase the latest special effects or piggyback in a formulaic manner on someone else's vision. Pornography is a particularly offensive example of a movie lacking any integrating perspective. Other movies might purposely blur their vision in the hopes of attracting a disparate audience, one with conflicting views of reality. But such movies often prove self-defeating. Without a foundation on which the story is built, the movie falls flat.

It is on first reflection incredible that we can view a story about someone or something else that takes place in a different place and time and yet say, "This is important to me." Or, "I agree." Or perhaps, "Wonderful." But such responses by the viewer are fully understandable when it is recognized that a movie is built on someone else's view of reality—on "an irreducible kernel of human nature, a particular case of a fundamental underlying problem we all struggle with in defining ourselves."[28] Part of the power of the film *Titanic* (1997) was its ability to make its worldview, its *Weltanschauung,* more explicit through the device of a "story within a story." As the movie opens we hear Rose telling her story to Brock Lovett, the undersea adventurer who had discovered the sunken vessel. And again at the end of the film, Rose finishes the narration, giving us to understand that this has been her understanding, not only of the story, but of life itself. The movie is not just a disaster film; it is a love story in which one person sacrificed his life that another might live. And the results proved transformational over a lifetime.

Just as we relate what we do and who we are by telling our own stories, and just as we seek to connect the fragments of our lives by placing them into some greater whole, so a movie provides us alternate narrations on reality. The recognition that movies have an informing vision, or worldview, embedded in the shape of their stories is a natural point of connection for any person wanting to explore the relationship between theology and film. These filmic visions need not be intentionally Christian to be significant for the Christian, only rooted in life itself. In fact, without themselves being Christian believers, filmmakers can even use the Christ story as a root metaphor concerning reality. Ken Kesey and Milos Forman do this, for example, in *One Flew over the Cuckoo's Nest* (1975). It is enough that the moviemakers find in the Christ story, or some other informing vision, a hint of the shape of the authentically human.

An example of the critical use of story to understand a movie will prove helpful at this point. How does the consideration of a movie's plot, character, atmosphere, and tone, together with an analysis of the film in terms of the artistic critical circle (the film, the filmmaker, the viewer, and the movie's worldview) aid the critic in understanding the center of power and meaning of a movie story?

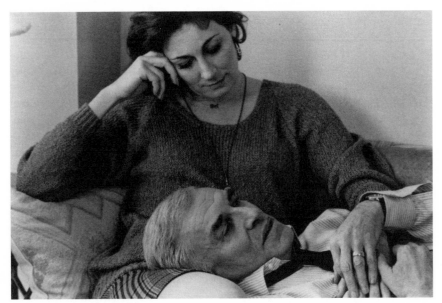

Judah (Martin Landau) tries to end his affair with Dolores (Angelica Huston), before having her killed. *Crimes and Misdemeanors* (d. Allen, 1989). Photo by Brian Hamill. ©1989 Orion Pictures Corporation. All rights reserved.

Narrative Criticism: An Example

Crimes and Misdemeanors (1989)

Woody Allen's *Crimes and Misdemeanors* interweaves two main *plots*. In the first, Cliff, played by Allen himself, is an insecure, struggling documentary film-maker whose topics include terminal diseases and natural disasters. He falls in love with an attractive producer only to lose her to his materialistic and ego-centric brother-in-law, Lester, a TV producer. In the second story, Judah, an oph-thalmologist, tries to end an affair with Dolores, but cannot; has his brother arrange for her to be killed when she threatens to expose him; is racked with guilt; but comes to realize that he has gotten away with the act and guilt fades. Allen says about the film, "There are certain movies of mine that I call 'novels on film,' and *Crimes and Misdemeanors* is one of them, wherein a number of char-acters are being dissected and a number of stories are going on at the same time."[29]

Underlying these interwoven story lines is the conviction that life is amoral, however we might want it to be otherwise. This is not portrayed as a value judg-ment; it is simply a given. Here is the movie's *atmosphere*. We might go to the movies in hope of feeling "reel" life, or we might wish that religion could offer real answers, but the reality is what Judah's brother tells him: "This is murder. You paid for it. Engineered it. It's over. Forget it!" As the movie unfolds, we see a killer go on to live a "successful" life; a lonely woman abused through a relationship started through the personal ads; a saintly rabbi go blind; a wise philosopher who speaks of love commit suicide; and the wrong man "get the girl." Ben, a rabbi friend and a patient of Judah's, says to him at one point, "Our entire adult lives, you and I have had this conversation regarding life. You see it as harsh. I see it as having a moral structure with real meaning and forgiveness and some kind of higher power or there's no basis to live." Judah responds sarcastically, "You're talking like you do to your congregation." In this movie "crimes" have no "punishment"; that would take the existence of a moral code. There are only "misdemeanors."

Like one of the movie scripts that is discussed in the film, life seems simply "made-up"—and not very well. Success often goes to the wrong people (e.g., Lester). As the philosophy professor Levy recognizes, "The universe is a pretty cold place; we invest it with our feelings." But Levy commits suicide. How then should we live? The *characters* explore various options, but they boil down to two: "reel life" and "real life." Cliff wants his niece to learn from stories and is always taking her to the movies. But he is a hopeless romantic, out of touch with life. Judah imagines a conversation with the rabbi in which he tells him, "You live in the kingdom of heaven." Ben is content as the movie ends, but he is both literally and metaphorically blind. Judah also recalls a conversation around the table when he was a boy in which his father said, "The eyes of God see all." To which Judah responds, "Do you prefer God to truth?" But even Judah wants to project some meaning onto life (to "invest it with our feelings"), so much so that his brother must chide him, "I'm not so high class that I can avoid looking at reality." One option is to live by some higher principles, but that leads in this movie to suicide (Levy), blindness (Ben), failure (Cliff) and guilt (Judah). Such "reel life" doesn't work.

A second option that the characters test is the attempt "to get away with murder," whether figuratively or in reality. Accept reality for what it is. But this is next to impossible, it seems. Cliff's brother-in-law Lester has no principles other than success, and he is a buffoon. But Lester wants a documentary made about his life that will show him as the man that he projects himself to be. Fame and fortune (and women) come easily, but the movie's point of view suggests that life must be more than crass materialism. Even Lester rejects such a view of reality. Judah also "gets away with murder," but he too is eager to create his own set of values. His choices have consequences, even as he comes to realize that there is no one to punish him for his mistakes if he doesn't punish himself. Work, family, and friends remain important. Here is his value frame.

In telling *Crimes and Misdemeanors*, Allen uses a variety of techniques to project an understanding of life, given the amorality with which it presents itself. (Here is the story's *point of view*.) He frequently juxtaposes scenes from old movies (the "reel") with the "reality" that is happening in the story. In this way, the two options—the reel and the real—are always before the viewer. Allen also uses eyes as a primary metaphor. The camera often focuses on the eyes of the characters. The movie is about people who see and those who don't. Rabbi Ben is going blind; Judah, an ophthalmologist, helps us see life clearly. Cliff tells his young niece, "Don't listen to . . . your school teacher. . . . Just see what they look like." The movie is full of others making movies about what they see. When Judah drives through the tunnel in his car and comes out into the brilliant light, he is able to again see clearly and recognize that if he does not judge himself, no one else will either. The film would have us believe that if we see life clearly, we will observe that the only meaning there is, is the meaning and values we invent. Reality has no inherent meaning.

Yet this is not all that the audience sees either, for the movie ends on a positive note. Despite life's amorality, there are "compensations—friends, family, love, art." Ben might be blind, but he is dancing with his daughter at her wedding as we again hear Levi in a voice-over. "Most human beings seem to have the ability to keep trying and even find joy from simple things like their family, their work . . . future generations." Interestingly, Allen changed his original ending to the movie after seeing the first cut. He first had a scene with Cliff and Jenny, his young niece and only real friend. Cliff is telling her that little girls are the hope of the world. Allen also toyed with juxtaposing cuts from *It's a Wonderful Life* (1946). Allen wants his viewers to feel life's ambiguity and tugs, but continue to hope. It is important that people create some meaning, even if we realize that in a larger sense these are merely fictions of consolation.

In ways such as this, the film critic who is using the elements of story—plot, atmosphere, character, and tone—might analyze this movie. But the critic can also put the movie into dialogue with Woody Allen, its auteur, with his worldview enfleshed in the film, and with the viewers' own understandings that they bring to the experience.

With more time and space, we could profitably compare and contrast *Crimes and Misdemeanors* with Allen's other films. *Hannah and Her Sisters* (1986) comes to mind. One can find similarities of theme, character, atmosphere, and tone throughout Allen's *oeuvre*, his body of films. But helpful as well is to listen to Allen's own commentary on the making of this film. Consider the following:

I think that at best the universe is indifferent. At best! Hanna Arendt spoke of the banality of evil. The universe is banal as well. And because it's banal, it's evil.[30]

My own feeling about Ben is that, on the one hand, he's blind, even before he goes blind. He's blind because he doesn't see the real world. But he's blessed and lucky because he has the single most important lucky attribute anyone could have, the best gift anyone could have. He has genuine religious faith. . . . The worst kind of adversity can be surmounted with faith. But as the author, I think Ben is blind even before he's blind, because he doesn't see what's real in the world. But he's lucky, because he has his naiveté. [31]

I grew up at a time when you go to the movies and your basic movie was Fred Astaire or Humphrey Bogart. All those wonderful larger-than-life people. This was such a glamorous time, as portrayed in films, and so great a contrast to life outside, that it was a pleasure to be in there and a monstrosity to be outside. [32]

Allen's comments both confirm and extend our analysis. Particularly interesting is his statement about the "argument of the movie" (i.e., its worldview, or *Weltanschauung*): "No higher power is going to punish us for our misdeeds if we get away with them. Knowing that you have to choose a just life or there will be chaos, and so many people don't do that that there *is* chaos."[33] Does Judah choose a just life? Perhaps. He has returned to his family and his work, but is justice satisfied with his variation of Lester's definition of comedy: tragedy + time = comedy? As Judah tells Cliff what is assumed to be a fictitious "murder story" (but which is actually the story of what has happened), he concludes, "Now he is scot-free; his life is back to normal." Cliff asks, "Yes, but can he really ever go back?" To which Judah responds, "Well, people carry sins around with them . . . but with time, it all fades."

For the religious Jewish or Christian viewer, the choice that Allen portrays between faith and truth seems to cast the issue wrongly. It need not be an either/or decision—faith or truth. Allen's is only one vantage point a viewer might adopt. There is another. As the writer of Ecclesiastes recognizes, life is amoral, death ubiquitous, and ultimate meaning a mystery. Here is the harsh truth of reality. But even though wrong oftentimes goes unpunished, it is not naive to find meaning in accepting the small joys and fragile spaces of God's gift of life. Like Allen, the writer of Ecclesiastes demolishes the easy optimism of "reel" life—whether that be wealth, fame, wisdom, or pleasure (Eccles. 1–2). This same observer of life's mysteries nevertheless recalls God as his Creator and writes concerning "real" life:

Go, eat your bread with enjoyment, and drink your wine with a merry heart; for God has long ago approved what you do [cf. Gen. 1]. Let your garments always be white; do not let oil be lacking on your head. Enjoy life with the wife whom you love, all the days of your vain [or short] life that are given you under the sun, because this is your portion in life and in your toil at which you toil under the sun.

Ecclesiastes 9:7–9

Allen states that he would like to believe but cannot. His understanding of Judaism is that it is rooted in a moral code, in the reality of a universe with answers. And he, like Freud, rejects such a possibility as wishful thinking. Both Ecclesiastes and Job suggest a different possibility, however: not an answer to life's enigmas, but a divine answerer who meets us in life. We cannot comprehend, but we can apprehend the divine presence. We need not jettison faith for truth, or truth for life. There is a fragile but real co-inherence.

becoming
a film critic

Siskel and Ebert became household names in America by using their thumbs. Two thumbs up on their weekly television show reviewing current films meant a movie was worth seeing; two thumbs down, avoid it like the plague. More elaborate reviewing schemas are used in newspapers across the country, but the goal is similar: to express personal satisfaction or dissatisfaction with a current release. The *San Francisco Chronicle*, for example, uses pictures of a little man sitting on his chair watching the movie. If the movie is judged to be a dog, the little man is snoring; if it is okay, the man is watching; if it is good, the man is clapping; and if it is a "must see," the man is standing on his chair clapping wildly as his hat comes off. Such judgments by reviewers have become the staple of journalism, and they are repeated informally by moviegoers themselves who share with friends over a cup of coffee their opinion of the latest movie. Such judgments serve an important function in helping potential viewers know which movies to see.

Film criticism, however, has a different goal than simply the negative or positive evaluation of a film. It seeks to initiate a process of inquiry and reflection in order better to understand a movie. It does this by commenting on a movie's style and story, its structure and theme. Moreover, film criticism explores the connection a movie has both to its creators and to its audiences. The best film criticism seeks comprehensively to ask, "How is it that the movie is (or is not) a meaningful experience?"

If theologians, both amateur and professional, are to avoid reading into movies what is not there, they must learn something of the craft of viewing and reflecting; they must develop their critical skills. The church has been involved in film criticism throughout the past century and has even addressed some of its distinct aspects. Richard Blake argues that the church itself initiated film criticism: "In fact, it would not be much of an exaggeration to claim that the churches actually invented film criticism, as opposed to the reviewing carried by the daily papers, in the first years of the century."[1] Churches were concerned about the social impact (public morality) of film. They also saw the catechetical (Christian education) function that movies could provide through their interpretation of life. Here is film criticism in its infancy.

We have already considered in the last chapter how we might understand a film's power and meaning by concentrating on the narrative shape of the movie itself. In this chapter, we will look in an analogous way at four particular aspects of film criticism: *genre criticism* examines the common form and mythic shape of film; *auteur criticism* attends to the author; *thematic criticism* compares film texts; and *cultural criticism* focuses on a film's social context. We can diagram these four methods by again using an artistic-critical circle:

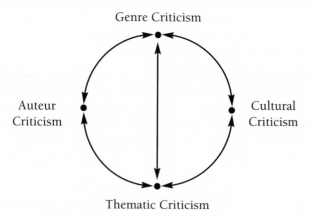

Figure 7.1 Film Criticism Options

It is to these four critical approaches that we now turn.

Genre Criticism

When we go to Blockbuster to rent a video and ask our companions whether they would like to see an adventure film, a comedy, a sci-fi, a thriller, or perhaps a romance, we are acknowledging that many movies fit into certain categories—into genres, a system of orientation for both the filmmaker and filmviewer, a means of communicating expectation and convention. These expectations need not correspond exactly to real life, but only to a viewer's previous experience with like movies. *The Thomas Crown Affair* (1999), for example, is hardly realistic with regard to its surface story, but it doesn't matter. The movie is a suspense story, a "thriller" about a heist. The organization of its surface details is like others of the genre, including a previous version of the same story, and allows its audience to identify with the movie at a deeper level.

When movie viewers fail to recognize a film's genre, their interpretation becomes skewed as the film is taken literally and its meaning wrongly reduced to its face value. This is what happened for some when watching *Thelma & Louise* (1991), for example. Not recognizing its road movie genre and thus its fable-like quality that centered on the changing relationship between the two women, the film was judged harshly by some as painting women into a corner in which their only liberation was suicide.

Each genre carries with it a characteristic set of conventions. Its subject matter, style, and values are standardized. Thus genre becomes a convenient way of selecting material, determining the narrative's strategy, and organizing the story. If a hero is killed at the end of a Western, for example, the audience feels cheated. If a Disney fable is too dark or its values nontraditional, viewers feel betrayed. Genres provide a set of built-in satisfactions by taking on something of a collective ritual or game. Audiences come expecting a certain kind of pleasure (just ask the teenager who attends a slasher movie). Originality is, of course, part of the fun, but only as it intensifies the expected experience.

By organizing and synthesizing vast amounts of material, genres give viewers cues about how to interpret the story. They are not ironclad rules, but rather loose sets of expectations that provide direction. We all know who wears the white hat, for example. But if it is worn by another character, as in a Clint Eastwood film, we immediately take notice—it is an important part of the movie's originality and invites reflection as to its intended meaning.

Mediocre filmmakers merely repeat the formula; serious artists reinterpret. It was Aristotle who noted in *The Poetics* that the conventions of classical tragedy were basically the same whether they were used by a genius or a dolt. It is not genre that determines a movie's excellence, but what is done within a genre. Because filmmakers have only a limited amount of time to portray their story, they must rely on convention to convey meaning and give direction. Genre thus becomes a heuristic device pointing the audience to a film's meaning.

Genre criticism is interested both in a movie's text and in its context; it has both an internal and an external focus. With regard to the film itself, genre critics explore those formal and rhetorical patterns that give shape to the movie's meaning. The very structure of a Western, for example, conveys an understanding about the shape of life. Genres are a form of contemporary myth, giving expression to the meaning of everyday life. But critics can also focus on how shifts in the general characteristics of a genre reflect changes in the culture out of which it came. Having located the basic structure of a movie, its dramatic pattern, genre criticism also turns its attention to exploring the relationship between that genre and the world surrounding it. For example, a gangster film like *The Godfather* (1971) might be viewed as a way of exploring social unrest. Or an animated Disney film (e.g., *Tarzan* [1999]) might be interpreted as reinforcing conservative values.

The typical plot for a Western prior to World War II centered on the hero as rugged individualist who rode into town from the outside and solved the problem out of a sense of what was right, or perhaps for the love of a girl. In this way the West was won and community achieved (even if the lone hero had to ride off into the sunset). But through the 1950s and into the 1960s, American culture became more corporate and professional in nature. Thus it should come as no surprise that the typical Western plot changed with it. Now, the hero became heroes, and they worked for money. They were specialists (typically professionals who are for hire; sometimes even outlaws) who formed a group to solve the problem (consider *True Grit* [1969], *The Wild Bunch* [1969], and *Butch Cassidy and the Sundance Kid* [1969]).[2] American society had changed and the Western with it. The change in the structure of many (not all—genre is fluid) Westerns signaled a change in the attitudes and expectations of the movie audience. And this has continued. There are few Westerns being made today. The disillusionment within American culture allows little room for this classic, mythic struggle between good and evil, at least in this form. We all know too well the mixed motives for establishing civilization on the frontier, and the consequences that resulted.

Genre criticism thus opens out to auteur criticism on the one hand and to cultural criticism on the other. Genre allows the viewer to appreciate the directors' personal vision as they embellish and reinterpret the pattern. It also offers the critic a means of assessing cultural values and changes. Tom Ryall writes:

> When we suggest that a certain film is a Western we are really positing that a particular range of meanings will be available in the film, and not others. We are defining the limits of its significance. The master image for genre criticism is a triangle composed of artist/film/audience. Genres may be defined as patterns/forms/styles/structures which transcend individual films, and which supervise their construction by the film maker, and their reading by an audience.[3]

But though artist and audience are important, central to the use of genre is its ability to be used almost like myth. Genres carry an intrinsic worldview. They become stylized conventions to portray universal conflicts whereby viewers can participate ritualistically in the basic beliefs, fears, and anxieties not only of their age, but of all ages. As Orson Welles once remarked, "The camera is much more than a recording apparatus; it is a medium via which messages reach us from another world that is not ours and that brings us to the heart of a great secret. Here magic begins."[4] Genre films become iconic. That is, through repetition, a certain imagery, story line, and characterization become archetypal. Behind their repeated use, we sense some sort of pattern or model which gives shape to, or provides options for, interpreting reality. Here is the way human existence is structured at a central region.

In genre films, we are invited to explore dimensions of meaning that adhere to the patterns and conventions themselves. In a musical, for example, the viewer moves back and forth between narrative and musical presentation. The song and dance numbers become a stylized means of portraying the meaning and intention of the larger situation. Aware of this, viewers do not expect the songs to carry the plot further, but look to the production numbers to convey primary meaning. They function something like the soliloquies of Elizabethan drama ("To be, or not to be? That is the question"). It is foolish to judge *The Sound of Music* (1965) for being untrue to the facts or Pollyanna in content; this is to miss the genre's intention. Rather, one must listen to the music in the production numbers. If we do, we too will discover that "the hills are alive with the sound of music."

Shane (1953)

The movie *Shane* provides an example of the way genre criticism works. It is one of the great Westerns of all time, largely because of the clarity and simplicity with which it interprets the classic ingredients of the Western genre. Will Wright says simply, "*Shane* is the classic of the classic Westerns."[5] For Wright the plot of a typical Western will unfold as follows:

1. The hero enters a social group.
2. The hero is unknown to the society.
3. The hero is revealed to have an exceptional ability.
4. The society recognizes a difference between themselves and the hero; the hero is given a special status.
5. The society does not completely accept the hero.
6. There is a conflict of interests between the villains and the society.
7. The villains are stronger than the society; the society is weak.
8. There is a strong friendship or respect between the hero and a villain.
9. The villains threaten the society.
10. The hero avoids involvement in the conflict.
11. The villains endanger a friend of the hero.
12. The hero fights the villains.
13. The hero defeats the villains.
14. The society is safe.
15. The society accepts the hero.
16. The hero loses or gives up his special status.[6]

Shane follows this pattern closely. Filmed against the backdrop of the Grand Teton Mountains and starring Alan Ladd as Shane, the movie begins with the hero wearing spotless buckskin as he rides down from the mountains into an

"Eden-like" valley. There he is spotted by young Joey across a still pond, where a deer is peacefully drinking, even though Joey is playing with a toy gun. Shane asks for water at the farm of Joe and Marian Starrett, who perceive him as a threat and force him to leave at gunpoint. But after the Riker brothers ride up and threaten Starrett in order to get him off his land so their cattle can use it for grazing, Shane returns wearing a gun and announces he is a friend of the Starretts. Scaring off the Rikers, Shane is now invited for dinner and offered a job on the farm.

The next day Shane goes to town for supplies and is harassed by the Rikers' men. Shane avoids a fight, however. Later that evening, when a group of the farmers meet to plan their response to the Rikers, Shane is present, but he is accused of cowardice by one of the farmers. When all the farmers go to town on Sunday, Shane goes along and intentionally returns to the saloon where he had been harassed. This time he fights a cowboy named Chris and defeats him. The Rikers try to neutralize his opposition by offering Shane a job, but Shane refuses. When the cowboys in the saloon attack Shane, Joe Starrett comes to his defense, and together they defeat the cowboys. Realizing something must be done, the Rikers send for a gunfighter, Wilson.

After arriving in town, Wilson soon forces a showdown with one of the farmers and kills him. This is followed the next day by the Rikers burning down one of the farms. Dispirited, the farmers get ready to leave the valley, but Starrett persuades them to stay one more day. Trying to take matters into his own hands, Starrett then decides to go to town to kill the Rikers. Marian asks Shane to try to stop him, for her own pleas have failed. Told by Chris that Starrett is heading into a trap, Shane again puts on his gun and tells Joe to stay home. When the farmer refuses, Shane must knock him out. Saying his goodbye to an adoring Marian, Shane rides to town where he outdraws Wilson and kills him and the two Riker brothers. Shane tells Joey, who has followed him to town, that the valley will again have peace, but that he must be going. Wounded in the chest, Shane rides out of town back up the mountain, while Joey calls out after him, "Come back, Shane! Come back!"

Is this simply a repetition of the formula? After all, it fits almost perfectly Wright's description of the classical Western plot. But as Jean Renoir, the French director and critic, once observed, "The marvelous thing about Westerns is that they're all the same movie. This gives a director unlimited freedom."[7] And it is the freedom that director George Stevens displays that both distinguishes the movie and heightens the meaning of this story. Stevens wants us to see the story's mythic qualities. There is more to the film than the slow and stylized plot. Viewers are struck by the mystical quality of the movie.

In his article "The Drama of Salvation in George Steven's *Shane*," Robert Banks points out a number of ways in which the screenplay varied from the novel from which it was taken.[8] For example, in the book by Jack Schaefer, there is no opening descent from the mountain by our hero, nor is there a return back up the mountain at the end. In the book there is no idyllic, Eden-like opening setting into which evil intrudes. Although according to the book Shane's clothing is dusty, in the movie his buckskin is spotless, in contrast with Wilson's black outfit. In the film, Shane's gun represents his extraordinary ability, but he puts the gun away to work on the farm. Only when forced to defend his friend does he put it back on. It is Shane furthermore who preaches a kind of Sermon on the Mount to the farmers, reminding them of what is at stake. As he rides into town for the final time, Stevens frames the scene in such a way that the cemetery crosses seem to follow him for a time as he rides. Again, as he speaks to Joey one last time after the fight in which he is wounded, Shane reaches out and touches Joey on the head, in effect consecrating him to continue in his stead. And then of course, Shane has come into the valley to live with Joe (Joseph) and Marian (Mary). Stevens has cast the confrontation between farmer and rancher, between frontier and civilization, between good and evil, as a variation of the Christ story. Shane has come into a tarnished Eden to restore it to its rightful self.

Geoffrey Hill sees other mythic archetypes in the movie. In particular, he finds parallels with the Cain and Abel story. The story pits gatherers against hunters, farmers against cattle herders, nesters (homesteaders) against ranchers, vegetarians against meat eaters, matriarchies against patriarchies, domesticators against warriors. Shane rides into the valley wearing buckskin, but he soon changes into clothes made from fiber. He tries to shed his gun but ultimately cannot. And as with the Cain and Abel story, the result is human violence. Like Cain, Shane ends up a wanderer.[9]

In ways such as these, George Stevens, the director, has given us a multi-layered story that invites our deeper gaze. An allegorical treatment of either the Christ story or the Cain and Abel saga is not intended. It would be wrong to overinterpret the film. But allusions abound that add a universality and depth to the portrayal. Moreover, Stevens has done more than this. Not only has he recast this Western to heighten its mythic, quasi-messianic meaning, but also he has done it in a way that ties it into what many in the 1950s thought of as the American myth. He has sought not only to connect the story to its ancient past but to plant the movie in its present soil. His success is perhaps evident in the fact that hundreds of American babies were named Shane soon after the film came out. Joe and Marian recall not only Joseph and Mary but George and Mary of the classic American film *It's a Wonderful Life* (1946). Quoting John Wiley Nelson, Banks summarizes the American dream:

Evil intrudes from outside the essentially good society: people are basically good not evil, but some have yielded to their baser instincts; this breaks social relations and threatens social institutions, such as the family, community or nation; the source of deliverance is also external: it comes through a mysterious, celibate individual with special powers; the outcome is preservation of the family-community-nation, and the future guarantee of schools, churches, law and order.[10]

The similarity with *Shane* is again clear. Though people are weak, they are basically good. Though a community is present, it is the work of a strong individual who preserves order. And the religious is present mainly to preserve family–community–nation. ("In God We Trust" was put on our coins by Eisenhower.) It was not until our seemingly invincible hero John F. Kennedy was shot that this mythic balloon popped. Future generations would come along and question whether there ever really had been a Camelot (cf. the movie *Pleasantville* [1998]), but at the time *Shane* was produced, the American dream reigned supreme.

Shane is a classic American film, not simply because it follows the Western script, but because Stevens creatively used this genre to tie his story into those archetypal biblical stories that provide it depth and texture. He also effectively brought his story forward into the present and expressed it in a way the Eisenhower era in America could affirm. The result was a movie that spoke with power and meaning about the nature and possibilities of humankind. However, many students in my classes today find the movie quaint, for we no longer live in the days of *Leave It to Beaver* and *Father Knows Best*. That innocence was shattered by the assassinations of John F. Kennedy and Martin Luther King, to say nothing of the Vietnam War. But though the movie lacks existential and visceral power for contemporary viewers, *Shane's* archetypal patterns continue to fascinate viewers. Its classic confrontation of the forces of good and evil still speaks to people today.

Auteur Criticism

It is said that the philosopher George Santayana, while teaching at Harvard University, was asked by an undergraduate what courses he would be offering the next semester. He replied: "Santayana I, Santayana II, and a seminar in Santayana III." The creative person, whether philosopher or artist, has a consistency of vision. This holds true for the film world as well. Many moviemakers both return to the same small group of themes time and again and express these in a similar manner. One can describe a typical Van Gogh, a Vermeer, a Miro, or a Winslow Homer. One can also speak of a Woody Allen movie or one by Milos Forman. It is not simply marketing that causes the producers to include in a movie's credits "A Peter Weir Film." There is in a Weir film both a unique visual style and a worldview that is expressed in recurring themes. And people come to experience this as it is expressed afresh in each new film he makes.

David Bayles and Ted Orland, two working artists, have written a personal reflection on the perils and rewards of making art. Among their other observations is their belief in the constancy of interior issues for the artist: "We tell the stories we have to tell, stories of the things that draw us in—and why should any of us have more than a handful of those? The only work really worth doing—the only work you *can* do convincingly—is the work that focuses on the things you care about. To not focus on those issues is to deny the constants in your life."[11]

The validity of this neo-romantic notion has been argued over the centuries. Does the work of art express not only an outer surface but an inner emotion, one arising out of the soul of the artist? Michelangelo thought so, as did Wassily Kandinsky, who speaks of the capacity of the inner life of the artist to evoke a similar emotion in the observer: "The inner element, i.e., emotion, must exist," he argued, "otherwise the work of art is a sham. The inner element determines the form of the work of art."[12]

Auteur criticism begins with the talent or person behind the work of film and seeks to understand the movie in that light. Such reflection is made more difficult for the film critic by the fact that moviemaking is a collaborative process. There are producers, writers, directors, camera crew, editors, actors, lighting and sound people, composers, costumers, casting agents, and more. The credits at the end of a film speak for themselves. Yet there is often an organizing or unifying force behind a film, typically the director, whose creative vision shapes the story. When filming *One Flew over the Cuckoo's Nest* (1975), for example, Milos Forman fired noted cinematographer Haskell Wexler, not because of his lack of competence, even brilliance, but because they were unable to come to a shared vision as to how the story should be portrayed on the screen. It was Forman's vision that needed to prevail. Though painful, such evaluation is necessary for a film's coherence. Lacking this, a movie often flounders, becoming a mere pastiche of competing interests. (Some believe that independent filmmakers are often more successful today than studios, for there is less likelihood of the compromise of the creative process by competing interests and personalities.) Not all movies lend themselves to auteur analysis, but many do. When the creative effort of a moviemaker is dominant, a recognition of the auteur allows new insight into the power and meaning of the movie itself.

Although cases have been made for the producer, or the scriptwriter, or even the actor as auteur, the dominant personality in the making of a movie is usually the director. One can lose the individual movie by considering only the whole corpus of a director's work; one can also overlook individual brilliant movies that have no parallels in a director's other works. But used with a modicum of common sense, auteur criticism helps one uncover the full significance of an individual film. We can speak of a Bergman film or a Fellini film. Charlie Chaplin, D. W. Griffith, Alfred Hitchcock, Akira Kurosawa, Stanley Kubrick, Spike Lee, Luis Bunuel, Steven Spielberg, Robert Altman, Krzysztof Kieslowski, Gillian Armstrong—the list of directors with a body of work that invites analysis and intertextuality (a conversation between the movies, or "texts") could go on and on. Most moviegoers, for example, can identify a typical Woody Allen movie with its thematic stress on the romantic, a large dose of skepticism, a slightly hopeful ending, a nostalgic look at the joys of family, and a repeated return to memories and to youth as holding sacramental meaning. Viewers can also note his self-deprecating humor, his use of film and music from the past, his sight gags, and his humor that does not mask an underlying sadness and tragedy.

Just as there are internal criteria (what are the film's components) and external factors (what does its particular shape reveal about the cultural context in which it was produced) that genre critics consider when analyzing a film, so auteur criticism can have both an inner and an outer focus. On the one hand, it seeks to identify a consistent vision of reality expressed through similar themes and visual style across a range of the director's movies. Critics look for a personal signature attached to the movies themselves that extends across theme, cinematic style, structure, and even worldview—assumptions about the nature of life, itself. On the other hand, auteur critics also explore the biographies of directors, as well as their own interpretation and commentary on their work, in the hope of uncovering the cultural and ideological context of the films. Movies reflect the social and personal histories of their makers. Some critics have wanted to deny such external referents as intrusive, wanting simply to stay inside the world of the movies themselves. But under pressure from marginalized groups (whether distinguished by race, gender, sexuality, or religion) to recognize their unique contributions within the industry, biography has been increasingly reinserted into the critical process.[13]

Smoke Signals (1998)

The importance of the auteur's biography for an understanding of a movie can be seen in the movie *Smoke Signals*. Billed in the advertisements as the first feature movie written, directed, and acted entirely by Native Americans, the film's style and meaning are best understood in this light. Adapted from four short stories by Sherman Alexie out of his collection *The Lone Ranger and Tonto Fistfight in Heaven*, the film won two awards at Robert Redford's 1998 Sundance Film Festival. Interestingly, the writer Alexie is quoted as saying, "I love the way movies have more power than books. They continue the oral tradition [of our heritage], the way we all sit around the fire and listen to stories."[14] Chris Eyre, the director, has taken the short stories and, with Alexie's help with the screenplay, has captured this oral tradition well.

The film opens on the Fourth of July, 1976, the night Thomas Builds-the-Fire is orphaned. It tells the tale of two modern-day Coeur d'Alene Indians, Victor Joseph and Thomas Builds-the-Fire, who leave their Idaho reservation twenty years later to go by bus to retrieve the ashes of Victor's alcoholic father.

Arnold Joseph has died in Arizona, years after abandoning his family, and forgiveness does not come easily. Victor is good-looking, self-righteous, and stoic. He has sealed himself off in anger since his father left him as an adolescent. Thomas—geeky, happy, and forever talkative—is the storyteller trying to understand his friend's pain (and perhaps his own). It is Arnold Joseph who binds these otherwise dissimilar twenty-year-olds together. Not only is he Victor's father, but he is also the one who saved the infant Thomas from the fatal house fire that orphaned him that July Fourth evening.

From such a skeletal plot description, one might presume the movie to be dark and sentimental; it is not. Humor abounds, and this humor is portrayed from a Native American perspective. The weather report on "K-REZ" always begins, "It's a good day to be indigenous," and its traffic report typically says, "One car went by earlier." Frustrated with Thomas's non-stop talking, Victor tells him to "Get stoic. Look like a warrior." He also accuses Thomas of learning his "Indianness" from *Dances with Wolves* (1990). We see young Native Americans poking fun at themselves.

Smoke Signals is a genre "road picture" whose structure needs only a "destination" to work. Otherwise, the story allows for freedom and improvisation along the way. The need to recover the father's ashes is the plot excuse for the bus trip to Arizona, but the real movement occurs as the two men discover life's meaning and possibilities through their growing friendship. Dialogue is the heart of the movie, but it is never preachy. The film uses humor and a fondness for Indian culture to help viewers better understand both today's Native Americans and themselves. Through the use of storytelling so typical of Indian culture, *Smoke Signals* weaves together fantasy and realism in a series of flashbacks and fast-forwards, often narrated by Thomas. In the process not only are Thomas and Victor able to accept their past and present, but we as viewers are enabled to discover our stories as well.

The director, Chris Eyre, describes the movie as a "universal story about fathers and friends and forgiveness." He has used the tradition he knows best (Native American), but the movie is meant to transcend culture. Its final soliloquy is a moving poem by Dick Lorrie: "How do we forgive our fathers / Maybe in a dream. . . . Do we forgive our fathers in our age or theirs? Or in their deaths? Saying it to them or not saying it?" These are questions for any time or place.

Yet *Smoke Signals* is also a Native American movie. The life history of its collaborators, Chris Eyre and Sherman Alexie, is crucial to the film. *Smoke Signals* is more than just a metaphorical story with universal meaning. The movie is political despite itself; it is about getting to know the American Indian in our midst. These auteurs show us three typical ways that Native Americans have learned to cope with the largely indifferent if not hostile world around them—quiet anger, ingratiating storytelling, and alcohol. In *Smoke Signals* no answers are presented; the life of the Native American does not allow for this. But the viewer achieves insight nonetheless. We are a long way from Tonto (Spanish for "stupid") and the Lone Ranger in this Native American film.

Woody Allen

The movies of Woody Allen have also been analyzed in terms of his ethnicity. Lester Friedman sees Allen's Jewish characters as "bouncing from one trauma to the next with barely a moment to catch their breaths." They are "the schlemiel endlessly and vainly searching for love and respect."[15] While this is true, the Allen stamp on his films is evident in other ways as well. In particular, many of Woody Allen's movies have a common theme—that of the relationship between the "real" and the "reel"—between life and art, between fiction and reality. Complicating this theme are both Allen's own presence as an actor within his movies and the way in which Allen, the writer, deals on screen with issues that seem to parallel his own life and experience. This causes his movies often to be viewed autobiographically, the line blurring between his own life and the movies he directs. Allen, of course, denies any one-to-one parallel, even while continuing to invite such comparisons. What are we to make, for example, of the fact that many of Allen's movie characters seem to be fascinated with young girls (cf. *Crimes and Misdemeanors* [1989]), given his public affair and subsequent marriage to Mia Farrow's adopted, teenage daughter? Allen has said in an interview,

> Most people . . . can't understand an act of imagination. So every film I make, they feel is an autobiography. . . . They always think that my stories and ideas are based on reality. Therefore I have to explain to them, that *Annie Hall* wasn't, that *Manhattan* wasn't, that *Husbands and Wives* wasn't.[16]

But Allen encourages this confusion. Allen's movies cannot be reduced to autobiography, but the relationship between his art and his life is clearly present. At times his movies imitate life. At other times they provide a commentary on it. Perhaps they even presage it. It is from the stuff of his own life that his imaginative worlds are created.

Crimes and Misdemeanors (1989) portrays the constant interplay between reel life and real life. When Cliff is asked to make a documentary of the slick Lester, for example, he does so by comparing Lester first to Mussolini and then to a talking mule. Lester is understandably upset, saying, "The idea was to show the real me!" Yet the "real me" is in fact presented in the documentary. Lester is a womanizer, someone who can fire a writer with cancer because he is no longer funny; someone who is narcissistic and self-indulgent. Cliff's visual metaphors are closer to the truth, closer to reality than Lester knows. Reality is Reel-ality—or is it?

Allen revels in blurring the lines. For example, he often has real-life figures make cameo appearances in his movies. In perhaps his most famous use of a person playing himself, he has Marshall McLuhan suddenly appear in *Annie Hall* (1977) from offscreen to silence an intellectual bore who is pontificating while in line at the movies. Or in *Broadway Danny Rose* (1984), the story is told by real life, retired, stand-up comics sitting around a table at a New York deli. That they are telling the story of Danny adds both reality and unreality to the narrative, for their shaggy dog story might well say as much about them as about Danny.

Allen also uses edited photographic images to move back and forth between the reel and the real. In *Zelig* (1983), for example, Zelig/Allen is the son of a Yiddish actor who assumes the characteristics of whomever he meets, so much so that he is nicknamed "The Human Chameleon." As a baseball player he meets major sports heroes, and as a Nazi he distracts Hitler during a rally. Zelig hugs Josephine Baker and James Cagney, clowns with Jack Dempsey, and poses by the side of Calvin Coolidge. The scenes are shot in a pseudo-documentary style using old film clips so that the viewer actually suspends judgment and accepts that these are real events. To add to the ambiguity, we hear New York intellectuals and critics, such as Susan Sontag and Irving Howe, together with Saul Bellow and Bruno Bettelheim, discussing Zelig and his significance. They both provide possible interpretations of Zelig, and warn us against overinterpretation. Is he the ultimate conformist? Zelig's existence, the narrator says in a voice-over, is "a non-existence. Devoid of personality, his human qualities long since lost in the shuffle of life, he sits alone quietly staring into space, a cipher, a non-person, a performing freak." Do we agree?

In *The Purple Rose of Cairo* (1985) Allen returns to this theme. But this time he uses the technique of a movie-within-a-movie. We see a character in the movie-within-a-movie, Tom Baxter, stepping off the screen in a theater in New Jersey and then competing with the actor who is playing the part, Gil Shepherd, for the affection of Cecilia. Here Allen is making explicit what all art points to—its role in entering into the very lives of its audience. Gil recognizes the absurdity of the situation and argues, "Tell him you can't love him. He's fictional! You want to waste your time with a fictional character? I mean, you're a sweet girl. You deserve an actual human." But Cecilia is addicted to the movies, in part because of the abusive life that she must endure in her marriage. She is addicted as well because "Tom's perfect!" She says, "I . . . I . . . I just met a wonderful new man. He's fictional, but you can't have everything." Here is her escape.

Ultimately, it is not perfection that Cecilia chooses, but real life. She explains to Tom, "See, I'm a real person. No matter how . . . how tempted I am, I have to choose the real world." And so with Woody Allen's full irony, she chooses the real world . . . not of New Jersey and her abusive husband, but of Hollywood! When Gil says to her, "Come away with me to Hollywood!" she does. When her estranged husband finds out that she is leaving him to go to Hollywood, he yells, "Go, see what it is out there. It ain't the movies! It's real life! It's real life, and you'll be back!" For Monk, her husband, reality is the neighborhood in New Jersey and his wife, who is to serve him. There is reality and there is reel-ality. Which is preferable? We are left unsure. Even the photography itself reinforces the ambiguity of the choice, for the movie-within-the movie—also called "The Purple Rose of Cairo"—is black and white, while the movie itself is in color.

In one of his short stories, "The Kugelmass Episode," Allen tells the story of a professor who loves Madame Bovary so much that he enters into Flaubert's novel.[17] Allen repeatedly retells classic stories in his films. We have "Oedipus Wrecks" from *New York Stories* (1989; cf. *Oedipus Rex*), *Crimes and Misdemeanors* (1989; cf. Dostoyevsky's *Crime and Punishment*), *Love and Death* (1975; cf. Tolstoy's *War and Peace*), *A Midsummer Night's Sex Comedy* (1982; cf. Shakespeare's *A Midsummer Night's Dream*). Again, we have portrayed the real and the reel. By replaying these old stories, by re-entering them (sometimes most literally), Allen provides himself the categories for both seeing and understanding life itself. But can we really replay these stories? In his movie *Play It Again, Sam* (1972), which takes its title from the movie *Casablanca*, Allen has Ilsa ask Rick to "play it," referring to the song "As Time Goes By." But of course time has gone by, and the words of the song become a contrast to the reality of the situation. One can't go back.

Jesus of Nazareth (1977)

Auteur criticism also proves useful as we consider *Jesus of Nazareth* by the Italian director Franco Zeffirelli. In order to tell the story, Zeffirelli rearranged episodes of the four Gospels spatially and chronologically so as to center on Jesus' arrest. It is in the vicinity of the temple that Jesus now teaches, heals, and blesses, not in the countryside of Galilee. By relocating the events of the story, Zeffirelli makes it clear to the viewer why Jesus was arrested by the authorities—he is a threat to the system, both ecclesial and political. And Zeffirelli is not apologetic about doing this, for any director, he believes, ends up giving the viewer a personal point of view through his reaction to and sensitivity toward the material at hand. New Testament scholar Joel Green has even called Zeffirelli another "Gospel writer, an evangelist."[18]

Why did Zeffirelli make the movie? This is what he has written: "I was interested in the possibility of telling the story fully and clearing up unknown areas in our faith, plus the political stories behind them. I felt that I was putting an end to centuries old misunderstandings about the Jews and Jesus, that I was destroying medieval attitudes."[19] Given that the movie was to be shown over television for seven hours of playing time, Zeffirelli believed that it was his opportunity and moral responsibility to take a popular approach in the telling of the Jesus story, one aimed at a mass audience. In his memoirs he even speaks of his divinely ordained mission. Given the crisis of traditional values and beliefs in the West, and given his sincerely held Catholic beliefs, Zeffirelli hoped his film might help believers and unbelievers alike to realize how much they are losing by giving up traditional beliefs. Thus Zeffirelli identifies an explicitly didactic intention for his movie.

Wanting both to express his simple piety and to speak to viewers worldwide, Zeffirelli does not give his movie a Marxist slant as Pasolini had done with his. His will not be a messiah of the poor who does justice. Neither will he risk losing his audience by portraying too high a Christology. Zeffirelli omits, for example, the temptation in the desert, the Transfiguration, and Jesus' walking on the water. Wanting also to avoid portraying too human a Jesus, Zeffirelli omits most of the suffering connected with Jesus' death. Instead, he seeks a more moderate and pious approach. Zeffirelli desired to reach as wide an audience as possible without offending them, and he succeeded admirably. His desire for tastefulness can be seen in the looks (and the reputations) of the actors he chooses and in the nonviolent(!) presentation of the crucifixion. It is evident in the careful compositions of the scenes that take on almost the quality of religious paintings. It can be observed in the extreme piety with which he depicts Joseph and Mary. As a result of these choices, his did in fact become the most popular of all the professional movies that have been produced on Jesus.

The cost of his choices was high, however. By popularizing and sanitizing the Jesus story, Zeffirelli ran the risk of watering down the gospel. Lloyd Baugh summarizes his critique (and mine) in these words:

> Intended for a mass television audience, Zeffirelli's Jesus does not disappoint that public: superficially characterized, rendered inoffensively, materially mysterious and sentimentally human, surrounded by attractive supporting personalities and a well-unified and smoothly-developing narrative, he is an ideal domestic Savior. In the end, however, and precisely because he is so domesticated, this Jesus has little to do with the mystery of Jesus Christ of the Gospel.[20]

Thematic Criticism

Jon Boorstin writes, "Movies can be made without themes. They're made all the time by producers who don't believe they need an emotional line to their film. They think a film can be about the greatest train robbery of all time or about saving the Super Bowl from terrorists. But I can't think of a movie that works that hasn't had a theme."[21] Themes empower the story; they also help the moviemaker decide during editing what to include and what to leave out. Even if a scene works well, if it does not enhance the theme, it should end up on the cutting room floor. It could be that an action sequence will draw viewers into the theater, but it might also sidetrack the audience from the story.

Boorstin illustrates his observation by considering the Western *The Magnificent Seven* (1960). The story needs to be about more than simply seven guys rescuing a town from bandits. Such a concept does not propel the action forward in a meaningful way. But once the filmmaker decided that the movie was about bravery, then the process of constructing the film could proceed. The seven men then became different examples of bravery or cowardice. There is a cocky beginner who has never been tested; an old pro who is afraid he has lost his nerve; a strong, silent type; someone filled with his own importance; and so on. The gunfights become ways of testing these individuals, and the plot moves the characters toward their final confrontations. There is the same amount of action as in a cowboy movie lacking in theme, but now the audience is drawn into the story. They are not bored by the gunfights, for these confrontations reveal something of the nature of bravery, not only theirs but ours as well.

Thematic criticism is often used by psychologists as part of their counseling practices. A growing number of counselors are using movies with human themes to help clients achieve personal insight into their own situations. Such movie therapy allows the therapist to ask patients about their emotional responses to what they saw. Did a patient see similarities to her own situation? Were the obstacles identical to his own? Could the strategies be transferable?[22]

Recognizing the value of movies as a tool for self-awareness, Mary Ann Horenstein has co-authored *Reel Life/Real Life: A Video Guide for Personal Discovery*.[23] She writes that she realized the power of film to heal after her first husband died when she was just forty-one. When she went to see Jill Clayburgh in *An Unmarried Woman* (1978), she saw on the screen a woman who had gone through everything she was going through. She too was angry and hurt and refused even to speak to men at first. But Clayburgh's character, who had been married for sixteen years before her husband left her, gradually finds help in a support group and from a persistent suitor who is patient with her. From this personal beginning, Horenstein and her three co-authors expanded their list of movies that they believe say something meaningful about a topic to over seven hundred films. Each movie teaches us something about ourselves and the world in which we live. These movies are reviewed and grouped into chapters that address specific topics or interest areas. "Substance abuse," for example, has a list of thirty-four films that are reviewed. Some of the chapters deal more with topics (e.g., "Feisty Women") than with themes, but the intention of the book is clear. Basic to the design of the book is the belief that "a viewer can watch an individual face a similar life situation and vicariously live that experience, with all the attendant emotions."[24]

It is thematic criticism perhaps that the church has used most often. Roger Kahle and Robert Lee's *Popcorn and Parable* (1971), for example, grouped movies according to nine theological topics: relationships, faith, reverence for life, sin, evil, freedom of man, nature of life, alienation, and celebration. Reflecting the interests of the early seventies, as well, was Neil Hurley's book *Theology through Film* (1970). In one chapter, for example, Hurley discusses "Grace on the Screen." As in the other chapters, he first reviews a number of movies that have grace as a theme and then turns to consider six principles about grace that surface from his overview. Other chapters take up the themes of "man as inner center," freedom, conscience, sex, evil, death, sacrificial love, and the future.

A more recent volume by Sara Anson Vaux concentrates on nineteen movies, organizing them according to their most prominent theological themes—alienation, integrity, authenticity, home, vocation, purity of heart, celebration, and healing. She sees each film as being a deliberate attempt "to communicate a concept of a moral universe—a sense of order and meaning that affects the ways we live on and with our earth; a search to determine right or wrong behavior; and a grasp of how we should behave toward one another."[25] Each film takes its life from its search for a deeper meaning lying behind life's events and encounters. By concentrating on a movie's theme, Vaux believes the viewer can connect with its creator's purpose and organize the complex perceptions a movie provokes.

Even when other forms of movie criticism are used by theological critics, thematic criticism often remains central. The excellent collection of essays entitled *Explorations in Theology and Film* (1997) addresses several theological themes and suggests the intertextual methodology of the book: mutuality, salvation, Christology, violence, liberation, Jesus, the human condition, spirituality, grace, and hope.

One Flew over the Cuckoo's Nest (1975)

Thematic criticism refers to the content of the movie. Its focus is on the movie itself, rather than on the moviemaker, the audience, or the embedded worldview. The critic looks for a movie's theme and then compares it with how a similar theme plays out in another text. Most often that companion text is another movie, but once one decides that intertextual dialogue has meaning, there is no reason that a film might not also be compared, for example, to the novel or play from which it was adapted. For example, Milos Forman's Academy Award winning movie *One Flew over the Cuckoo's Nest* is based on the novel of the same name by Ken Kesey. In both the movie and the novel, the theme has to do with individual freedom over against institutional control.

Kesey's cult classic tells a mythic tale through the voice of a huge American Indian. Big Chief is a paranoid schizophrenic who goes in and out of the fog and whose vitality has been reduced to impotence. The reliability of his narration is, thus, left in doubt through most of the novel. It is not until he is challenged and cajoled into wholeness by Randall McMurphy that the fog lifts. McMurphy is portrayed as a TV cowboy, someone larger than life who wears boxer shorts with white whales on them. The narrative has a mythic shape as

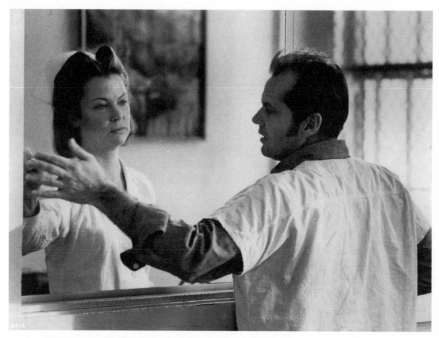

Randall McMurphy (Jack Nicholson) challenges Nurse Ratched's (Louise Fletcher) control of a ward of the mental hospital. *One Flew over the Cuckoo's Nest* (d. Forman, 1975). ©1975 Fantasy Films and United Artists. All rights reserved.

the garden is contrasted with the machine, freedom with order, masculinity with maternal dominance, individuality with community. Nurse Ratched, who runs the ward, is both controlling and controlled. When her femininity is literally exposed at the end of the novel, she is shown to be the woman that she is. Similarly, McMurphy's sacrificial death on behalf of the self-referrals in the mental asylum is told as a secularized Christ story in which McMurphy offers his life so that the men on the ward might live. Kesey wants his readers to take control of their lives, to tell their own story, to make their own film of their life. The message is that we cannot let the "Combine" control our lives.

Milos Forman's film adaptation has much in common with the novel. In both we see the mythic struggle between Randall Patrick McMurphy and Nurse Ratched, a struggle between masculine freedom and maternal power. While the opening credits roll, we are given through music and image the fundamental metaphor which will unite the film. We hear the simple music of the Indian culture as images of nature move across the screen. Then we enter into the highly artificial environs of the mental hospital, where baroque music is playing in the background to help keep the inmates calm. The struggle will be between garden and machine, the natural and the artificial, the simple and the ornate. The oppressive structures of the hospital establishment are much like the "Combine" that Kesey describes. It thrashes the men it controls. Into this world McMurphy inserts himself, and by the movie's end, the result is the liberation of Chief Bromden, an Indian healed in spirit and emboldened bodily through the antics and friendship of McMurphy. Bromden has the courage to break free as he throws a water cooler through the window and escapes into the night.

In telling his story, Forman discards the surrealistic for the real, the mythic for the political. The narrator is no longer the "crazy" Indian. Rather it is now the system itself that is judged insane as the realistic story unfolds. And McMurphy is no longer a mythic cowboy figure and certainly not a very developed Christ-figure. Rather he is a con man who nevertheless comes to care about those in the ward with him and chooses to stand up to the evil system as incarnate in Nurse Ratched. As in other of Forman's movies, this all too human hero dies for his efforts. (Cf. Coalhouse Walker in *Ragtime* [1981]; Mozart in *Amadeus* [1984]; and Berger in *Hair* [1979]. In *The People vs. Larry Flynt* [1996], Flynt does not die but is paralyzed.) But rather than his death being the salvation of all fifteen of the "self-referrals" as in the novel, only Big Chief leaves. The movie ends with the system of the hospital reasserting its control over the others. It is only Big Chief who takes his destiny into his own hands.

For Forman, the head nurse is not to be considered as evil herself. She believes that what she is doing is in the best interests of her patients. That is what makes her character so chilling. In an interview, Forman has said,

> I have never met anyone who walked up to me and said, "Watch out. I'm a very bad person. . . ." So (in making this film), I start with the assumption that everyone is good and then say, "Ok, now let's watch everybody." When the film is over, the audience can judge who was right and who was wrong. Nixon, Stalin—I'm sure these men were convinced that they were doing the best from all points of view, including the moral point of view, and that is always the main subject of art.
>
> For instance Nurse Ratched. She believes deeply that she is doing right. And that is where the real drama begins for me. That's much more frightening than if you have an evil person who knows he's doing wrong.[26]

Though Forman has called the movie a political film about America, few will fail to see it also as a Czechoslovakian critique of Stalin. Forman has captured well the horror of a system that hides its conforming power under the guise of concern for the well-being of others. Perhaps Forman would respond that though his life story has sensitized him to the issue in unique ways, it is fanaticism and conformity in any guise that is his enemy. As he commented in his memoirs:

> We invent institutions to help make the world more just, more rational. Life in society would not be possible without orphanages, schools, courts, government offices, and mental hospitals, yet no sooner do they spring into being than they start to control us, regiment us, run our lives. They encourage dependency to perpetuate themselves and are threatened by strong personalities.[27]

It is the hospital system that ultimately is responsible for McMurphy's death. The rebel has no place. Institutionalism and conformism is a continuing threat.

Chasing the Sacred

At the City of Angels Film Festival in Hollywood in 1998, the theme was "Chasing the Sacred." Among the films screened were *Jesus of Montreal* (1989) and *The Apostle* (1997). On the surface these were very different movies. One was set in the rural South; the other in a large Canadian city in the North. The one dealt with a particular religious subculture, the Pentecostal church; the other looked at a secularized society in which religious values and beliefs had become largely irrelevant. Both dealt with the formation of a community, although the one was ecclesial while the other was artistic. But beneath the narrative differences there exists in these two films a common thematic concern, the mystery of vocation.

In *Jesus of Montreal*, Daniel Coulombe is hired by the priest of a local shrine to update the text of a passion play that is presented each summer in its gardens and then to produce it. Given a job to do, Daniel hires four actors who are called out from other professions, researches the historical Jesus, and then rewrites the story. He finally produces a new passion play emphasizing a very human Jesus. But Daniel's job becomes a vocation, as he lives into his role. The very events of his life become a mirror image of the Christ-figure he plays. He is forced to oppose the religious authorities at the Shrine, for example. Reacting to the sexist abuse that Mireille (Mary) must endure during an audition for an advertisement, Daniel also overturns the tables of equipment in the studio temple. Having captured the attention of the city with his performance, he is taken by a media lawyer (Satan) up to the top of a tall skyscraper and tempted with an alternate career. "This city is yours, if you want it." After a final supper of wine and pizza (bread), the actors put on their last performance. When the authorities try to close down the play, there is a scuffle; and in the free-for-all, the cross on which Daniel is hanging as he portrays Jesus is knocked over, and Daniel's head is crushed. After his death, his organs are transplanted in order that others might live, and a theater is established in his memory. Daniel has lived into his calling to be like Christ. And as a result the lives of his "disciples" (the four actors who are part of his ensemble) are transformed. Montreal is in need of spiritual renewal; its worship of mammon has proven destructive to the human spirit. Not all respond to the "savior" who arrives, but for those who do, there is hope and newness of life.

The Apostle tells a similar tale of vocation, of someone called to be an unlikely savior. From the opening sequences of the movie where we first see a boy evangelist of twelve and then follow him into adulthood as he stops his car at a roadside crash to witness to a couple of teenagers who are dying, Sonny knows

Sonny (Robert Duvall) knows he is called to preach. *The Apostle* (d. Duvall, 1997). Photo by Van Redin. ©1997 October Films. All rights reserved.

he is called to preach. His license plate—SONNY—and his white suit suggest something of his personal vanity in being God's chosen servant. It is only after his temper has caused him to kill his wife's lover with the swing of a baseball bat that his calling takes on fresh meaning. Now he must flee town. Baptizing himself the "Apostle E. F.," the old Sonny seeks to live into his calling as a chastened man. His transformation is not immediate; he continues to flirt with women, and he fights with a heavy equipment operator who tries to interfere with his new church. But E. F. knows he "has done a lot more zigging than zagging" and is repentant. By the end of the film, he has confessed his past to his co-pastor, is giving baskets of food to the poor anonymously, has turned from his womanizing, and is peaceful when the cops finally arrive to arrest him. Not only does Sammy, the mechanic with whom he is living, come to faith through his witness, but as the credits roll, we see E. F. on a prison work detail by the side of the road, witnessing again to his fellow inmates. He is at peace with his calling.

These two movies invite dialogue and comparison. Both are about the "redemption" of a person as that individual lives into his calling. E. F. is baptized "the Apostle" and he proves to be just that; Daniel, like his apocalyptic prophet namesake, preaches a message of judgment to his society, as he too lives into his role as the Christ. The salvation that is preached, moreover, is social in character. The needy are given food, whether through soup kitchens or Thanksgiving baskets. The emerging church must function outside the normal religious circles—their leaders have been kicked out of the established church. Yet Daniel's and E. F.'s testimony and life-witness produce disciples, and new faith and life are the result. Throughout the process of their growth into wholeness, there is an incarnational mystery about these leaders. It is almost as if the "hound of heaven" is chasing them. They might have "sought the Lord, but afterward they knew, they were found by thee." Such is the nature of "vocation."

Cultural Criticism

Movies help shape their audience's view of reality. Why else would advertisers buy time on television? By offering viewers a slant on life, they both reflect the reality of an age and help define it. Because movies provide such a powerful representation of reality, their effect on the audience is profound (whether it eventuates in demonstrable change or not). It is also true that people see film differently depending on what they bring to the experience. Gender, education, age, race, and social location all matter. So does the composition of the audience in which one views a movie. Moviegoing is, after all, a community event.

No one today disputes that a movie's story has a powerful impact on its audience. On complex issues, however, it is difficult to isolate the influences. Take, for example, the shooting rampage at Columbine High School in Littleton, Colorado, in 1999. Soon after the killings, John Broder and Katharine Seelye reported on a meeting President Clinton convened in Washington to study the growing problem of teen rage. Gathered at the White House were entertainment executives, representatives of hunting groups and gun manufacturers, clergy, educational officials, nonprofit organizational leaders, law-enforcement officials, and students. Broder and Seelye began their article by saying, "When violence strikes yet again in the school yard, Washington's search for villains is never far behind. Democrats tend to finger guns and their powerful lobby, the National Rifle Association. Republicans are more inclined to blame Hollywood and the glorification of natural born killers in movies, music and video."[28] In reality, it is both of these and more. After originally trying to defuse the blame and to caution against censorship, Hollywood seems to be realizing that the public outcry about violence in Hollywood is growing. Full-page ads have been taken out in major newspapers across the country decrying the sharp escalation in violence and explicit sexual content in television, movies, music, and video games. Many feel children are being robbed of their normal childhood innocence. And since the Columbine killers actually fantasized about what kind of movie their story would make and argued over whether Quentin Tarantino or Steven Spielberg would do a better job as director, Hollywood is unable blithely to remove its name from the list of responsible parties.

The cultural message about violence is mixed, however. There is a continuing openness to certain stories where violence is central, particularly when it is shown in a larger context or given a comic-book veneer as in many action movies. Consider the popularity of wrestling on television, for example. Similarly, *The Matrix* (1999), an action movie filled with violence but clever in its visuals and thoughtful as a cyber-thriller story, made $171 million at the domestic box office soon after the Columbine shootings. *Three Kings* (1999), a movie rooted in the violence of the Gulf War, nevertheless showed the consequence of violence. In *The Green Mile* (1999), violence was similarly critiqued.

Fight Club (1999), however, even with the drawing power of Brad Pitt, could not overcome its violent premise and viewers stayed away. Its box office take was less than $40 million, despite massive publicity. *8MM* (1998), starring Nicolas Cage, did no better a year earlier. The trajectory is becoming clearer. Consciousness has been raised. Many people want violence to be toned down, and some studios are heeding the calls for voluntary restraint. Amy Wallace reported in the *Los Angeles Times* that Disney will no longer use guns in future movie ads. Warner Brothers eliminated all gunplay from the trailers of *The Matrix* for its international release. And early drafts of *Big Momma's House* (2000), starring Martin Lawrence, were altered to get rid of a violent motorcycle chase that was to open the movie. The producer, David Friendly, said, "We talked about it, post-Columbine, and decided the scene was inappropriate to the movie and inappropriate for the time. We said, 'This movie doesn't need it, we don't want it, let's take it out.' And it cost too much, anyway."[29]

Cultural criticism looks at film in terms of its social and psychological contexts. It studies the life cycle of a film from production to distribution to reception. With regard to a movie's reception, for example, it desires to know what effect a movie has on its viewers, whether in attitude, emotions, or behavior. It also considers whether the differing social situations or competencies of an audience give to the movie experience a different viewing. This process can be illustrated with reference to the Japanese movie *Shall We Dance?* (1996). I saw the movie twice—once in a largely Anglo audience and once with a predominantly Asian audience. The difference was startling. While Anglos enjoyed the simple yet elegant parable of a decent, hardworking middle manager in a Japanese company who discovers a new *joie de vivre* through ballroom dancing, the Japanese American audience laughed uproariously through much of the movie at the incongruity of such a situation. It was almost inconceivable to them. For the Anglo audience, the opening subtitles told us that in Japan ballroom dancing is regarded with great suspicion and dancing before others is embarrassing. But for the Japanese audience, such instruction was unnecessary. They knew this existentially, and their knowledge added greatly to the enjoyment of the movie.

Movies are made most often for the majority population. After all, the purpose of the movie "industry" is to make money. It is not surprising, then, that there is stereotyping of various minority groups. The results, however, are unfortunate. Cultural criticism studies these effects on the population. To give but one example, the American Indian has been subject to consistent caricature in the movies. *Smoke Signals* is the rare exception. More typical is a film like John Ford's *The Searchers* (1956), which presents Indians as brutal killers, perhaps even subhuman. They are portrayed as deserving all the vengeance that Ethan Edwards (John Wayne) can muster. In the film, Edwards even shoots out the eyes of a dead Comanche in order to prevent him from entering the spirit world.

As part Cherokee Indian, I never wanted to play cowboys and Indians when I was a child, because I knew from television and the movies what my role was supposed to be. Edward R. Murrow, in a speech to the Radio and Television News Directors' Convention, expressed my frustration well:

> If there were to be a competition in indifference or perhaps in insulation from reality, then Nero and his fiddle, Chamberlain and his umbrella, could not find a place on an early afternoon sustaining show. If Hollywood were to run out of Indians, the program schedules would be mangled beyond all recognition. Then some courageous soul with a small budget might be able to do a documentary telling what, in fact, we have done and are still doing to the Indians in this country. But that would be unpleasant. And we must at all costs shield the sensitive citizens from anything that is unpleasant.[30]

Feminist criticism has grown up around a similar awareness with regard to how women are portrayed in the movies. Laura Mulvey, in one of the most reprinted essays in film criticism, argues that a person's pleasure at the movies is related to issues of gender. In particular, the viewer's gaze (like the camera's) is fixed on the female characters as a male might watch the action. While the male star is an object of identification for the audience, the female star is most often defined as a passive sexual spectacle.[31]

How spectators view movies might be more complex than Mulvey's 1975 study indicated. It is possible, for example, to bring an oppositional gaze to the cinema, something the African-American critic bell hooks has pointed out insightfully.[32] But Mulvey was certainly right to identify gender representations as a problem in Hollywood. I heard a leading director speak of his current movie that once again romantically linked an older man with a younger woman. When asked why he was interested in making movies that elevated the human spirit and yet continued to treat women as sexual objects who could be discarded as they grew older, his only response was to say that this was the industry norm. He felt he could do certain things to challenge the studios, but this was one area he felt he was helpless to fix. (And this from a director who had grossed over one billion dollars on his last four films!)

Working Girl (1988)

The movie *Working Girl* provides an instructive example of cultural criticism. It tells the story of Tess McGill (Melanie Griffith), a secretary on Wall Street who longs to move up the ladder. Smart and ambitious, she has gone to night school. However, it is not only her brains but also her chutzpah and down-to-earth sensuality that allow Tess to escape her Staten Island digs. Afraid she is stuck at the bottom of the ladder, she gets her break (so to speak!) when her boss is laid up out of town with a broken leg. Asked to watch over her apartment, Tess discovers that her boss (played wonderfully by Sigourney Weaver) has stolen her idea for a proposal to one of their major clients. Furious, Tess takes over for her boss, even wearing her dresses and ultimately stealing her boyfriend. Crashing a wedding reception in order to pitch her idea to the client, she succeeds in getting a hearing. When her boss storms into a subsequent meeting claiming the idea was hers, Tess is rescued by Jack Trainer (Harrison Ford), the boyfriend. Everyone realizes it was Tess's original idea; she is hired by the executive she has helped; and as the movie ends, Tess is set up in her own executive office.

When it was first shown in the 1980s, the movie was meant to be a progressive portrayal of women in the workplace. When Tess is asked by her new secretary what is expected of her, she responds, "I expect you to call me Tess. I don't expect you to fetch me coffee unless you're getting some for yourself. And . . . the rest we'll just make up as we go along." But today many students in my classes find the movie's depictions stereotypical and demeaning to women. The egalitarian ending seems like sugarcoating on a movie that stereotypes gender and class.

Why is it, some ask, that Melanie Griffith must appear partly undressed (she is described as having "a mind for business and a bod for sin")? Why is it that the only way portrayed for a woman to compete in a man's world is to become a masculine shrew or an immoral seductress? And why must Tess become a damsel in distress, rescued in the end by Jack Trainer (note his last name)? Is this movie little more than a throwback to the 1940s secretary movies where a stenographer takes off her glasses, lets down her hair, and gets her man? The newspaper ads for the movie, for example, showed Melanie Griffith peeking out coyly from behind Harrison Ford and Sigourney Weaver. Perhaps nothing more needs to be said than to note the double entendre of the movie's title, *Working <u>Girl</u>*.

As one critic noted, we have in this movie a film of the Reagan-Bush era where there is a kinder "inside trading" and a gentler sexual discrimination. Many of my students would agree. Rather than a thoughtful treatment of women's rights, we are given a "Cinderella," rags-to-riches story in which the heroine uses deceit and seduction to accomplish her goals. Here is hardly a model for the career woman of the new millennium.

Mike Nichols, the director, has made a career of being sensitive to the audience's attitudes and changing mores. His *The Graduate* (1967) spoke for a generation. *Catch-22* (1970) and *Silkwood* (1983) were also strongly influenced by their cultural context as they sought to give expression to the hopes and fears of the audience. Now again with *Working Girl,* Nichols captured something of the 1980s with its crass materialism, its increasing class differentiation, and its continuing chauvinism. His yuppie fable of the American dream has the feel of the Reagan era. The goal is for the rich to get richer; and, if others must be left behind, it is because some are more deserving. And it is okay to bend the rules and use your feminine wiles; sometimes nothing else will work. Many viewers at the time found such depictions acceptable. The 1990s would prove to have their own ethical challenges, but they would not be framed in the same way. Nichols's gender and class stereotypes are, in part, a product of his casting the story as a "Cinderella" fable, but whereas his reinforcement of materialistic and sexist attitudes still worked in the 1980s (the movie was very successful), they seem dated—if not demeaning—to many today. The culture has not necessarily improved, but it has moved on.

Genre criticism, auteur criticism, thematic criticism, cultural criticism—the toolbox that movie critics have at their disposal is varied and rich. Used alone, such criticism can deceive the viewer. Auteur criticism, for example, when done in romantic isolation can falsely minimize any social determinates, positing an objectivity that is ill-founded. We have seen this in our discussion of the growing effect of violence on our culture. But cultural criticism, similarly, when used too exclusively, can reduce a person's response to a movie to sociology. But together, such approaches help us unpack a movie's power and meaning and prepare the way for honest and constructive theological criticism. Film criticism, that is, is the first step toward a total criticism. It is to this completing task that we now turn.

responding to movies theologically

8

Even the most commonplace things are tinged with glory.

W. H. Auden

Every year in the class on theology and film that I teach, there are students who come to the dialogue with such strong religious commitments that they cannot view a particular movie on its own terms. They are quick to judge its ethics or its images from an imposed point of view. I recall one student, for example, who could not get beyond the fact that Charlie Chaplin's character in *City Lights* (1931) was drunk. She could therefore see nothing of his pathos and compassion, let alone take note of the themes of sacrifice, hope, and providence that were central to the movie. However ultimate one's theology is, it is the penultimate—the movie itself—that demands our initial attention. It is for this reason that I have postponed until now a discussion of theological criticism.

T. S. Eliot cautioned that whether a piece of literature was worthy or not could only be decided on aesthetic grounds. Here is ground zero with regard to a person's response to any work of art. Eliot then went on to assert that the subject of literature (and film) was ultimately too important not to be completed from a theological perspective.[1] Personal evaluation, including theological dialogue, has its place as in any human encounter, but it must follow the act of first looking and listening. Having been open to receive the images (the "testimony") of a film, one needs to take the cinema with sufficient seriousness to complete the critical act by engaging in dialogue and reflection with it. Movies seek to affect us wholly, and we are affected whether we admit it or not. What the effect is, together with how the film portrays life's power and meaning, should be the subject of our conversation, reflection, and evaluation.

It is this completing act of criticism that we will focus on in this chapter. Film's root metaphors, informing vision, and axiological perspectives make claims on us and invite both our analytical and our experiential responses. We cannot escape responding to film from our own perspective, our own center of power and meaning. Even "objective" critics do this, as we know. The potential use of an outside criterion by the critic (or of the critic as outside criterion) is not unique to the theological enterprise. Feminist criticism and Marxist criticism, for example, also bring an outside standard to bear on a film, and the responses are most typically made by feminists and Marxists. There is a personal dimension to the evaluation.

Theological criticism, similarly, seeks to engage a movie from perspectives that come out of, but move beyond, the movie experience. It seeks a dialogue between filmic elements and convictions and Christian experience and belief. It can include issues of class, politics, and gender, but it is by no means limited to them. Rather, it is the visual story of a movie with its particular narrative elements that invites communion on its own terms through theological dialogue. In the movie *Grand Canyon* (1991), Travis, the Steve Martin character, reflects, "Everything you need to know about life is in the movies." His remark rings true. It is a movie's portrayal of "life" that invites, if not demands, our theological response. In the process, Christians can help viewers more generally to be sensitized to such theological issues.

The Theological Critic

As Christians, we can take two basic approaches to movies. We can either reflect analytically on or respond experientially to what we have seen. I have spoken of this in terms of engaging a movie's meaning and power. As with all art, movies both invite discourse and become at times a revelatory event.[2] Theological critics of film speak of movies as being both a medium for "critical analysis of theological ideas and a medium to "provoke religious experience,"[3] as allowing theological questions and as being sacramental. They understand movies as both discursive (being about something) and presentational (being something).[4] Of course, it would be wrong to draw this distinction too starkly, for there are a range of meanings within any film that overlap with a range of experiences (though these are limited by the movie's own portrayal).

We might diagram these possible critical responses by using a matrix:

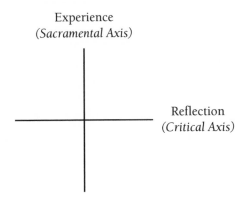

Figure 8.1 Theological Responses to Cinema

Each axis is a continuum suggesting a variety of possible theological responses. We can label the two points of the sacramental axis "The Holy" and "The Human." Here is a continuum along which we experience revelatory events. For the critical axis, we can describe the two end points as "Staying within the Movie Itself" and "Learning from a Theological Partner." This continuum suggests how we respond to movies analytically:

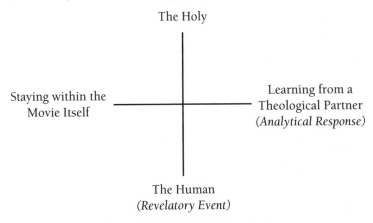

Figure 8.2 Matrix of Theological Responses

Martin Buber's distinction between "I-Thou" and "I-It" relations provides something of an analogy here. He writes, "There is no I taken in itself, but only the I of the primary word *I-Thou* and the I of the primary word *I-It*."[5] Buber understands the character of all human existence as being-in-relation. With regard to the world of cinema, the viewer exists in relation to it. But that relationship is of two types—the one analytical and the other experiential. We relate to the living world around us either as subjects ("I-Thou") or as objects ("I-It"). We enter into a shared presence, or we measure and judge. The sphere of relationship that Buber is particularly interested in is that of personal presence, that which ultimately opens one to the eternal. It is the sacramental axis, one rooted in revelatory event, that is his focus. But a critical perspective also has its role. It allows the world of work to function and provides perspective on our experiences.

To use other language, there is first order and second order understanding. We can learn as we encounter something or someone directly, and we can understand by reflecting on the experience. In our discussion in chapter 2 of the history of the church's relationship with Hollywood, we noted a general trend during the era of the Code for the church to relate to films critically, assessing their ethical impact. In more recent decades there has been a growing trend to see the human and aesthetic dimensions of film, that is, to seek an encounter with cinema. In our discussion of theology, we noted that the word "theology" can stand for our understanding "of" God or our understanding "about" God. Here, again, the analytical and the revelatory axes are distinguishable.

The Experiential Axis

In our current American climate, the revelatory, that which concerns spirituality, and not the analytical, that which suggests dogma, seems of particular theological interest. The experiential is in ascendancy throughout our culture. Transcendence, furthermore, is of two types. The one is an encounter with the sacred itself, with that which lies beyond the natural but which gives meaning to it. For the Christian, this is an attribute of God, indicating that the divine is outside of and independent of the world. Regardless of the religious tradition, phenomenologists of religion point out that the encounter is always a mystery that is at one and the same time inviting and yet awe-inspiring, fascinating and yet evoking of dread. Rudolf Otto used the word *numinous* to label this sacred other that is encountered. As he investigated how people worldwide described their experience with the numinous, moreover, he noted that it was always a mystery that simultaneously invited and repelled. Think of Moses at the burning bush or Isaiah in the temple. Here was a *"mysterium: fascinans et tremendum."*[6] Transcendence, in this sense (what we might call Transcendence A) refers to something independent of ourselves and our cultures. It is one pole of the experiential axis, one I have labeled "The Holy."

By its very nature, there is no way to identify which films will be the occasion for experiencing the miraculous, for encountering such mystery. But stories that dramatize the human search for ultimate meaning seem more often to be the vehicle of divine manifestation. *Dead Man Walking* (1995), for example, is more than a story about Sister Helen Prejean's work as a counselor to inmates on death row. It is also the story of her struggle with the soul of Matthew Poncelot, the condemned murderer who awaits execution. *Babette's Feast* (1987), *Breaking the Waves* (1996), *The Passion of Joan of Arc* (1928), *The Green Mile* (1999), and *Becket* (1964) are the kind of movies that seem uniquely able to mediate the holy, to be the occasion for epiphanies. (I say this knowing full well that epiphanies are never coerced.)

Transcendence can also be spoken of in terms of the human possibility of exceeding our limitations, of experiencing wholeness within brokenness, of glimpsing how life was meant to be but is not (what we might call Transcendence B). In the vernacular, we sometimes get a glimpse of Humpty-Dumpty put back together again. T. S. Eliot writes of this as "the still point of the turning world."

> At the still point of the turning world. Neither flesh nor fleshless;
> Neither from nor towards; at the still point, there the dance is,
> But neither arrest nor movement. And do not call it fixity,
> Where past and future are gathered. Neither movement from nor towards,
> Neither ascent nor decline. Except for the point, the still point,
> There would be no dance, and there is only the dance.
> I can only say, *there* we have been: but I cannot say where.
> And I cannot say, how long, for that is to place it in time.
>
> T. S. Eliot, "Burnt Norton," *Four Quartets*[7]

Wallace Stevens speaks of the same experience as "a self that touches all edges."[8] Within our all too fragmented lives, we occasionally rediscover life as a whole, if only for a moment. Here is the other pole of the experiential axis, what I have labeled "The Human" in order to suggest its this-worldly focus.

A number of movies come to mind that seem able to mediate what I am labeling "The Human (Transcendence B)": *Grand Canyon* (1991), *Tender Mercies* (1983), *Places in the Heart* (1984), *Sling Blade* (1996), *Secrets & Lies* (1995), *Driving Miss Daisy* (1989), *Forrest Gump* (1994), *Awakenings* (1990), and *Life Is Beautiful* (1998). But again, any filmic story that portrays human experience truthfully has this spiritual capacity. Such movies, in the words of writer Anne Lamott, "deepen and widen and expand our sense of life; they feed the soul."[9]

Transcendent human experiences (Transcendence B) are not confined to the traditional religious sphere but occur throughout life's activity. Peter Berger finds such "rumors of angels" in the human activity of play, for example.[10] One of John Updike's characters, David Kern, speaks of these human experiences as "supernatural mail on foreign soil." David's transcendent experience took place as he helped a cat, which had been hit by a car, die. At the time, he was on his way home from the hospital where his wife was giving birth to their daughter.

Death and life came together as a moment in time, but out of time. David concludes, "The incident had the signature: decisive but illegible."[11] The experience was transformative for Updike's character in conveying a sense of the sacramentality of life. Though such encounters are personal in nature, they are never simply subjective or aesthetic. Rather, they are a revelation about Reality itself.

What unites these two otherwise disparate understandings of transcendence—what we are labeling The Holy and The Human—is their common recognition of some "Value More that exceeds our current possession."[12] That is, they are revelatory of something beyond ourselves. David Hay recounts his findings after asking people to describe that "personal experience of the presence or power of whatever is conceived as ultimately real, whether named God, the gods, . . . or anything else."[13] In his surveys, he discovered that when given the opportunity and taboos were allowed to be broken down, three out of four individuals recognized that they had had such experiences. For some, these transcendent experiences were what we are labeling holy. For others, they were human. But however described, they demanded the individual's total involvement, were intensely real, were responses to a perceived "given," and had consequences for their practical lives. Many who were interviewed had not chosen to talk about these experiences before, fearing misunderstanding or rejection. But for most people, transcendence was a known experience.

Hay observes that his findings match the evidence we have from comparative religion, where it can be noted how

> literally anything or any occasion can be associated with a sudden moment of religious awareness. . . .
> . . . [T]here are records of such moments during childbirth, at the point of death, during sexual intercourse, at a meal, during fasting, in a cathedral, on a rubbish dump, on a mountain top, in a slum: in association with a particular plant, stone, fish, mammal, bird and so on *ad infinitum*. . . . [T]hough it is worth repeating that there seems to be no way of "switching them on."[14]

It is this experience of a "reality not ourselves" that suggests for Wallace Stevens an affinity between art and religion. Writes Stevens, "And the wonder and mystery of art, as indeed of religion in the last resort, is the revelation of something 'wholly other' by which the inexpressible loneliness of thinking is broken and enriched."[15] Nathan Scott speaks similarly as he writes that "the truth of the matter is that both art and religious faith share a common intention to summon us into the presence of what is other than, and transcendent to, the human mind; and, in this, they provide each other with a kind of mutual confirmation."[16]

Julius Lester, who teaches Judaic studies at the University of Massachusetts at Amherst, tells of his experience while teaching a course on religion and Western literature. His testimony is true of the power of story more generally. He says that his students are often bristling with cynicism but want to believe. After reading Eliot, Baldwin, Hesse, and Potok, "students who have not been to mass since coming to college are going again. Jewish students who go to synagogue only on Rosh Hashanah start attending Shabbat evening services. Students who do not come from a religious tradition find themselves, like the Psalmist, seeing God in nature." He concludes:

> I harbor no illusions that many of them will be able to sustain their nascent experiences of transcendent meaning. But I respect these new beginnings, regardless of how brief they may be. The students have cared enough about God to suffer the terror of His absence and they are now willing to suffer the terror of His presence.[17]

What is true for the other arts is true also for film. In the opening chapter, I offered my testimony of the power of story, together with the testimonies of Paul Woolf, Christoph Meili, Catherine Sittser, and Gregory Elmer. What these personal witnesses have in common is a transcendent experience. Such revelation cannot simply be reduced to the subjective, however personal its expression. What these witnesses encountered was a "reality not ourselves."

In a special issue of the journal *Image* that was devoted to the topic "Screening Mystery," guest editor Ronald Austin asked a number of writers, filmmakers, and screenwriters to discuss the films that most powerfully influenced their spiritual lives. The testimonials of the contributors included experiences of what I have labeled both Transcendence A and Transcendence B. Cecelia Gonzalez, co-chair of the City of Angels Film Festival, recalled a childhood memory when she encountered God while watching a movie under the stars in Havana:

> It was black and white on the screen under a black sky full of white stars. I leaned over the second floor stone balustrade toward the church courtyard. My heart strained at its moorings as the film came alive on a large sheet strung between two pillars. This is indeed a strange tribute, for I don't remember the name of the film, and in my nine-year-old memory only fragments survived, yet I know that the God alive in the film whose holy presence stopped the soldiers from desecrating his church, was the same amazing God who danced with us children in that history-paved patio, the God who made me weep.
>
> One summer night in old Havana, the sky, the screen, and the sanctuary were all framed inside the hollow of tiny hands.[18]

Here is what I am labeling Transcendence A.

Arthur Hiller answered the same question by recalling a more this-worldly transcendence (Transcendence B):

> The film *Open City* had a strong effect on me spiritually. Granted, I saw it shortly after returning from flying missions in World War II with the Royal Canadian Air Force, but it still stays with me by showing me it is still possible to keep your faith and good-

ness while undergoing one of the most unjust and emotionally wrenching disasters of this century. The scene where Anna Magnani chases after the truck while the fascist troops drag off her friend and priest still haunts me.

It is such an affirmation of the human spirit that it raised my expectations of myself and helped me to realize that doing what is right is essential even in the worst circumstances.[19]

We might distinguish between the experiences of Otto and Gonzalez on the one hand and Eliot and Hiller on the other by contrasting the miraculous and the marvelous; the supernatural and the truly natural; or perhaps the experience of mystery and the experience of compassion.

Screenwriter Paul Schrader seems to have distinctions such as these in mind when he distinguishes between (1) movies that either inform the viewer about the Transcendent or reveal the Transcendent in human reflection and (2) movies "which relate the human experience of transcendence, which *express* not the Transcendent but the human who experiences the Transcendent. . . . The terms 'Transcendent,' 'transcendental,' and 'transcendence' represent a hierarchy of the spiritual from the Other-oriented to the human-oriented."[20]

Schrader argues that such experiences must be kept distinct. I have chosen rather to place them all on the experiential continuum running from the Other-directed ("The Holy") to the human-oriented ("The Human"). I have done this, for our experiences of the Transcendent and transcendence often overlap or move back and forth seamlessly. For example, in describing the grotesque characters of Fellini's *Satyricon* (1969), Harvey Cox speaks of the need to compare Fellini with Hieronymous Bosch: "Both pour on the monstrous and the grotesque first because they want to zap us into an encounter with another reality, *and* because they want us to see perverts, cripples, idiots, sadists, and weak-kneed pushovers as our brothers and sisters."[21] Nevertheless, although the miraculous and the marvelous, the wonder-filled and the fully human, merge at times in practice, they can be described as opposite poles on the experiential axis. We as viewers will witness to our own experience of the mixture.

The Human (Transcendence B)

Human portrayals in film have greater theological connotations than we often realize. The human and the theological, in fact, are so intertwined that to speak authentically of the one is to engage the other. Recall the words of Jesus when asked what was the greatest commandment? He responded that we should love the Lord our God. But then he immediately added, "And a second is like it: 'You shall love your neighbor as yourself'" (Matt. 22:39). For Jesus, the supernatural and the natural conjoined. Stories that portray the truly human bind their viewers with the religious expressions of humankind. They awaken a holistic sense in their viewers, providing windows of meaning. Movies are evocative, portraying life's great experiences (e.g., love, birth, work, death) or their opposites, so that the gift of life becomes known by its negation. Here is one pole of the experiential axis.

Ken Gire remembers experiencing such a moment while watching the movie *An Officer and a Gentleman* (1982). The film portrays the story of a Naval Aviation recruit who must make it through boot camp in order to get his wings and fly for the Navy. Though he has done well in flight school (or perhaps because he has done well), he is singled out by the drill sergeant as someone who needs to be broken. While the other recruits are given the weekend off, the Richard Gere character is made to stay on the base and run an obstacle course. The drill sergeant is in his face, yelling at him, taunting him, and trying to make him break. Finally, while Gere is doing sit-ups in the rain, the drill sergeant tells him that he is through, discharged from the Navy. And these words break him. In his tears, Gere pleads, " You can't do it to me. I got nowhere else to go. . . . I got nowhere else to go." The scene had a profound impact on Gire. Here was an expression of his own humanity too. He writes:

> When I was going through my own grueling experiences in the wilderness and being forced to give up what I loved doing most, that scene came back to me in a powerful way. I knew what Richard Gere's character felt. I knew the determination he had to get his wings and the fear he had of not getting them. I knew the rigors of the obstacle course and the agony of endless repetitions of meaningless exercises. I knew because I was the new recruit doing sit-ups in the rain before a stern and unrelenting drill sergeant. "You can't do it to me," I remember crying out to God. "I got nowhere else to go. . . . I got nowhere else to go."[22]

In *An Officer and a Gentleman*, Gire had experienced a concrete story, but he had also been invited to transcend that reality. Through the portrayal of the human, Reality had also been discovered. Because the movie was both particular and universal, it proved to be a source of ongoing inspiration and insight.

For me, it was the Academy Award winning film *Life Is Beautiful* (1998) that provided such an experience of human transcendence. As a father with one daughter in college and one about to launch her adult career, I was moved deeply by the portrayal of a father's love for his child. Here was a sacrificial and yet joyous love that was boundless. Here is how I should have been more often with my daughters. Here is what it is to be a Father. Life is beautiful within the loving embrace of a family; it is worth any sacrifice to love those near to us.

The movie's story is simple and warm, horrific and yet humorous. Using the language of both slapstick and romance, Roberto Benigni, the co-writer, director, and lead actor, tells the story of a young peasant who comes to the city to work. It is 1939 and anti-Semitism is growing. But Guido, a Jew, is oblivious to his danger. He is in love, and life is beautiful. In one of the funniest courtships portrayed on film, Guido wins Dora (played by Benigni's real-life wife), a school-

teacher with social standing. The couple's love is genuine and contagious, and their son, Joshua, lives in the wonderful embrace of their love.

Then both Joshua and Guido are arrested and shipped to a concentration camp. The thought of Joshua suffering in fear is more than Guido can bear. The second half of the movie shows the extreme measures that Guido takes to protect his child. (There is an equally moving story of how Dora, who is not a Jew, volunteers to go to the camp in order to be with her family.) Guido plays an elaborate game to protect his son from the horrors of the prison. The extent of Guido's love for his boy brought tears to my eyes, as did the commitment Dora and Guido have to each other. In a scene reminiscent of *The Shawshank Redemption*, Guido risks his life to play music for Dora over the camp's loudspeaker. It was magnificent to watch and to hear. In fact, my wife and I went out and bought the CD so the memory could linger. Guido will do anything for Dora and Joshua, and the compelling power of his affection is reciprocated.

Guido (Roberto Benigni) protects his son, Joshua (Giorgio Cantarini), from anti-Semitic hatred by making a game with him. *Life Is Beautiful* (d. Benigni, 1998). Photo by Sergio Strizzi. ©1998 Miramax Films. All rights reserved.

The transition from town to concentration camp is heart-stopping. But the contrast works; the joy and innocence of the opening scenes only make the pathos of the second setting more heartfelt. Some have questioned the appropriateness of linking laughter with the unthinkable. Is not the Holocaust beyond humor? But such a response misses both the genre and the intention of the movie. For this film is not about Italy in 1939 or Germany in 1945. It is, instead, a celebration of a father's love, even in the midst of unspeakable tragedy and pain.

The movie begins by saying that it is going to tell a fable. It thus invites the viewer to see Reality behind, and in, reality. The humor in *Life Is Beautiful* was inviting; the horror of humankind's inhumanity was chilling. But the sacrificial and trusting love between a boy and his father was compelling. Ultimately, in this film the father's love became paradigmatic of what a parent's love should be; it was even analogous to the Father's love (1 John 3:1: "See what love the Father has given us, that we should be called children of God; and that is what we are"). To hold your child in your arms (or to be held in your parent's arms) is transformative. In the words of Joshua as the movie ends, "We won."

The Holy (Transcendence A)

The other experiential pole I have labeled "The Holy." Here the transcendent is disclosed through the material of reality, but in such a way as to manifest a reality that does not belong to this world.[23] Or, to put the matter more simply, movies are a window through which God speaks. The experience of the holy cannot be programmed. It is a gift. However, some movies seem to predispose their viewers to receive such an experience. They are sacramental. Some of my students speak, for example, of having a mystical encounter through seeing the baseball movie *Field of Dreams* (1989). Few, if any, speak similarly about *Bull Durham* (1988), even though the movie begins with the Susan Sarandon character's monologue about the "church of baseball."

A movie that Andrew Greeley says ushered him into the presence of the divine was *Places in the Heart* (1984), the film for which Sally Field won an Academy Award in 1985 for best actress. The movie ends in a Baptist church in a small Texas town during the Depression. The congregation sings "Blessed Assurance," and then there is a communion service. Writes Greeley, "As the cup and wafers are passed through the congregation and the camera examines the faces of each of the communicants, we become aware that all of the characters in the story are present, the good and the bad, the venal and the heroic, the living and the dead, the killer and the victim." All are brought together as one by Jesus. This moving and vivid portrayal of "the communion of the saints" became the occasion for Greeley to again meet God. Although the meaning of the scene is so blatantly accessible that in the hands of a less skilled filmmaker it would seem trite, "the sheer, gentle beauty of the scene" rescued it for Greeley from any charge of moralizing. Greeley concludes, "Film in the hands of a skilled sacrament-maker is uniquely able to make 'epiphanies' happen."[24]

Greeley describes Eric Rohmer's *My Night with Maud* (1969) and Bob Fosse's *All That Jazz* (1979) as being similarly sacramental for him.[25] He believes movies to be particularly suitable for the creating of epiphanies, for they have an inherent power to affect the imagination. I am reminded of C. S. Lewis's book *The Pilgrim's Regress*, when Lewis portrays John hearing words near the Canyon: "For this end I made your senses and for this end your imagination that you might see My face and live."[26] Greeley argues that God discloses himself to us through the experiences, objects, and people we encounter in our lives. He writes that "grace is everywhere."[27] One must be concerned about the poor, thinks Greeley; but one must also be concerned with the arts, for the artist is a potential sacrament maker, one who can reveal the presence of God within creation itself. Here is the theological basis for our experience of the holy in film.

Greeley's experience with *Places in the Heart* was necessarily unique to him (it was *his* experience), but it is also shared by others. My colleague and the series co-editor, Bill Dyrness, speaks of this same film as changing his consciousness. He writes, "I doubt I will ever think about the church in the same way after that final scene."[28] Some movies have a sacramental intention that opens viewers repeatedly to experiences of grace. This was my experience as I watched *Becket*; it proved to be similar for Father Gregory Elmer. Similar, that is, and yet distinct, for how God spoke to Father Elmer was different from how I heard my call into ministry.

That movies affect people differently not only has something to do with the varied background and life experiences of the audience. It not only has to do with the mystery of the Holy Spirit's presence. No, movies' effect on their viewers has also to do with the nature of story itself. For stories are not received simply as a string of linear facts. Rather, stories create images, they give us "pictures inside our heads" to which we respond. Joseph Sittler, the Lutheran theologian, recognized something of the unpredictability of story in his comments on the gospel story. He noted that the four Gospels are full of phrases like "and suddenly . . . and on the way he met . . . now it happened that . . . there stood before him a man."[29] It is "in the midst of the many-threaded, wild unsystematic of the actual," he wrote, that "the not-expected was crossed and blessed by the not-possible."[30] It is in the "not-expected" that movie viewers are often graced by the "not-possible," as God meets us and speaks to us through movies.

The Critical Axis

Movies, like life itself, are first experienced, then reflected on. They affect the heart, then the head. And one's gut-level response becomes itself part of what is later reflected on.[31] It is for this reason that we have turned to consider the experiential axis first. It is our encounter with the movie itself that should control all else. Faithfulness to the concrete experience of the movie's story is the first criterion for effective theological criticism. Such movie-centered criticism can be confirmed and extended through the use of genre analysis, auteur criticism, thematic dialogue, and cultural critique. A totally idiosyncratic viewing of the shape or meaning of a film, particularly if it is then used as the basis for theological dialogue, should be thought suspect. The adequacy of any critical response to a movie must be measured by the film itself.

There is also the possibility of saying more, of bringing the engagement with film into conversation with one's second-order theology. To reflect analytically and constructively on a movie's meaning is to treat the film with the seriousness that its creators intend. If the movie is meant to be simply entertainment, mere escapist fare, theological conversation is of course pointless. But so too is any film criticism. What we have is the equivalent of pulp fiction or dime store romances. Just as there are bad novels and trite paintings, so there are confused or hackneyed movies. But for any film that seeks to connect with its viewers with regard to the human condition, or to offer a vision of transcendence whether human or divine, theological criticism is both appropriate and even necessary.

As with the experiential axis, we can again view the critical as having two poles, one interior to the movie itself and the other exterior to our experience with a film. These I have labeled "Staying within the Movie Itself" and "Learning from a Theological Partner." The one seeks to find within the movie itself a standard for theological judgment. No outside, or ultimate, ground for critiquing the movie is appealed to. The other uses theological resources from outside the film itself to better understand or judge it, although these outside resources cannot be used to skew the first-order experience of movie viewing itself.

Again, in practice these two forms of theological criticism often overlap, with both internal and external theological criteria being brought to bear in analyzing a film's meaning. For example, there are a significant group of movies that have a purely fictional character who has substantial resemblance to the Christ-figure (e. g., someone who comes into a society from the outside and through suffering love redeems other[s]). *Cool Hand Luke* (1967), *E.T.* (1982), *One Flew over the Cuckoo's Nest* (1975), *Sling Blade* (1996), *Babette's Feast* (1987), and *Titanic* (1997) are all such films. Here the theological dialogue needs to take both critical poles into account. That is, the portrayal of the Christ-figure by the movie adds new understanding to who Christ is. It needs to be considered on its own terms. At the same time, because the biblical portrayal of Christ has been used metaphorically, the Christ story can clarify the character's situation and add depth and authority to the characterization. It too has a place at the critical table.

Perhaps because of the history of heavy-handed theological and moral judgments being levied by the church with regard to Hollywood, there was a time when some theologians were content to limit themselves to internal criticism alone—to only consider film as film and to offer no external theological evaluation. Ernest Ferlita and John May's early work, *Film Odyssey: The Art of Film as Search for Meaning* (1976), is perhaps an example. Having discussed the human search for meaning in a brief opening chapter, they then turn to consider a number of movies that take up this theme. They argue:

> The theological critic of contemporary culture . . . is an eye specialist rather than a painter. The painter gives us an impression of the world as he sees it; the ophthalmologist strives to bring our vision back to the norm so that we can see life as it really is. By exposing the visual structures of a limited number of films, we hope that our reader will sharpen his own capacity for interpreting other films of quest and for discerning in them whatever meaning the form suggests. . . . We go directly to the painting or the film, not of course to stay with the artist's world, but to allow his vision to direct ours to discover anew life's meaning, even if we must in Shakespeare's words "by indirections find directions out" (*Hamlet* 2.1.65).[32]

Though theological dialogue is their ultimate stated goal, the book remains at the level of "ophthalmology."

Autonomous theological criticism has its place; it can be extremely helpful in focusing the viewer's attention on the center of power and meaning of a movie. Richard Blake's book, *Screening America*, is one such example. Written by a Jesuit priest who was for fifteen years the film reviewer for the Catholic journal *America*, the book discusses five classic American films, each representing a particular identifiable genre—the screwball comedy, the gangster film, the Western, the detective story, and the horror film. In the process, Blake not only reveals much about American culture but also much about the nature of the human condition. He does not bring external biblical or theological judgments to bear on the movies in view. But his Catholic sensitivity to a movie's sacramental potential is evident. At a more popular level, the same might be said of Roger Ebert. His film reviewing, thumbs up included, is filled with an implicit Catholic perspective.

While "autonomous" criticism was perhaps necessary for a period when the church and its theologians tended to be artistically insensitive, it is less than the total criticism which T. S. Eliot argued for so successfully. Having assisted viewers to better see the religious import of a film, theological critics can go on to engage the film's center of meaning from their own theological perspective. The importance of this final critical step has been increasingly recognized over the last decade or so, in particular by a group of scholars trained in biblical studies. In the preceding chapters, we have had occasion to refer to several of these scholars who are presently engaged in critical conversation with film. Robert Jewett, Bernard Brandon Scott, David Rhoads, and Larry Kreitzer are also New Testament scholars by training.

These biblical scholars speak of the needed dialogue between film and Scripture using different metaphors and descriptors. Rhoads argues for a needed critical intertextuality. Jewett speaks of film as a "conversation partner" with Scripture. Scott seeks a "critical correlation," while Jewett also wants to apply an "interpretive arch" that is rooted on one end in the biblical world and on the other in the world of cinema. Kreitzer argues the need to "reverse the hermeneutical flow" between Bible and culture, letting film and novel inform and instruct Scripture. However it is expressed, for all these biblical scholars, movies need to be brought into conversation with the Bible in order that both Scripture and movies might be illumined.

Again, in their book *Screening the Sacred* (1995), Joel Martin and Conrad Ostwalt define theological criticism as a dialogue between movie themes and Christian categories. Most of John May's more recent writing also fits into this category (cf. *Image and Likeness* [1992] and *New Image of Religious Film* [1997]). So, too, does Clive Marsh and Gaye Ortiz's edited volume, *Explorations in Theology and Film* (1997), where Marsh speaks of a needed negotiation between film and theology; and chapter after chapter illustrate the enterprise. There is possible a fruitful dialogue between movies on the one hand and the sources of Christian reflection on the other.

In order to understand better the nature of theological criticism as practiced analytically, two examples of theological film criticism will prove instructive. Both involve popular Hollywood movies. They were written for a general Christian audience. I wrote the first in 1995. It seeks to put the film *The Shawshank Redemption* (1994) into conversation with the biblical Book of Ecclesiastes.[33] In this meditation on friendship, film and theology have become conversation partners, each throwing light on the other. Here the model is that of dialogue, or intertextuality. The film's verbal script and visual images are put into dialogue with a thematically similar text from Scripture.

The second example of theological criticism I wrote in 1999, as the last year of the old millennium dawned.[34] Here, there is a reverse hermeneutical flow, as the images of a group of Hollywood apocalyptic movies are used to inform and critique the church and its theology of end times (or lack thereof). Both essays are examples of film criticism being completed by its engagement with theology.

A Meditation on Friendship

Two are better than one, because they have a good reward for their toil. For if they fall, one will lift up the other; but woe to one who is alone and falls and does not have another to help. Again, if two lie together, they keep warm; but how can one keep warm alone? And though one might prevail against another, two will withstand one. A threefold cord is not quickly broken.

Ecclesiastes 4:9–12

The Shawshank Redemption (d. Darabont, 1994) was one of five films up for an Oscar as best picture of 1995. Because it lacked the popular appeal of *Forrest Gump*, it lost. But the movie should not be missed. Set in Shawshank Prison, the film portrays human possibility within the impossibility of that impersonal world.

In particular, the movie is a story of human friendship—the friendship of Andrew Dufresne (Andy) and Ellis Redding (Red). Red has been sent to prison for a crime committed in his youth twenty years earlier. Andy, a bank vice-president, has been recently and wrongly convicted of the murder of his wife, who was found in the arms of her lover. Red is an African American; Andy is white. Red has little education but lots of street smarts. (He is the guy who can get anything smuggled into the prison.) Andy has lots of education but lacks prison savvy. (He is beat within an inch of his life by the prison "sisters.")

Red (Morgan Freeman, left) and Andy (Tim Robbins) develop a friendship as inmates of Shawshank Prison. *The Shawshank Redemption* (d. Darabont, 1994). Photo by Michael Weinstein. ©1994 Columbia Pictures Industries, Inc., and Castle Rock Entertainment. All rights reserved.

The movie begins by showing Andy's wife's murder while the radio plays, "If I didn't care more than words can say. . . . If this isn't love then why do I thrill? . . . Is it love beyond compare?" And the viewer senses the full irony. No, it is not love beyond compare that Andy's wife and her lover have. It is a vulgar, desperate, mutually self-centered affair that ends in a double murder. But the question "Is it love beyond compare?" remains in one's mind and frames the movie. Andy and Red come to care deeply for each other. Their friendship becomes, in fact, a love beyond compare.

At Shawshank, the old prison librarian, Brooks, is let out after fifty years in that jail, so that the government will not have to pay for his final years. Brooks is afraid to leave. He says, "These walls are funny. First you hate them. Then you get used to them. Then you need them." When he is paroled, Brooks tries to live as a free man, but he is lonely and frightened. Finally, he writes a note back to the prison ("I don't like it here. I've decided not to stay") and then hangs himself in his rooming house. With no friends, he cannot cope.

Woe to the one who is alone and falls and does not have another to help.

As Red becomes older, he too becomes fearful that he has become "institutionalized." He is scared that he will be cast out of the prison when he is too old to readjust to the outside. Wanting to give hope to his friend, Andy shares with him a dream he has. When he gets out of prison, he wants to go to a little town in Mexico on the edge of the Pacific Ocean—Zihuatanejo. He will buy a little hotel and an old boat that needs fixing up.

Andy says to Red, "A place like that could use a man who knew how to get things." Red says he is too old for such dreams, but Andy persists: "Red, if you ever get out of here, do me a favor. Go to a hayfield near Baxton [and Andy describes the place] and look for a black rock and find what is buried there." And Red agrees.

These two friends do get out. Andy first; Red sometime later. Red, like Brooks, gets a job, but almost despairs of fitting back into society. There is an important difference, however. Red has promised his friend to go to the field in Baxton. So as a final act of desperate courage, Red goes and does, indeed, find what is buried there. Andy has left him some money and a note, saying, "Remember, hope is a good thing." The film ends with Red traveling south to Zihuatanejo, where he finds his friend on the beach repairing an old boat.

"If I didn't care, more than words can say. . . . Is it love beyond compare?" The shallow words of the radio song have faded, but they are replaced by the profound actions of two men whose friendship is life-giving and life-sustaining.

Two are better than one, because they have a good reward for their toil. For if they fall, one will lift up the other.

Human friendship is one of the Creator's great gifts to humankind in helping us deal with life's problems, or so the writer of Ecclesiastes teaches and the director of *The Shawshank Redemption* portrays. For the prisoners, there are issues of injustice, of oppression for those lacking power. The writer of Ecclesiastes outlines similar wrongs, ills typical of ancient Israelite society but which sound jarringly familiar. The Preacher writes of the tears of the oppressed (4:1), of jealous competition as the real fuel of most hard work (4:4), and of the compulsiveness of the rich, who are never satisfied (4:7). What is the antidote for our vain toil? For our work that so often proves little more than a chasing after wind?

Though one might prevail against another, two will withstand one. A threefold cord is not quickly broken.

We need each other. The Lord God once said, "It is not good that the man should be alone; I will make him a helper as his partner" (Genesis 2:18). This simple creational truth is foundational. The Preacher knew nothing of God's ultimate plan of redemption in Christ Jesus, but he was well-versed in Genesis (as the text of Ecclesiastes reveals through multiple allusions and references). Reflecting on who we were created to be and therefore on who we are, the writer of Ecclesiastes could thus point beyond the impasse of society's futile work. He could point beyond our vain self-interest to something more primary.

Our habits of the heart so feed our individualistic spirits that a commitment to the common good has flagged in our society. We have asserted our self-sufficiency so uncritically that we have placed our very lives in jeopardy. On the national level, we risk reducing our democracy to single-interest politics. Our own agendas must take priority. At the church level, we feel little compunction against leaving for another congregation that can better meet our needs. Our identification with a body of co-believers has become shallow, if not nonexistent. In the home, marriages are failing as both partners go their separate ways, putting personal fulfillment ahead of other common aspirations. Our collective self-interest is proving meaningless, little more than a chasing after wind.

How can we once again discover the importance of others as Red and Andy did? Dietrich Bonhoeffer, writing from his prison cell in Nazi Germany, penned these words to his friend Eberhard Bethge:

> Who is there . . . in our times, who can devote himself . . . to music, friendship, games, or happiness? . . . I believe that within the sphere of this freedom friendship is by far the rarest and most priceless treasure, for where else does it survive in this world of ours, dominated as it is by [work, marriage, and state]. It cannot be compared with the treasures of the mandates, for in relation to them it is *sui generis*: it belongs to them as the cornflower belongs to the cornfield.[35]

The cornflower to the cornfield—friendship to work. The cornfield requires tilling. The obligation and the opportunity to work is still ours. But alongside the cornfield is the cornflower that sustains.

* * * *

Thinking about the Millennium

As we approach Y2K (year two thousand), movies dealing with the end of history have proliferated. Besides entertaining us with their nonstop adventure and eye-popping special effects, these films should challenge the church and its thinking (theology) if we would but observe and consider. For the typical, current end-of-the-world movie both rejects the established approaches to life and its solutions (including, by implication, the church's) and recasts our apocalyptic dreams and projections in secular terms.

Some of these recent movies are post-apocalyptic, that is, they deal with events after the destruction of the world as we know it. Kevin Costner's *Waterworld* (1995) is a good example of this genre (even if a bust of a film!). Its story is played out amidst a world covered in water because of human stupidity and greed.

A second group of films, and perhaps the more prevalent, portray events that threaten to bring about the world's end. Some malevolent force (asteroids in *Armageddon* [1998]; aliens in *Independence Day* [1996]; and dinosaurs in

Veteran astronaut Spurgeon Tanner (Robert Duvall, center) confers with the shuttle crew. *Deep Impact* (d. Leder, 1998). Photo by Myles Aronowitz. ©1998 by Paramount Pictures and DreamWorks LLC. All rights reserved.

Godzilla [1998]) is about to bring about our destruction. To avoid it, we will need the best of both human ingenuity and technology. But humankind is capable, even if barely: we ultimately must take responsibility for ourselves and our posterity. Though there is carnage and loss, life will continue. Or so the script suggests.

The 1998 movie *Deep Impact* (1998) is a good example of our current doomsday movies. As the film opens, Leo Biderman, a high-school student on an astronomy field trip, discovers a comet "the size of Mt. Everest." It is about to collide with the earth—that is, to make a deep impact. What will people do, given this "ELE"—Extinction Level Event? Throughout the rest of the film we observe the response not only of Leo but of Jenny Lerner, an inexperienced but ambitious MSNBC reporter, and ultimately of the president of the United States, Tom Beck (played convincingly by Morgan Freeman). The government has been secretly working on a survival plan; it is building a spaceship called Messiah to intercept the comet, plant nuclear devices beneath its surface, and skillfully blow the comet to smithereens. It would be wrong to give away the story, which involves choosing a million people by lottery to repeople the planet (animals "two by two" will also be squirreled away in the underground fallout shelter in Missouri). But several observations can be made without giving away the particulars of the ending (the larger pattern we already suspect: "though there is carnage and loss, life will continue!").

First, linear thinking is out. Planning, organization, technology—these are insufficient by themselves. Jenny Lerner uncovers the asteroid threat by mistaking ELE for Elie, a supposed lover of a senator, and she is hailed as an investigative genius. Just as septuagenarian John Glenn joined six younger astronauts aboard discovery last October for a space flight, so Spurgeon Tanner (Robert Duvall) is the older former astronaut involved in accomplishing the Messiah Project (most of these films are not too subtle in their meaning!). Although the younger crew members resent him at first, believing he is educationally outdated and along only for P.R. reasons, Tanner proves indispensable. The others might be better able to handle the necessary technology, but leadership, wisdom, and an aesthetic sense are equally necessary, particularly when plans inevitably fail. A highlight in the film is when Tanner goes to comfort a young colleague in the doomed spacecraft by reading *Moby Dick*.

We are reminded of *The X-Files*, where both Fox Mulder's intuitive, even irrational, grasp of reality (his sister was abducted by aliens when he was a small child, which opened him to believe in anything and everything) and Dana Scully's no-nonsense rationalism (she is the clear thinker, the scientist/medic) must be used if catastrophe is to be avoided. There is no retreat from our technological age, in either the TV or film episodes of this ongoing saga. But equally sure is the realization that the scientific rationality of our modern age has come to a dead end and must be supplemented. Guidance must come from multiple sources.

In his inaugural lecture as Professor of Practical Theology at Aberdeen University, John Drane points to this need to go beyond rationality and coherence as a major theme in the film *Armageddon*.[36] If there is a way of preserving planet Earth, it will not be through the normal rules of reason and rationality. It is not NASA or the Pentagon who will save us. In fact, at one point in the movie, the NASA director tells his colleagues that if they feel like praying, "now would be the time." It is not the government that will save us, but Harry Stamper, the world's greatest oilfield driller. His strategy will be totally illogical but also ultimately successful.

What are we to make of this? As I write this essay, *Time* magazine's cover story is about the herbal medicine boom with its so-called alternative remedies. The film *Patch Adams* is about to be released with Robin Williams playing a doctor who dresses in clown outfits in order to assist the healing of his patients (much to the consternation of the chief of the medical staff). Jesse "the Body" Ventura is in Hollywood to celebrate his recent election victory over Hubert Humphrey Jr. as governor of Minnesota. Is there any who would doubt our culture's denial of system and coherence alone? I think of the image of Ken Starr in his grey suit and impassive face, sitting on his briefcase to increase his stature and trying to convince a group of legislators and the wider population that logic should prevail or our system is in trouble. But as we approach the millennium, it is logic and mysticism, Prozac and St. John's Wort, poetry and physics, a good (successful) president and a bad (sinful) person that together hold sway. There is no longer a system to be trusted. Loose ends will remain. But success can be found in using both the intuitive and the rational.

A Secularized Evil

There is a second aspect of *Deep Impact*'s apocalyptic vision that is also worth noting. Evil is now secularized. It is not the satanic that is a threat as much as it is a comet (in other movies, you can substitute global warming, viruses, and even aliens). Moreover, it is not a sovereign God who initiates the apocalypse, but natural causes hastened by human blundering and capriciousness. In the biblical vision of the apocalypse, the righteous are raised—they escape the final annihilation. But in this Hollywood version, good and bad people alike are threatened. It is not so important to be among the righteous as it is for human ingenuity and heroism to link with technology in order to save the day.

What are we to make of such a "natural" apocalypse? Conrad Ostwalt, speaking at a recent conference on religion and film, has suggested provocatively that Americans are increasingly substituting Hollywood doomsday films for the more typical Christian apocalyptic vision.[37] With the evangelical church becoming mainstream within our society, we have difficulty portraying world destruction at the hands of a sovereign God. After all, we like the world we live in. So outside of certain religious groups on the cultural margin, a real apocalyptic consciousness is largely missing from contemporary Christian thought. The church's voice has grown silent (when was the last time you heard a sermon about the world's imminent end at the hand of a righteous God?). Enter Hollywood to deal with our millennial fears.

Perhaps Ostwalt has overstated his case. But only slightly. While some theologians predicted one hundred years ago that this century would be the "age of eschatology," few are speaking that way about the next. Typically, we continue to believe that the end times will come, but this is not preached or taught as often as other aspects of the Christian story. A minister friend wrote his master's thesis on "gehenna" (Mt. 18:9) and the "lake of fire" (Rev. 19:20; 20:10). His doctoral dissertation was on angels in the eschaton. But that was in the 1970s, when Hal Lindsey's first book, *The Late Great Planet Earth*, went through multiple printings and the Soviet Union was still the threat from the north. Now my minister friend has moved to a large evangelical megachurch, and his first lengthy sermon series was on wisdom for life from the Book of Proverbs. The focus of his ministry has become that of helping people live Christianly. This is what an upper-middle-class congregation needs (and expects). But in the process, has the congregation not lost something of the story—God's story? The denouement is absent; the ending is lacking.

Do we live in the full consciousness that God will bring this age to a close? Do we want to hear an apocalyptic, end-time message? God will overcome evil and establish his universal kingdom forever. If God's message about the ending of his story is no longer being heard vibrantly within the church, is God using Hollywood to challenge us to recover a sense of the apocalyptic? Most of us go to see *Deep Impact* or *Godzilla* with popcorn in hand and then head for the pizza parlor with our children. These movies are simply escapist fare. But could it be that these futurist, fantastic images also have the magical capacity to inspire once again our imagination with regard to the end times? Or speak our fears about the future? It would not be the first time God has used unconscious agents to accomplish his purposes. Whether a complacent, middle-class church wants to hear such a message, the final act of God's story will happen.

Maranatha. Lord, come quickly.

9

an example: the movies of peter weir

As the twentieth-century's art form, movies continue to play a prominent role as we enter the new millennium. In many ways they are our world's *lingua franca*. Just ask your kids! Though some are mere entertainment and diversion, many are not. Movies can widen our exposure to life and provide alternate viewpoints as to its meaning and significance. Movies recreate experience and awaken it to life. They reveal what an unaided eye might otherwise miss. This is why the artistic craft of a film, the means by which it portrays its story, is so crucial. Moviemakers and moviegoers alike ask the question, "Does it work?" And the answer is largely an aesthetic one.

Movies also have their ethical dimension, both by what they do and by what they don't. The discussion about sex and violence on the screen is pertinent, even if at times shrill. So, too, is the variety of portrayals of what it means to be human today. For through the stories they present, movies help shape the lives of their audience. That is, the "real" and the "reel" come together in the experience of the viewer. Perhaps the advertisement that declares "We are what we eat" overstates, but its truth with regard to movies is incontrovertible—"We are what we watch."

While movies are both aesthetically powerful and ethically affecting, they have seldom been thought to be a conversation partner for theology. It is this deficiency that *Reel Spirituality* has sought to address. Most of us recognize that we are being shaped emotionally and cognitively by what we see on the screen, but we seldom consider the realm of the spirit. Despite the truth of the spiritual's lyrics "He's got the whole world in his hand," we seldom notice God's sacramental presence in the ordinary experiences of life, including our moviegoing. We fail to hear God speak. For this reason, we rarely respond theologically, whether critically or experientially. That is, Hollywood and the Christian faith are kept distinct, even if it is occasionally recognized that both help give shape to what we think and feel, and to how we act.

Movies image life. Through editing and framing, sound and special effects, they give expression to memorable stories. As an art form, we might even say that they tell *our* stories. It was C. S. Lewis who recognized that "the story does what no theorem can quite do. It may not be 'like real life' in the superficial sense, but it sets before us an image of what reality may well be like at some more central region."[1] In their particularity, movies have the capacity to portray something universal about life and to convey it convincingly.

Reel Spirituality is about seeing and responding, about encountering stories that both interpret us and are interpreted by us. On the one hand, as John Ruskin put it, "The greatest thing a human soul ever does in this world is to see something and tell what it saw in a plain way."[2] Seeing and telling, however, cannot remain dispassionate if they are to be appropriate to the invitation of the movie story itself. For movie stories provide an interpretation of life, inviting movieviewers to respond to them from their own perspective concerning life's power and meaning. In other words, one's response to a movie (with its governing convictions) needs to be completed from a definite theological perspective. Such communion is called forth by the very artistic shape of the movie.

Movies offer meaning with regard to the facts of life. They make a claim, provide a perspective, and portray a reality. In order to help us see what they see, I have suggested a variety of critical approaches to movie viewing. As stories, movies invite reflection on their formal characteristics—their plot, characterization, atmosphere, and point of view. At one level, a movie story is to be experienced, not analyzed. But by reflecting critically on where the power and meaning of a given story is centered, the viewer can often see how best to enter into dialogue with it.

Alternately, a movie can be considered in terms of its theme. All good movies have a theme, an overall perspective, position, or point of view around which the content and images of the movie are chosen. A movie's genre provides it with a system of orientation as well as a means of communicating expectation. As such, genres give viewers cues as to the director's personal vision as well as to cultural values within the society. Auteur criticism explores how a particular movie can be illuminated by the similar themes and visual style that occur across the *oeuvre* of a director, as well as by the director's biography. And cultural criticism can help us recognize the context of the movie's creation, as well as the role of the audience as both recipients and active interpreters of a movie.

All of the above critical means help us unpack the power and meaning of a movie on its own terms. In thinking about how we might then complete the critical task by responding theologically to the movie's story, I have suggested that theology includes both the study "of" God (an experiential enterprise) and study "about" God (a critical task). Dialogue between filmic elements and convictions and Christian experience and belief can, therefore, be either experiential or reflective, spirit oriented or word oriented. Ideally it will be both. But in all cases, conversation between Christians and Hollywood should be two-way and open-ended, a dialogue and not a diatribe.

As we bring this study of the interrelationship of Christian theology and Hollywood movies to a close, a final example might be helpful in illustrating how these critical perspectives interact in practice. I have chosen to consider the movies of Peter Weir, and to respond critically and theologically to the stories they present.

Weir as Auteur

At the beginning of most of his films is the caption "A Peter Weir Film." This is not simply a marketing device or an expression of artistic ego. Audiences come to a Peter Weir movie expecting something specific, and their experience is filtered in that light.

Peter Weir came of age during the 1960s, sharing much of the anti-authoritarian and idealistic attitudes of his generation. In all of Weir's movies, the establishment is put on notice. Whether it is the army (*Gallipoli*, 1981) or the police (*Witness*, 1985), journalism (*The Year of Living Dangerously*, 1982) or television (*The Truman Show*, 1998), Appleyard College (*Picnic at Hanging Rock*, 1975) or Welton Academy (*Dead Poets Society*, 1989), New York liberals (*Green Card*, 1990; *Fearless*, 1993), Australian lawyers (*The Last Wave*, 1977), or American industrialists (*The Mosquito Coast*, 1986), Weir's movies oppose the power structure. Like other Australians of his era, Weir has been impatient with the enforced conformity of the older generation. He has questioned their alliances and structures and has opposed their intolerance. He has recognized there must be something more than the materialism they have fostered. As an alternative, in a number of his films he has explored the spiritual and the uncanny. Here is our beginning point for understanding Weir's movies.

Peter Weir usually puts his characters into closed situations or hostile environments. *The Truman Show* is paradigmatic. His solutions to the needs of his characters, however, are rarely structural or political. Weir is not a social commentator or ethicist. He has not produced movies to critique the military or challenge the legal system. In fact, though his films are situated in the public world, they are not so much interested in it as in the private world, the shadows that lie behind. His movies deal not as much with his characters' external circumstance as with their internal situation. While society's voyeurism is questioned in *The Truman Show*, for example, the movie is primarily interested in

Truman the person. Can he really be a whole human being in the artificial environment of Seahaven Island? While the political unrest and squalor of Jakarta are portrayed in *The Year of Living Dangerously*, Guy Hamilton's personal growth is the film's focus. *Picnic at Hanging Rock* reveals class issues, and *The Last Wave* brings to light the plight of the Aborigines. But neither film ultimately shows much interest in structural solutions. While *Witness* deals with a shooting within an Amish context and *Gallipoli* shows the horrors of war, neither are really about violence. Viewers will bring their own political agendas to Weir's movies and might even be moved to act politically by what they see, but that is not his movies' primary focus.

Rather, Peter Weir's movies are more mythic than realistic. Their specific contexts simply support the larger, more universal intentions of the films. In his storytelling Weir proves to be a romantic, someone convinced that individuals must take control of their own lives, break free from society's constraints, and create a new vision of what it is to be human. Weir presents to his audience a take on human liberation, and through it, a portrayal of what it is to be a whole person. Weir's heroes and heroines are not just people who are educated or cultured, but people who are at home in the world, particularly given its mystery. Weir would have us "seize the day," choose our love, go back to our jobs transformed, or else fail trying. It is a vision of life that he seeks to portray, not a solution to life's problems.

Weir began his career in the 1960s, just as the Australian film industry was coming alive after a thirty-year hiatus. An immigrant people who left all behind to come to a new land, Australians have often viewed themselves as largely without an identity, without a story. Weir thus set out in his early films to provide not a commentary on issues facing Australians, but a story by which they might celebrate their identity. He attempted to provide a myth by which Australians could envision themselves. In *The Year of Living Dangerously*, both Billy Kwan and Guy Hamilton are half-Australian, struggling with their identities. Billy says to Guy, "We're divided men. Your father an American, mine Chinese. We're not certain we're Australians. . . . [W]e're not quite at home in the world." Much of Weir's initial work focused on this issue: How could the Australian experience (nature's vast and hostile expanse, "mateship," an indigenous people, a difficult circumstance) be put to the service of something more fundamental, the providing of a sense of identity?

It is not just Australians who feel personal dislocation and dis-ease, however. Even though Peter Weir has shifted his location from Australia to Hollywood, and his style from "art-film" to studio movie, he has continued creating universal stories of human possibility. And new audiences have discovered his movies. Peter Weir has transcended his culture and has filmed stories that challenge and renew the human spirit. He would have us transcend our cultures and "seize the day."

Weir's Thematic Concerns

Peter Weir is a storyteller interested in life's central issues—death, nature, friendship, freedom, spirit, and the like. His films are rooted in particular times and places, but they focus on life's fundamental concerns: "What then must we do?" How can we "seize the day"? Is there a reality beyond our surface existence?

As Weir has portrayed on the screen the shape and possibility of human life, he has focused his individual movies on particular thematic concerns—death, Nature, "Dreamtime," Asia, "seize the day." That is, together with his screen-writers, he has organized and empowered his stories by focusing on a given perspective. *Gallipoli*, for example, is not so much about the massive defeat of Australian and New Zealander troops in 1915 on the Gallipoli peninsula in Turkey, as about the Australian phenomenon of "mateship." In the isolation of the outback, women stayed home to care for children, and men went off to work. In that context friendships between men developed that were close and innocent. These bushmen made up the core of the Australian army that fought in World War I. Their camaraderie and mutual support is what Weir tried to capture in his film. In an interview (1984), he said,

> It's often said of male filmmakers that we don't deal effectively with women. I think what's more to the point is that we don't deal effectively with emotion, with feminine aspects of the personality, which are also contained in the male. In a stridently heterosexual, macho society, these are doubly dangerous things to deal with, because they can be easily misconstrued.[3]

The tenderness of friendship is given central importance in *Gallipoli*, but it is an important theme in other of Weir's movies. In his romantic portrayal of what it is to be human, Weir would have us let the gentler, more intuitive side of our being surface (cf. *Dead Poets Society, The Year of Living Dangerously, Fearless, Green Card* [where the gender characteristics are reversed], *The Truman Show*). Weir would blur the distinctions between those male and female characteristics that we all possess, something he symbolized brilliantly in casting Linda Hunt as Billy Kwan in *The Year of Living Dangerously*.

Although *The Year of Living Dangerously* is on one level an adventure story about the political turmoil in Indonesia that characterized the 1970s and 1980s, it is actually about "Asia."[4] It is about the missing spiritual component that the West needs and which is evident in the East. In "Asia," there are the puppet-masters, those able both to balance left and right and to focus their attention on the shadows that the puppets create rather than on the puppets themselves. Billy Kwan, with one foot in each culture, is the appropriate guide into this culture for Guy Hamilton, a foreign correspondent for the Australian Broadcasting Service. As they explore Jakarta, however, Guy seems incapable of seeing anything but his career opportunities—anything, that is, but the puppets. When

Guy betrays the confidence of Jill Bryant and publishes secret information about an arms shipment that she has given him, Billy challenges him, saying, "You abuse your position as journalist." Guy has failed to respond to the spiritual, to the gift of friendship that Jill has offered. He has valued detachment over commitment, career over relationship. In the process, he has failed to see as Asians see. He has failed to look beyond the "puppets" themselves. As the movie ends, Guy, having begun to learn his lesson, risks his external eyesight and his career to pursue his love. He now has eyes to see other realities.

In his subsequent movies, Weir returns to this same theme: there is in the West a missing spiritual component. *Witness, Dead Poets Society, The Mosquito Coast, Green Card, Fearless*, and *The Truman Show* all explore the life of the spirit (the shadow). There is more than the surface realities of life, something his early movies also portrayed. One can substitute Anzac, Amish, or Aborigine for Asian. The concrete political reality is important but only as the occasion to delve beneath the surface to explore life itself.

Or again, Weir has said that in *Picnic at Hanging Rock*, "The grand theme was Nature, and even the girls' sexuality was as much a part of that as the lizard crawling across the top of the rock. They were part of the same whole; part of larger questions."[5] Hanging Rock is itself a volcanic eruption that has forced itself up from the earth's crust. It represents the untamed forces of nature. It is a symbol for a more ancient knowledge (like the Aboriginal "dreamtime" in *The Last Wave*) that provides the schoolgirls entrance into adulthood. The primitive power of Nature over ongoing life is announced with the credits. On the screen we read, "On Saturday 14 February 1900, a party of schoolgirls from Appleyard College picnicked at Hanging Rock near Mt. Macedon in the state of Victoria. During the afternoon, several members of the party disappeared without a trace. . . ." Nature simply engulfed them. No answers are provided in the movie about what happened or where they went. Not even a coherent story is related. Rather, Weir is content to present the problem. Nature does not always give up her secrets.

"*Picnic at Hanging Rock* presents humankind's total helplessness when confronted with the inexplicable."[6] Weir, once again, makes this his thematic center in *Fearless*. After miraculously surviving a plane crash, Max Klein, a successful architect, must somehow make sense out of the surrealistic nonsense of his life. But there is no sense, no rational solace to be given. Therapists are helpless. The promise of an insurance settlement is a profanity. There is no answer for the horror of death he has experienced. As the audience is allowed into Max's thoughts through a series of flashbacks dramatizing the horrific crash, we hear in the background the music of Henryk Gorecki's Symphony no. 3, a haunting piece composed in 1976 for performance at the magnificent St. Magnus Church near Auschwitz. If there is to be hope in such desperate circumstances, it will only be born of such sorrow.

Weir's Use of Genre

Weir seems to have chosen a new genre for each of his films, though usually to subvert it or to cross it with elements of other genres. *Fearless*, for example, is a disaster movie. But in order to emphasize that the real suspense is internal not external to his character, the disaster happens at the beginning of the movie, not the end. Weir would have us know that it is not the action of the "puppets" but the "shadows" they produce (cf. the Wayang in *Living Dangerously*) that is of paramount importance. In both *Picnic at Hanging Rock* and *The Last Wave*, Weir has written and directed a horror film, a fantasy that allows him freedom from the constraints of linear thought. (One might compare it to *The Blair Witch Project* [1999].) He can explore the inexplicable without being forced prematurely toward closure.

The variety of Weir's use of genre is impressive. *Green Card* is in the tradition of the screwball comedy, a romantic farce that creates an expectation in the audience that indeed the "opposites" will eventually come together. *Dead Poets Society* is a coming-of-age movie about male adolescents. The genre allows Weir again to explore the shape of the human and to portray the need for us to "seize the day." Dealing with the influence of an inspiring teacher, it also is able to portray the importance of someone to guide you on your journey (cf. Chris in *The Last Wave* and Billy in *The Year of Living Dangerously*). *Gallipoli* is a war movie that eschews the macho, redefining in the process what is appropriately masculine.

The Truman Show is of particular interest in that it confronts the boundaries between illusion and reality. It is one of a growing number of recent films dealing with a story within a story, such as *Pleasantville* (d. Ross, 1998), *Wag the Dog* (d. Levinson, 1997), *Illuminata* (d. Turturro, 1998), *Edtv* (d. Howard, 1999), and *The Game* (d. Fincher, 1997). In each case, "the real" and "the reel," the actual and the simulation, are blurred. We are no longer sure what is rational and what is irrational. In *Pleasantville*, the mysterious Don Knotts character is fairly harmless, even if the closed society of the 1950s to which he leads the teenagers is anything but colorful or fulfilling of the human potential. *The Game* is more sinister. The simulations that are played are actually staged, and Michael Douglas is a pawn. And with the character of Christof in *The Truman Show*, the unknown power turns destructive.[7] In each case the "shadows" behind the "puppets" are hardly spiritual in nature. They are simply human manipulation. But these movies also hint at something more, as our spirits cry out for a Reality by which to judge the "real."

Perhaps Weir's most successful use of a genre to reflect his larger mythic interests is his film *Witness*. The movie is a Western(!), now transposed into Amish territory. John Book, like his counterpart Shane, enters a new community, a stranger to all in that society. He is given special status in the community, even while he is not fully accepted. There is a clear threat to the Amish society from the corrupt Philadelphia police, who have guns and power while the Amish have nothing. Book is friends with the enemy; in fact, he is one of them. Yet Book has rejected their corrupt ways. When the police threaten the Amish way of life and the safety of one of their children, Book defeats the cops in a scene reminiscent of *High Noon* (1952), bringing safety and peace to the community again. Book is a hero, but he must leave. His violent ways are foreign to the Amish and inappropriate for an ongoing relationship with Rachel Lapp. Saying goodbye, Book returns to Philadelphia. Here is an almost "pure" expression of the typical plot of the Western.

As with *Shane*, the shape of the plot allows a spiritual, idealized quality to show forth. There is something quasi-mystical, for example, in the movie's presentations of the barn-raising episode, in John's wearing the less "manly" clothes of the new community, in the chaste love between Rachel and John, in the contrast between rural safety and urban violence, even in the musical score of Maurice Jarre that echoes *Appalachian Spring* and evokes a past frontier. As with the Aboriginal culture in *The Last Wave*, the Anzac innocence in *Gallipoli*, and the Asian culture of *The Year of Living Dangerously*, the Amish community in *Witness* is cognizant of life's "shadow," that spiritual alternative to the corrupt materialism and heightened rationalism that has stifled the modern West. Though the Amish might need the protection of modern society from modern society, it is modern society that is in fact the more needy in this clash of two cultures.

Weir's Cultural Concerns

Peter Weir has portrayed in all of his movies a clash between two cultures, not in order to provide political insight, but to reveal a greater depth of meaning lurking behind and under these surface confrontations. In his early movies, Weir used such cultural conflict in the service of creating an Australian myth. The typical rationality of the West needed to be challenged, whether from Aboriginal alternatives or the outback example. In the confrontation, something of permanence shone through.

Since "moving" to Hollywood, Weir has continued to look for juxtapositions between, or within, cultures that can expose and counter the dehumanizing effects of modernity and allow the wonder of life to resurface. In *Green Card*, for example, we see the romantic immigrant challenging the modern, independent woman. In *Witness*, Rachel Lapp helps John Book see the pretense of Philadelphia, the "city of brotherly love." It is not as clear, however, what Book is to do about it. In *The Mosquito Coast*, Weir portrays the hollowness of the industrial North as Allie Fox, an eccentric inventor, flees the United States he says he loves, only to impose his alternative society, a jungle utopia, on the Mos-

Truman Burbank (Jim Carrey) lives his life in front of the TV camera. *The Truman Show* (d. Weir, 1998). Photo by Melinda Sue Gordon. ©1998 by Paramount Pictures. All rights reserved.

quito Coast's population. In *Dead Poets Society*, it is objectivist and pragmatic educational strategies that encounter Robin Williams's character's romantic passion, again with mixed results. Weir realizes that life is more complex than his romantic vision might long for. We cannot put Humpty-Dumpty back together again. Vietnam ended that dream. But the dream persists.

In all of his movies, Weir has what two social critics have labeled a "sixties within the eighties" (and nineties) mindset.[8] That is, like others within popular culture today, Peter Weir's artistic imagination continues to express the idealistic, anti-institutional, anti-imperialistic, and anti-authoritarian commitments of the sixties. He came of age in the caldron of nationalistic liberations, the women's movement, civil rights, and the opening of the East. It is not the politics of this period, or even the polemics, however, that has captured his soul, but its largely implicit spirituality. The yearning for wholeness, the vague recognition of Otherness, the desire to "make love, not war," the desire for personal fulfillment, a recognition of the value of the Dionysian and not just the Apollonian, a longing to be one with Nature—just as then, so now, it is this larger spiritual vision that is Weir's goal.

In *The Truman Show*, we again see Weir's "sixties in the eighties" (you may substitute the year 2000) mindset as he explores the virtual reality of our computer age. Recently on the *Today Show* (September 1999), I watched a news segment on a legal battle in Tampa, Florida, between the city council and a business using the Internet. Voyeurdorm.com is making over $300,000 yearly by broadcasting images from a "dorm" house where six female college students live. As with Truman Burbank, in every room there are webcams—cameras that post continuous pictures on Web pages—that show the coeds as they live together. Voyeuristic internet viewers pay $35 monthly to see the women taking showers, studying, eating, talking on the telephone, and so on. There is no privacy. The city council is arguing that "voyeurdorm.com" is an "adult" business in a residential section that is a violation of zoning codes. But the real issue is certainly much deeper than zoning codes or even the morality of adult entertainment. As in *The Truman Show*, we are being asked whether we can reduce human life to a sideshow. Is there not a sanctity, even a sacredness, to life that is somehow being violated?

Webcam sites are cropping up at campuses across the country. At Bradley University in Peoria, Illinois, the web site of sophomore Jim Crone got so many hits one night in the winter of 1999 that it crashed the campus computer system. Webdorm.com is supported by advertising and features students from around the United States. Have we voyeuristically turned our fellow human beings into "virtual reality"? If so, can we be far behind? The title of Neal Gabler's book *Life the Movie: How Entertainment Conquered Reality* has been brought to life.

Weir as Storyteller

Peter Weir sees himself first of all as a storyteller, not as a moviemaker. He believes that fiction "can give you a truth within its own set of lies."[9] Weir says,

> I belong to that tradition of entertainer or storyteller. There's this cartoon up on my wall of an old lady at a ticket box window saying, "I want my sense of wonder back." I like that idea. It's a desire to feel the sense of not knowing, that sense of danger and potential interlocked. It's very difficult to achieve, but the screen is one of the few places where it is possible.[10]

Elsewhere he says, "I think of myself as a storyteller, and I would have chosen another medium if films hadn't been available, presumably writing."[11]

While skill in the techniques of filming and a sensitivity to the cultural values of one's audience are important, these are not at the heart of filmmaking for Weir. Weir once gave a lecture in a media course where the instructor emphasized the technical functions of a film crew (hitting their marks with the camera or dressing a set). But Weir challenged such an approach, saying:

Right—let's get all this gear out of the way. This has got nothing to do with it, nothing. Let's just talk, about anything, everything, about stories, experiences. You've got too much of this gear. It's summoning up the ideas that's the hard thing—the inspiration, the passion. Without them, this stuff's useless.[12]

Plot

As he tells his story on the screen, Weir is less concerned with the power of his plots than with the reality under their surface. Weir wants to give back to the lady at the box office her sense of wonder. Over his career, Weir has shifted the perspective of his plots from European ambiguity and non-disclosure to Hollywood's linear and predictable narrative conventions. But the neat closure is still usually avoided (Keating is fired; Book returns to Philadelphia; and Bronte stays in New York).

In the usual Weir movie, middle-class and WASP characters are driven by forces they don't understand and encounter something inexplicable and mysterious, usually from another culture (the Amish, a Frenchman, a near-death experience, a loving embrace from a non-actor, the East, and so on). Through this experience, the inadequacy of white, Western culture is made clear. The mysterious confronts the individual, for which the typical, rational patterns of understanding prove ineffective. The otherness that is encountered is not sinister, although it is often perceived as a threat to WASP civilization. Instead, this clash of cultures provides an opportunity for a character's personal growth.

Character

Weir's characters are typically newcomers from an outside world who encounter a new culture and struggle to understand it. They are firmly planted in the rational world. They are lawyers, reporters, teachers, policemen, and social activists, who encounter something alien. In the process they are offered the opportunity for human growth. In *The Mosquito Coast*, Allie Fox goes into a Central American jungle, while in *The Last Wave*, David Burton explores the underground world of the Aborigines. In *Witness*, similarly, John Book finds himself in the closed religious community of the Amish. But Weir also varies the shape of these cultural confrontations that bring the possibility of growth and insight to the characters. In *Dead Poets Society*, Weir has the more spiritually sensitive character enter a less spiritually open context. John Keating, a poet, teaches at Welton Academy, where discipline and tradition threaten to squeeze out the humanity of his students. In *The Truman Show*, Weir alters the scenario once again by having Truman unaware that his culture is alien, while still longing for another. Still again, in *Fearless*, the alien culture turns out to be Max's own, Max now having survived a near-death experience in a plane crash. But in each case, character development revolves around this clash of two cultures.

In order that a character might achieve insight and personal growth, a mediator is sometimes present. This individual remains outside society's norms and embodies the values and heart of the particular film. Just as the Aborigine Chris Lee serves this role for David Burton in *The Last Wave*, helping him to move between Aboriginal and white Australian cultures, so Billy Kwan, half-Asian and half-Australian, is able to assist Guy Hamilton in *The Year of Living Dangerously*. These individuals are almost Christ-figures in their life-giving and sacrificial love. But usually such persons are less all-knowing or spiritually alive, and their lives are not put at stake. Georges, a lovable but oafish Frenchman, is the catalytic figure for Bronte in *Green Card*, while Lauren/Sylvia is an actress with a conscience in *The Truman Show* who causes Truman to want something more. Moreover, while John Keating's charisma proves catalytic for his student John Anderson in *Dead Poets Society*, another student, Neil Perry, commits suicide.

For Weir, while insight is often mediated by another, it remains highly personal, even individualistic, in its achievement. The center of Weir's vision is not on the "savior" figure, but on personal and spiritual growth in his characters, particularly in an individual's own encounter with mystery and otherness. Weir remains strongly individualistic in his vision of life.

Atmosphere

It is not his plot, then, or even his characterizations (though the star power of Richard Chamberlain, Mel Gibson, Harrison Ford, Robin Williams, Jeff Bridges, and Jim Carrey should not be discounted) that propel Weir's movies forward. Rather, the source of power and meaning in his movies is the atmosphere he creates, the sense of otherness that controls the story and drives it ahead. This is more than a mere mood; it is the inalterable backdrop against which his story is played out. There is a spiritual presence—that which produces a sense of wonder, which the old woman in Weir's cartoon desired—that is the real star of his films.

Peter Weir shows us that there is something more out there, something far more powerful than civilization is prone to admit. Here is the deeper meaning of the Wayang in *The Year of Living Dangerously*, of Hanging Rock, poetry, barn raisings, and the French. The Amish recognize its presence, as do the Aborigines and the Anzac. Near-death experiences provide access to it, as does the death of a mate. There is something outside the "bubble" of our civilized but routinized life, as Truman Burbank is set on discovering. For Weir, even the absence of mystery propels forth a sense of its presence. Here is Weir's romantic portrayal of life, one that is neither naive nor uncritical, but which nevertheless sides with innocence, myth, nature, and the uncanny.[13]

Point of View

The primal otherness of Weir's movies is conveyed to his viewers primarily through his stories' point of view, the implied narrator's attitude toward the story's subject and audience. Weir often begins to paint a backdrop of mystery and otherness even as the opening credits roll. In *The Last Wave*, for example, the movie opens with an Aborigine artist drawing mysterious symbols on the roof of a cave. The scene changes to a small town in the Australian desert where torrential rain and golf-ball-sized hail fall from a cloudless sky as the grade-school teacher tells her Aborigine children, "We are witnessing nature at work." This linking of Aborigine myth with unusual and violent weather continues to set the tone of the storytelling throughout the remainder of the movie. There is something larger than human life and activity to which we are beholden.

In *Witness*, we are first introduced to the pastoral life of the Amish as waving grain gives way to a small rural settlement. The initial look is of the nineteenth century, complete with horse and buggy and old-fashioned costume. But the title that is superimposed on the screen, "Pennsylvania, 1984," jars its viewers back into the present. There is created in this way a strong dreamlike atmosphere that invites our curiosity. The opening is both evocative and enigmatic. Again, in *Fearless*, Weir sets up the film's perspective through the opening scene. We are shown the nightmarish aftermath of the crash of an airplane. People are wandering through a cornfield in slow motion. From the air, the site of the crash has an almost surreal quality to it. Max is seen wandering aimlessly, holding a baby. The scene is one of devastation beyond belief. The remainder of the movie is Max's (and our) response to what we have seen. It is almost more than we can bear. In ways such as this, Weir uses the movie's point of view to make central in his stories its atmosphere—the spiritual otherness that lies beyond the plot and character development, giving shape to them.

Weir has commented on the influence of painting in helping him capture a perspective. Before many of his shots, Weir will develop a folio of postcards, photographs, advertisements, and paintings to help him with the framing and lighting. For example, Sydney Nolan's paintings of Gallipoli were influential in helping Weir create mythlike figures and a dreamlike effect in *Gallipoli*. For *Picnic at Hanging Rock*, Weir studied the impressionistic paintings of the Heidelberg School in Australia at the turn of the twentieth century with their sunlit landscapes and natural realism. Such landscapes contrasted starkly with the Victorian stereotypes of the period, with their imposed and buttoned-up values. This became the clue for Weir's framing of the movie.

In *Witness*, the influence of the Flemish painters, particularly Vermeer, is evident in certain scenes (for example, when Rachel is taking a sponge bath or when she is nursing John back to health). There the framing of the images through the doorway and the delicate lighting are evocative of something transcendent. Weir has acknowledged this Flemish influence, noting that he went to an exhibition of Dutch masters, which opened in Philadelphia during the filming of that movie. It is perhaps not too exaggerated to say that the real story in many of Weir's films is told through images such as these. It is these "landscapes of the soul" that we remember and which provide the viewer a rich source of meaning.

It is not just Weir's skill in painting archetypal scenes, however, that provides his movies' particular point of view. Music also contributes much to the shaping of his movies' perspective. In fact, Weir has commented,

> Music is the fountainhead, the source of all my inspiration, in a way, if you can generalize. It certainly doesn't have anything to do with words and such. Storytelling is my trade, my *craft*. But music is my inspiration; and my goal, my metaphor, to affect people like music. The images should float over you like music, and the experience should be beyond words.[14]

Weir first used his music to this effect in *Picnic at Hanging Rock*, with its eerie evocation of the natural and yet mystical through the use of panpipes. Or consider *Witness*. When Rachel and John Book dance in the Amish barn to Sam Cooke's "What a Wonderful World That Would Be," we ache for them and yet feel their otherness. And, as the barn raising proceeds, Maurice Jarre's echoing of Aaron Copeland's *Appalachian Spring* helps rivet its images in our souls, reminding us of another time and place when communal values were cherished and family was judged central.

In *Green Card*, Weir juxtaposes a flute concerto by Mozart which is heard as Bronte takes care of her apartment's rooftop garden with the street sounds of the city. Yet it is the absence of any music—just the dripping of water—as Bronte returns to her garden after Georges leaves which signals that there is something missing in her life that Georges has uncovered. Their romance cannot be long in coming! In this comedy of manners, the music of life must again sound forth!

Weir's most powerful use of music to provide a point of view that evokes a sense of wonder, however, is in *Fearless*. Max's dislocation is reinforced by the playing of such popular music as U2's "Where the Streets Have No Name." It is not until the sequence at the end of the movie, though, when a flashback is shown of the inside of the plane during the crash that a sense of transcendence is achieved. The mystery of death and life is conveyed in part through the use of blue light and slow motion. But it is the music, Henryk Gorecki's, Symphony no. 3, sometimes called the "Symphony of Sorrowful Songs," that transports the viewer. Gorecki chose for the text of his first movement a fifteenth-century Polish lament of Mary, the mother of Jesus ("My son, my chosen and beloved / Share your wounds with your mother . . . Although you are already leaving me, my cherished hope"). The symphony's text continues with a prayer that was found inscribed on the wall of a cell in the Gestapo's headquarters in Zakopane. And it concludes with a Polish mother's folk song lamenting the loss of her child who "lies in his grave and I do not know where though I keep asking people everywhere." It is this last movement that Weir has chosen to use in the film. But the cumulative power of the three movements is simply overpowering in the context of this story. Who will bear our sorrows? Music critics speak of this symphony as evoking "a hope born of sorrow that is not itself sorrow."[15] Here is the wonder of *Fearless*, too. The music and the image have joined to portray a hope beyond sorrow. As Laura pleads with Max not to die, he opens his eyes. "I'm alive," he gasps. And they hug. Life begins anew from out of the ashes.

In ways such as these, Weir's artistic stamp helps provide a point of view for each of his films. One notes his preference for close-ups of long duration on a character's face to create intimacy or to show contrasts. His use of slow-motion and soft-focus shots to create almost a metaphysical quality. His fascination with water as reflecting primal forces, whether peaceful or chaotic. His choice of blue light to project an atmosphere of mystery. His long visual sequences with little or no dialogue. His care in providing music as background and commentary. His fascination with light. His seeing through a window or door. All of these stylistic devices are characteristic of a Peter Weir film and add to the sense of presence that he seeks to evoke.

Beneath the often calm exterior of civilized life, Weir would have us to see lurking a sense of the "other." Even when the superficial presence of life would seem to deny that there is anything other or more (as in *Green Card*, or better in *The Truman Show*), the very absence of mystery suggests a sense of its presence. There must be more to life than the television set of Seahaven Island. Although Georges might be an oaf, he is open to life's rhythms and is willing to accept their surprises. Bronte is slower than her viewers to see the light, but it happens.

Responding Theologically

Having experienced Peter Weir's stories on the screen, how are we to put these into conversation with God's Story? How are we to dialogue, critique, and learn from his film stories, even while the Christian story remains normative? Nathan Scott reminds us:

> But this normative story that comes down to us from a time long ago is likely to become something desiccated and moribund, if it is not being kept constantly in a lively interplay with all that issues forth from the important storytellers of the age. For, apart from this kind of confluence, the normative story will have no chance to discover new idioms and narrative strategems whereby it can be retold in fresh and arresting ways: nor will it have a chance to gather the kind of new vitality that can come only, as it were, by its "proving" itself against those stories that offer some radical challenge to its essential validity.[16]

Scott is correct. Christian theology can be made stronger both as it is challenged by and itself challenges Weir's vision of life. Let me, in particular, suggest three different approaches which this theological dialogue might take, each reflecting a different place on our theological/critical matrix:

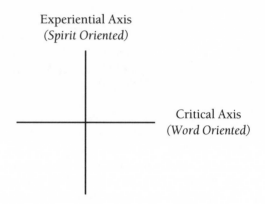

Experiential Axis
(Spirit Oriented)

Critical Axis
(Word Oriented)

Figure 9.1 Response Matrix for Weir's Films

The Critical Axis

STAYING WITHIN THE MOVIE ITSELF

In the typical Peter Weir film, a clash of cultures is portrayed, in which an outsider finds himself in an alien setting. In the face of a universe that they (we) can't control (the chief obstacle being death itself), Weir's characters begin to ask, "What then must we do?" They become aware that life has layers of meaning of which they were previously unaware. They begin to see the "shadows" or perhaps to explore the uncanny and the mysterious. They realize that they must get beneath the banality of culture in the West, for life is precious and valued. As Weir's heroes/heroines encounter life's terror and joy, they discover their humanity and find the courage to "seize the day." Truman Burbank is perhaps the quintessential example of such a person, but Guy Hamilton in *The Year of Living Dangerously*, John Book in *Witness*, Frank Dunne in *Gallipoli*, Bronte Parrish in *Green Card*, and Max Klein in *Fearless*, might also be viewed as examples.

This wider work of "Spirit/spirit" (this is my language; Weir leaves the experience nameless) is problematic for many contemporary Christians. For the Christian church, the experience of spirit is too often limited to a focus on the Holy Spirit as the Spirit of redemption and sanctification. It is given, that is, a specific Christological focus. There is too scant mention in Christian theology of the Spirit's presence in nature, in culture's activity, or even in human relationships. And there is little recognition of the human spirit's ability to discern the shape of human life apart from the teaching of the church. Weir's films can help us recover this creation-based theology. The intimations of Spirit/spirit found in his movies are real expressions of grace and have strong biblical warrant, if we would but listen.

The spiritual center of life as created is the theological heart of the Book of Ecclesiastes, for example. Weir's films can help us recover this creation-based perspective. The writer of that book, Qoheleth (the Preacher), portrays the vanity of seeking life's meaning and purpose in wisdom, riches, or pleasure. Here, one might almost think, is a critique of the West similar to the one Weir portrays. Materialism and rationality make no difference to one's ultimate fate, for death is the great leveler (Eccles. 2:14–16); greed, the real motivator (4:4). Life proves oftentimes amoral (8:9–14), and God's will remains mysterious (3:11; 6:12). And yet, for Qoheleth, life's fragility does not negate its fragrance. As a gift from God, life must be viewed as good (5:18–20). There is nothing better than to enjoy life (2:24–26; 3:12, 22; 8:15), for it is a gift from God (9:7–10; 11:7–10).

Here is the lesson Max Klein learns at great personal cost. So too, John Book and Truman Burbank. Despite the superficiality and banality of life as it presents itself, life's joys are precious and to be protected. The call of Spirit/spirit is dialectical. Though observable life is often evil and finally incoherent, life is sacred and to be valued. The anguish of Weir's characters, as for Qoheleth, is in knowing how to embrace this paradox. At times, Qoheleth's experience causes him to hate life (2:17; 4:2). But he also commends life, for it is God's gift (3:13). The days of our life, the ability to eat and drink and find enjoyment in our work, even our very spirit are spiritual gifts. Weir shies away from the use of theological language, and his vision of common grace is not Christian in its particulars. But then, neither is "common grace."

The movies of Peter Weir can help the church recover something of life's mystery and grace. They provide images of the larger life of the Spirit/spirit, with all its terror and attractiveness. In a less overtly religious style they reflect that paradox of existence that Elizabeth Barrett Browning captures so well.

> Natural things
> And spiritual,—who separates those two
> In art, in morals, or the social drift,
> Tears up the bond of nature and brings death,
> Paints futile pictures, writes unreal verse,
> Leads vulgar days, deals ignorantly with men,
> Is wrong, in short, at all points. . . .
> . . . .
> Earth's crammed with heaven,
> And every common bush afire with God:
> But only he who sees, takes off his shoes,
> The rest sit round it, and pluck blackberries.
> . . . .
> Not one day, in the artist's ecstasy,
> But every day, feast, fast, or working-day,

The spiritual significance burn through
The hieroglyphic of material shows,
Henceforward he would paint the globe with wings,
And reverence fish and fowl, the bull, the tree,
And even his very body as a man.

Elizabeth Barrett Browning, "Aurora Leigh," book 7[17]

LEARNING FROM A THEOLOGICAL PARTNER

Weir's romantic vision, an expression in part of the 1960s in which he was raised, reminds me of the writings of another student of the same era, Sam Keen. A former professor of theology and popular lecturer and writer in psychology, Keen's first book (and also his best), *Apology for Wonder*, presented an argument for "wonder." Keen paints a bleak picture of contemporary Western life much like Weir's, and then turns to consider the rediscovery of life's sacredness in the quotidian, the everyday and earthy. By considering Keen's "diagnosis" and "solution" to modern humanity's ills, we might be able better to understand the dialectic at work in Weir's films.

Keen believes the typical Westerner lives under a Promethean illusion, attempting to evade the reality of our transience. He speaks of our "scrubbing compulsion of the mind."[18] Through wealth, competition, politics, and a youthful façade, we seek to hide our "dis-ease" from ourselves. We seek order, reasonableness, and discipline. Yet, we remain impotent. This "masculine" image makes it impossible to appreciate the more "feminine" modes of perceiving and relating to the world. Sterile both in our environment and in our attitudes, Western "man" does not participate sensually so as to create authentic life.[19] Think of Guy Hamilton, John Book, and Max Klein, three of Weir's characters who discover their lives to be hollow. Think, too, of the parents and administration of Welton Academy, or even of Bronte Parrish, a woman who has learned the manipulative lifestyle of a man's world.

Instead of such self-defeating rationalizations, Keen believes we should ask ourselves where we have trembled or been fascinated. Perhaps it is through an experience of nature, at the ocean or on a mountain. Sometimes it is when we are truly in community. Keen recalls when the civil rights protesters sang "We Shall Overcome" with Martin Luther King. It might happen in our sexuality. Or our panic. Or when somebody tells their story and suddenly it is also "my" story. For Keen, such experiences are sacred. They are also often the heart of Weir's portrayals as we have seen.

Keen believes that we must rediscover our ability to wonder, and we do this through story. Story helps integrate past, present, and future. For Keen this story will not be external to us, but one that focuses on our own experiences. It is one's own biography, one's own experience, which will testify to the holy.[20]

Here too is Weir. Truman Burbank is no longer to live the script that others have produced for him. We see him walking through the door into a new life as the movie ends. After his near-death experience, Max must similarly walk through the tunnel into a new light and write a fresh story with Laura, his wife. Bronte realizes that her ordered and scripted life is bankrupt. She has been living another's script. At the end of *Green Card* she is given the invitation to begin her story anew in France with Georges. Jill gives a similar invitation to Guy in *The Year of Living Dangerously*. Even though John Book will return to Philadelphia to live anew his story, he has become a changed man through his encounter with Rachel and the Amish, someone now committed to making that urban center a "city of brotherly love."

Third, Keen argues that we must become "dis-illusioned," that is, we must shed those illusions that would have us possess rather than admire, exploit rather than enjoy, grasp rather than accept.[21] It is the poet within us that must come forth. We must live with ambiguity and open-endedness. As John Keating illustrates and Keen affirms, even a touch of madness is allowed, but only a touch. Sam Keen writes,

> Dionysus becomes the god of destruction and insanity if he keeps his worshippers in the wilderness with the promise of endless ecstasy rather than sending them back to the quotidian with a renewed vision of what might be possible if the community of man gave up warfare and began dancing together. We must listen to madness to find the seed of wisdom it contains, but we must not make madness an ideal.[22]

Accepting with wonder life's mystery, learning afresh to tell our stories, and forsaking our illusions of dominance and rationality—here is Sam Keen's therapy/theology. And such a romantic vision for life's possibilities is not dissimilar to that provided by the movies of Peter Weir. But can one call this theological? Keen calls himself an ex-theologian, and Peter Weir has certainly not provided his viewers an explicitly Christian vision. It would be dishonest to baptize either one a "Christian." Yet for both, their phenomenological approach to the mysterious and wonder-filled has much to teach Christians. It harkens back to the seminal description of the sacred in Rudolf Otto's *Idea of the Holy*.[23] In that book, Otto argues there is a *mysterium* due to the presence of the Other which has two defining characteristics: it is *tremendum* (awe-inspiring and frightening) and *fascinans* (compelling and desirable). Described in this way, such experiences can be fostered by the puppet world of the East, by the innocence of the faith of the Amish and the "mateship" of the Anzac, and even by the brief encounter with someone who treats you as the person you are (whether a bit actress or a Frenchman needing a green card). There are, in other words, both "religious" and "nonreligious" experiences of the sacred. Or in the traditional language of Christian orthodoxy, there is special revelation, but there is also general revelation.

The Experiential Axis

The spiritual path in Weir's movies can be walked with or without a commitment to any organized religion, and certainly independent of any overt Christianity. There is a breadth and an openness to his vision. Here is his strength and his weakness, theologically. On the positive side, as the opening chapters of the Bible portray, humankind is both dust and breath, body and spirit. Weir would help us experience something of the spiritual in an otherwise materialistic age—portraying the life of the Spirit/spirit, giving us in T. S. Eliot's words images of

> the waterfall, or music heard so deeply
> That it is not heard at all, but you are the music
> While the music lasts.
>
> T. S. Eliot, "The Dry Salvages," *Four Quartets*[24]

This is an important artistic gift. Weir's filmic vision engenders spirit reaching out to spirit (Spirit?).

But while such experiences are central to a spiritual life and thus important theologically, they also remain incomplete. To finish quoting T. S. Eliot's meditation:

> These are only hints and guesses,
> Hints followed by guesses; and the rest
> Is prayer, observance, discipline, thought and action.
> The hint half guessed, the gift half understood, is Incarnation.
>
> T. S. Eliot, "The Dry Salvages," *Four Quartets*[25]

Eliot reminds us of what Weir has ignored: prayer, observance, discipline, thought and action. In his movies, the spirituality rarely moves beyond the level of feeling. Guy Hamilton leaves the poverty of Jakarta for Jill. There is little if any discipline in Robin Williams's character. Max, Bronte, and Truman follow their instincts, but we have no clue as to how life will develop. We are, as with Truman, left at the open door. And certainly there is nary a hint of Incarnation. Eliot is correct.

To use more conventional theological language, Weir rejects the objectification of the Spirit, whether through word or concrete action. And this is an error in spirit and Spirit. Head, heart, and hands ultimately need integration and were created together. Similarly, Christian theology links Word and Spirit; it rejects any gnostic mysticism. It is important to discover the Spirit's signature on life. But to borrow an image from John Updike, if the signature of the Spirit's "supernatural mail" is "decisive but illegible," we are still left wondering, "What then shall we do?"[26] What will Truman do? What will John Book do in Philadelphia? Guy Hamilton gets his girl, but all else is unclear. The apostle John writes, "And the Word became flesh and lived among us, and we have seen his glory, the glory as of a father's only son, full of grace and truth" (John 1:14). This is T. S. Eliot's point about "Incarnation." Mystery remains, but it has taken shape in the person of Jesus so that there can be "prayer, observance, discipline, thought and action." Weir rejects such concretizing of the Spirit, for the church has so often been Spirit/spirit denying.

Australian journalist Guy Hamilton (Mel Gibson) and photographer Billy Kwan (Linda Hunt) are surrounded by political demonstrators. *The Year of Living Dangerously* (d. Weir, 1982).

But the consequence of his purging is severe—in the end nothing more is left than a vague romantic spirituality.

Having said this, having recognized that in and of themselves Weir's stories portray little beyond the vaguely spiritual (though even this "general revelation" should not be discounted), it is also the case that Christians and non-Christians alike have been moved to concrete action by the stories of Weir that they have experienced. His films invite our encounter with the spirit (Spirit) as few others do. Let me share one such theological encounter.

For my wife, Catherine Barsotti, seeing the movie *The Year of Living Dangerously* was a turning point for her, a conversion. Being immersed in the pain and poverty of Jakarta, seeing it both literally and figuratively through the eyes of Billy Kwan, she could not escape the question that Billy asked Guy. Quoting Tolstoy (who is quoting Luke 3:10), he asked Guy, "What then must we do?" Billy went on to tell Guy that Tolstoy sold all he had to relieve the suffering around him. In the movie, Guy is not persuaded, believing that government leaders and structures should be involved, not him. Billy himself had tried to respond personally, providing money for a young prostitute and her sick child. But when the boy dies from drinking polluted water, Billy can no longer avoid political involvement. Pounding out on his typewriter the same question, "What then must we do?" Billy decides to challenge Sukarno to feed his people. He hangs a banner over a balcony and is killed for his action. Let me quote Cathy directly,

"WHAT THEN MUST WE DO?" I left the theater with that phrase and the amazing eyes of the children of Jakarta burned onto the screen of my mind. In Luke 3, we first hear this question as John the Baptist is preaching repentance and calling the people to bear fruit worthy of their conversion. And when the crowd doesn't "get it" and asks "WHAT THEN MUST WE DO?" he tells them to live ethically and generously (i.e., "whoever has two coats must share with anyone who has none; and whoever has food must do likewise"; or to tax collectors, "collect no more than the amount prescribed for you"). In Luke 4 we hear Jesus echoing the same ethic and compassion as he begins his ministry with these words, "The Spirit of the Lord is upon me, because he has anointed me to bring Good News to the poor. . . . Release to the captives and recovery of sight to the blind, to let the oppressed go free. . . ."

A combination of people, events in my life, and the Spirit had prepared me to "see" this film. It became a turning point, a conversion. The next week I returned to my project at work, that of appraising a hospital, and I saw the world differently. Within weeks I applied for a leave of absence and within months left for Mexico to work as a short-term missionary. Six months after my return, I resigned my position at Bank of America to start my own appraisal business in which I would only work 30 hours/week so that I could give myself to the youth of my church and community, to the financial and political struggle to build a shelter for women and children in my city, and to study in the area of cross-cultural theology and ministry. The last 17 years have included a variety of tasks, jobs, ministries, and people. And it seems that Billy Kwan's, Tolstoy's, and the Bible's question still rings in my ears, "WHAT THEN MUST WE DO?"[27]

For Cathy, the "hints and guesses" of Weir's movie became incarnate as she heard her Savior speak. What followed was "prayer, observance, discipline, thought and action," for the "hint half guessed" became the "gift half understood." She heard her incarnate Lord compelling her to answer the question in concrete ways.

There are a variety of theological responses that one might offer to the movies of Peter Weir. I have provided but three. One's theological response can be either analytical or experiential, word oriented or spirit oriented. By first looking at how the spiritual vision is portrayed in Weir's movies and then comparing it with the Book of Ecclesiastes, I have sought to open the conversation. I have also turned to the theology of Sam Keen (and Rudolf Otto) as an initial, external source of insight into the heart of Weir's vision, believing that Weir's, too, is an "Apology for Wonder." My theological criticism of the films of Peter Weir evidences itself to be a two-way conversation, moving both from film to faith and from faith to film. Finally, I have illustrated the possibilities of an experiential theological criticism by relating the power of a Weir film to spiritually transform one life. We are affected spiritually by what we see.

Other avenues of dialogue are also open. Some might, for example, want to look at Weir's treatment of the explicitly religious, to explore Weir's portrayal of Asian or Aboriginal spirituality, or the pacifistic life of the Amish.[28] Such explicitly religious criticism is probably secondary to the central thrust of Weir's power and meaning, but it can also provide insight. How is the receptivity of Eastern and/or indigenous thought an important counter to the West's penchant to control? Which is more effective, the guns of the Philadelphia police or the political power of pacifism? Is the anachronistic way of life of the Amish or the Aborigines irrelevant to our modern lives? The dialogue might also proceed in this direction.

In C. S. Lewis's *Silver Chair*, two children are transported to the Green Witch's falsely empirical and bounded universe. Puddleglum, their traveling companion, challenges the Green Witch's realism:

> Suppose we *have* only dreamed, or made up, all those things—trees and grass and sun and moon and stars and Aslan himself. Suppose we have. Then all I can say is that, in that case, the made-up things seem a good deal more important than the real ones. Suppose this black pit of a kingdom of yours is the only world. Well, it strikes me as a pretty poor one. And that's a funny thing. . . . Four babies playing a game can make a play-world which licks your real world hollow.[29]

We have returned in our reflection one final time to consider the relationship between the "real" and the "reel." Peter Weir has done us the service of portraying on "reel" what reality might be at some more central region. His movies challenge that "black pit of a kingdom" which rationality and materialism assume to be the only possible one. His stories remain hints and guesses, but these should not be disparaged. He has provided the occasion for viewers to experience what in traditional theological language is called common grace. He has given us a *reel spirituality*.

All who have eyes, let them see.

notes

Introduction

1. d. = director, directed by.

2. Barry Taylor, address at the luncheon for Wilbert Shenk on the occasion of his installation as a professor at Fuller Theological Seminary, Pasadena, Calif., 13 April 1999, audiocassette.

3. John R. W. Stott, *Basic Christianity* (Downers Grove, Ill.: InterVarsity, 1971), 7.

4. Henry David Thoreau, *The Thoughts of Thoreau*, ed. Edwin Way Teale (New York: Dodd, Mead, 1962), 231, quoted in Ken Gire, *The Reflective Life: Becoming More Spiritually Sensitive to the Everyday Moments of Life* (Colorado Springs: Chariot Victor, 1998), 92.

5. Quoted in John C. Cooper and Carl Skrade, *Celluloid and Symbols* (Philadelphia: Fortress, 1970), 15.

6. During a panel discussion at the Nortel Networks Palm Springs International Film Festival (16 January 2000), director Milos Forman continued to voice just such a distinction: "In American films, entertainment comes first and soul-searching comes second . . . if at all. In foreign films, soul-searching comes first, and entertainment second . . . if at all." Jack Garner and Bruce Fessier, "Land of the Film," *The Desert Sun*, 18 January 2000, sec. D, p. 3.

7. See James Monaco for a distinction between film, movies, and cinema in *How to Read a Film*, rev. ed. (New York: Oxford University Press, 1981), 195. Though a distinction is sometimes made in more technical discussions, for our purposes the words *film*, *movies*, and *cinema* will be used interchangeably.

8. Edward Farley, *Theologia: The Fragmentation and Unity of Theological Education* (Philadelphia: Fortress, 1983), 7.

9. Ibid., 29–48.

Chapter 1

1. I am indebted to writer Ken Gire for showing me this film clip. He also will discuss it in his upcoming book: *Reflections on the Movies: Hearing God in the Unlikeliest of Places* (Colorado Springs: Chariot Victor, 2000).

2. Quoted by Robert G. Konzelman, *Marquee Ministry: The Movie Theater as Church and Community Forum* (New York: Harper & Row, 1971), 13.

3. The passion play featured thirteen tableau scenes, each a minute or so in length.

4. *The Temptation of St. Anthony* (d. Méliès, 1898) began with a monk reading a theological document when, suddenly, a naked woman appears. When the monk moves to greet her, however, she becomes a skeleton. Interestingly, St. Anthony is said to have had such temptations.

5. New York: Knopf, 1996.

6. John Updike, *The Centaur* (Greenwich, Conn.: Fawcett, Crest, 1962), 201.

7. Paul Woolf, "Turning toward Home," *Image: A Journal of the Arts & Religion* 20 (summer 1998): 116.

8. Ibid.

9. Ibid.

10. Stanley Hauerwas and William H. Willimon, *Resident Aliens, Life in the Christian Colony* (Nashville: Abingdon, 1989), 15–16.

11. K. L. Billingsley, *The Seductive Image: A Christian Critique of the World of Film* (Westchester, Ill.: Crossway, 1989), 53.

12. Amy Wallace, "'Ryan' Ends Vets' Years of Silence," *Los Angeles Times*, 6 August 1998, sec. A, p. 1.

13. Neal Gabler, *Life the Movie: How Entertainment Conquered Reality* (New York: Knopf, 1998), 9.

14. Clive Marsh and Gaye Ortiz, eds., *Explorations in Theology and Film: Movies and Meaning* (Oxford: Blackwell, 1997), 1.

15. Elia Kazan, *Elia Kazan: A Life* (New York: Knopf, 1988), 381.

16. Beverly Beyette, "A Modern-Day Schindler Faces the Consequences," *Los Angeles Times*, 19 August 1998, sec. E, p. 1; David Haldane, "Swiss Whistle-Blower to Attend Chapman," *Los Angeles Times*, 19 November 1998, sec. B, p. 5.

17. Gerry Sittser, *A Grace Disguised* (Grand Rapids: Zondervan, 1996), 173.

18. There is a coda to the story which Karen Covell shared with me. Speaking in October 1998 at a seminar in Hollywood that Karen attended, Linda Woolverton, the screenwriter of *Beauty and the Beast*, told of her struggle with executives at Disney to keep Belle as a reader, someone whose main love was books. Disney felt that reading was boring when portrayed on the screen. They wanted a more active hobby, something more physical in nature. Linda argued, however, that by making Belle an intelligent woman with a love for literature, the film could provide a stronger, more positive role model for young female viewers. Linda won the argument, and Catherine Sittser benefitted.

Chapter 2

1. For helpful discussions of early religious cinema, see John Baxter, *The Australian Cinema* (Sydney: Angus & Robertson, Pacific Books, 1970), 7–8; Ronald Holloway, *Beyond the Image: Approaches to the Religious Dimension in the Cinema* (Geneva: World Council of Churches, 1977), 45–59. I am dependent on Holloway for much of my discussion of the rise of cinema.

2. Holloway, *Beyond the Image,* 52.

3. Ibid., 53.

4. Quoted in Les Keyser and Barbara Keyser, *Hollywood and the Catholic Church: The Image of Roman Catholicism in American Movies* (Chicago: Loyola University Press, 1984), 20.

5. Ibid., 24.

6. James Skinner, *The Cross and the Cinema: The Legion of Decency and the National Office for Motion Pictures, 1933–1970* (Westport, Conn.: Greenwood, 1993), 18.

7. Quoted in Holloway, *Beyond the Image*, 118.

8. Quoted in Skinner, *The Cross and the Cinema*, 35.

9. Skinner, *The Cross and the Cinema*, 37.

10. Quoted in John R. May, "Close Encounters: Hollywood and Religion after a Century," *Image: A Journal of the Arts & Religion* 20 (summer 1998): 88.

11. For a fuller discussion of this period, see Gregory Black, *Hollywood Censored: Morality Codes, Catholics, and the Movies* (New York: Cambridge University Press, 1994); Frank Walsh, *Sin and Censorship: The Catholic Church and the Motion Picture Industry* (New Haven: Yale University Press, 1996); and Gregory Black, *The Catholic Crusade against the Movies, 1940–1975* (New York: Cambridge University Press, 1997).

12. Quoted by Ronald Austin, "Sacrificing Images: Violence and the Movies," *Image: A Journal of the Arts & Religion* 20 (summer 1998): 27.

13. Cf. Amy Wallace, "Do Movie Ratings Need New Categories?" *Los Angeles Times*, 10 August 1999, sec. F, pp. 1, 4, 5.

Chapter 3

1. The original categorization was developed by Robert Banks and has been expanded over several years by the two of us.

2. Hyman Appelman, introduction to *Movies and Morals*, by Herbert Miles (Grand Rapids: Zondervan, 1947).

3. Miles, *Movies and Morals,* 20.

4. Ibid., 20, 95.

5. Carl McClain, *Morals and the Movies* (Kansas City: Beacon Hill, 1970), 25.

6. Fax from Dr. Baehr to Todd Coleman, 3 October 1997.

7. Theodore Baehr, "A Cacophony of Prime Time Religions?" in *Religion and Prime Time Television,* ed. Michael Suman (Westport, Conn.: Praeger, 1997), 117.

8. Larry W. Poland, *The Last Temptation of Hollywood* (Highland, Calif.: Mastermedia International, 1988), 6.

9. *The Last Temptation of Christ,* trans. P. A. Bien (New York: Simon & Schuster, 1960).

10. Ibid., 146.

11. The Catholic Church's use of indulgences again made the news just a few months after *Dogma* was released. As part of its millennial celebration of the Jubilee, or Roman Catholic Holy Year, the pope ceremonially opened the doors of four basilicas where Catholic pilgrims could earn indulgences during the Holy Year (2000). This caused some Protestant leaders to decline sharing in what the pope had set up as an ecumenical event, the opening of the fourth basilica's doors. The archbishop of Canterbury and a representative of the Orthodox patriarch of Constantinople did participate, however.

12. Kevin Smith, quoted in Mick LaSalle, "Kevin Smith's Religious Experience," *The San Francisco Sunday Examiner and Chronicle,* 31 October 1999, Datebook, p. 50.

13. Patrick Scully, quoted in Teresa Watanabe, "Chasing Catholicism," *Los Angeles Times,* 10 November 1999, sec. F, p. 1.

14. Cliff Rothman, "*Dogma* Opens in New York to Protesters' Jeers, Audience Cheers," *Los Angeles Times,* 6 October 1999, sec. F, pp. 2, 4.

15. Donald J. Drew, *Images of Man: A Critique of the Contemporary Cinema* (Downers Grove, Ill.: InterVarsity, 1974), 106.

16. Ibid., 102.

17. K. L. Billingsley, *The Seductive Image: A Christian Critique of the World of Film* (Westchester, Ill.: Crossway, 1989), xii.

18. John Butler, *TV, Movies, and Morality: A Guide for Catholics* (Huntington, Ind.: Our Sunday Visitor, 1984), 10.

19. Michael Medved, *Hollywood vs. America: Popular Culture and the War on Traditional Values* (New York: HarperCollins, 1992), 242.

20. Mark Hulsether, "Sorting out the Relationships among Christian Values, US Popular Religion, and Hollywood Films," *Religious Studies Review* 25.1 (1999): 3–11.

21. Les Keyser and Barbara Keyser, *Hollywood and the Catholic Church: The Image of Roman Catholicism in American Movies* (Chicago: Loyola University Press, 1984), 94.

22. Ibid., 104, 106.

23. Michael Medved, "Want an Oscar? An 'R' Revs Up Your Chances," *USA Today,* 19 March 1999, sec. A, p. 9.

24. "Hollywood Makes Room for Religion," in *Religion and Prime Time Television,* ed. Michael Suman (Westport, Conn.: Praeger, 1997), 111–16.

25. Margaret Miles, *Seeing and Believing: Religion and Values in the Movies* (Boston: Beacon, 1996), 4.

26. Ibid., 15, italics original.

27. T. S. Eliot, "Religion and Literature," in *Religion and Modern Literature: Essays in Theory and Criticism,* ed. G. B. Tennyson and Edward E. Ericson Jr. (Grand Rapids: Eerdmans, 1975), 21.

28. R. W. B. Lewis, "Hold on Hard to the Huckleberry Bushes," in *Religion and Modern Literature: Essays in Theory and Criticism*, ed. G. B. Tennyson and Edward E. Ericson Jr. (Grand Rapids: Eerdmans, 1975), 55.

29. J. C. Friedrich von Schiller, *On the Aesthetic Education of Man*, trans. Reginald Snell (London: n.p., 1954), quoted in Herbert Read, *The Redemption of the Robot: My Encounter with Education through Art* (New York: Trident, 1966). Cf. Robert K. Johnston, *The Christian at Play* (Grand Rapids: Eerdmans, 1983).

30. Amos Wilder, *Theology and Modern Literature* (Cambridge: Harvard University Press, 1958), 29, quoted in Robert K. Johnston, "Christian Theology and Literature: Correlation or Co-Relation?" in *Collection of Papers Celebrating Professor Hiromu Shimizu's Retirement*, ed. Sachiko Yoshida (Kyoto: Apollon, 1991), 15.

31. Harvey G. Cox, "The Purpose of the Grotesque in Fellini's Films," in *Celluloid and Symbols*, ed. John C. Cooper and Carl Skrade (Philadelphia: Fortress, 1970), 91.

32. Carl Skrade, "Theology and Films," in *Celluloid and Symbols,* ed. John C. Cooper and Carl Skrade (Philadelphia: Fortress, 1970), 22.

33. Robert Jewett, *Saint Paul Returns to the Movies: Triumph over Shame* (Grand Rapids: Eerdmans, 1999), 20.

34. Robert Jewett, *Saint Paul at the Movies: The Apostle's Dialogue with American Culture* (Louisville: Westminster/John Knox, 1993), 7.

35. Ibid., 11.

36. James M. Wall, "Biblical Spectaculars and Secular Man," in *Celluloid and Symbols*, ed. John C. Cooper and Carl Skrade (Philadelphia: Fortress, 1970), 52.

37. Lloyd Baugh, *Imaging the Divine: Jesus and Christ-Figures in Film* (Kansas City: Sheed & Ward, 1997), 112.

38. Neil P. Hurley, *Theology through Film* (New York: Harper & Row, 1970), 3.

39. David John Graham, "The Uses of Film in Theology," in *Explorations in Theology and Film: Movies and Meaning*, ed. Clive Marsh and Gaye Ortiz (Oxford: Blackwell, 1997), 39.

40. Ibid.

41. Quoted in *Simon Birch*'s movie advertisement appearing in The *Los Angeles Times*.

42. Wall, "Biblical Spectaculars," 60.

43. Ibid., 56.

44. Thomas Martin, *Images and the Imageless: A Study in Religious Consciousness and Film* (Lewisburg: Bucknell University Press, 1981), 63.

45. G. William Jones, *Sunday Night at the Movies* (Richmond: John Knox, 1967), 40.

46. Neil P. Hurley, "Cinematic Transformations of Jesus," in *Religion in Film*, ed. John R. May and Michael Bird (Knoxville: University of Tennessee Press, 1982), 61–78.

47. Gerardus van der Leeuw, *Sacred and Profane Beauty: The Holy in Art*, trans. David E. Green (Nashville: Abingdon, 1963), 266.

48. Ibid., 337.

49. Ibid., 266.

50. John R. May, "Religion and Film: Recent Contributions to the Continuing Dialogue," *Critical Review of Books in Religion* 9 (1996): 105–21.

51. Ibid., 117.

52. Andrew Greeley, *God in Popular Culture* (Chicago: Thomas More, 1988), 250.

53. Ibid.

54. Hurley, *Theology*, x.

55. Martin, *Images*, 46.

56. Ibid., 52.

57. Ibid.

58. Paul Schrader, *Transcendental Style in Film: Ozu, Bresson, Dreyer* (New York: Da Capo, 1972), 3.

59. Ibid., 7.

60. Ibid., 3.

61. Ibid., 10.

62. Ibid., 11.

63. H. Richard Niebuhr, *Christ and Culture* (New York: Harper & Row, 1951).

64. Cf. Glen Stassen, Diane Yeager, and John Howard Yoder, *Authentic Transformation* (Nashville: Abingdon, 1996).

65. Martin E. Marty, foreword to *Hidden Treasures: Searching for God in Modern Culture*, by James M. Wall (Chicago: Christian Century Press, 1997), 7.

Chapter 4

1. Mark Noll, Cornelius Plantinga Jr., and David Wells, "Evangelical Theology Today," *Theology Today* 51.4 (1995): 495–507.

2. James Carey, "Symbolic Anthropology and the Study of Popular Culture" (unpublished essay), quoted by Margaret Miles, "Report on Research Conducted during 1994–95" (unpublished paper), 9.

3. Miles, "Report on Research," 10.

4. Walther Zimmerli, "The Place and Limit of the Wisdom in the Framework of the Old Testament Theology," *Scottish Journal of Theology* 17 (1964): 146–58.

5. Cf. Roland E. Murphy, "The Kerygma of the Book of Proverbs," *Interpretation* 20 (January 1966): 3–14.

6. Cf. Murphy, "Kerygma," 3–14.

7. Eduard Schweizer, *The Holy Spirit* (Philadelphia: Fortress, 1980), 47.

8. John V. Taylor, *The Go-Between God* (Philadelphia: Fortress, 1972).

9. C. S. Lewis, *Surprised by Joy* (New York: Harcourt, Brace & World, Harvest Books, 1955), 238, 180–81.

10. Paul Tillich, *On the Boundary: An Autobiographical Sketch* (New York: Scribner's Sons, 1966), 27–28.

11. Paul Tillich, *On Art and Architecture*, ed. John Dillenberger and Jane Dillenberger (New York: Crossroad, 1987), 12.

12. Peter Berger, *A Rumor of Angels* (Garden City, N.Y.: Doubleday, 1970), 45–75.

13. Robert Jewett, *Saint Paul at the Movies: The Apostle's Dialogue with American Culture* (Louisville: Westminster/John Knox, 1993), 67.

14. Klyne Snodgrass, "Justification by Grace—To the Doers: An Analysis of the Place of Romans 2 in the Theology of Paul," *New Testament Studies* 32.1 (1986): 79.

15. The lecture has been published in two different forms: first in Robert McAfee Brown, *The Pseudonyms of God* (Philadelphia: Westminster, 1972), 96–103, and years later in Robert McAfee Brown, *Persuade Us to Rejoice: The Liberating Power of Fiction* (Louisville: Westminster/John Knox, 1992).

16. Justin Martyr, *Second Apology*, 13.

17. Os Guinness, *Dining with the Devil* (Grand Rapids: Baker, 1993), 90.

18. Cf. NRSV rendering: "Do not be conformed to this world, but be transformed by the renewing of your minds, so that you may discern what is the will of God—what is good and acceptable and perfect."

19. Brown, *Persuade Us*, 35.

20. Ibid.

21. For a parallel discussion of Brown's methodology as it applies to literature, see Robert K. Johnston, "Christian Theology and Literature: Correlation or Co-Relation?" in *Collection of Papers Celebrating Professor Hiromu Shimizu's Retirement*, ed. Sachiko Yoshida (Kyoto: Apollon, 1991), 12–22.

22. Dietrich Bonhoeffer, *Letters and Papers from Prison*, ed. Eberhard Bethge, rev. ed. (New York: Macmillan, 1967), 104–5.

23. J. I. Packer, *Knowing God* (Downers Grove, Ill.: InterVarsity, 1973), 38–44.

24. Ibid., 43 (italics added).

25. Martin Luther, *Luther's Works* (Philadelphia: Fortress, 1958), 40:99, quoted in John W. Cook, "Picturing Theology: Martin Luther and Lucas Cranach," in *Art and Religion: Faith, Form and Reform*, ed. Osmund Overby (Columbia: University of Missouri, 1986), 26.

26. Cook, "Picturing Theology," 39.

27. See Richard A. Blake, *AfterImage* (Chicago: Loyola University Press, 2000).

28. H. Richard Niebuhr, *Christ and Culture* (New York: Harper & Row, 1951), 143.

29. Dietrich Bonhoeffer, *Ethics*, ed. Eberhard Bethge (New York: Macmillan, 1955), 101, quoted in David Baily Harned, *Theology and the Arts* (Philadelphia: Westminster, 1966), 148.

30. Harned, *Theology and the Arts*, 149.

31. Paul Tillich, *Systematic Theology* (Chicago: University of Chicago Press, 1951), 1:40.

32. Paul Tillich, "Art and Ultimate Reality," in *Art, Creativity, and the Sacred: An Anthology in Religion and Art*, ed. Diane Apostolos-Cappadona (New York: Crossroad, 1984), 219–35. This article was originally a lecture at the Museum of Modern Art, New York, 17 February 1959. I found helpful the summary of this lecture given by David Baily Harned in *Theology and the Arts*, 64–68.

33. D. W. Musser and J. L. Price, eds., *The New Handbook of Theology* (Nashville: Abingdon, 1992), 469.

34. John Goldingay, "Biblical Narrative and Systematic Theology," in *Between Two Horizons: Spanning New Testament Studies and Systemaitc Theology*, ed. Joel B. Green and Max Turner (Grand Rapids: Eerdmans, 2000), 132.

35. Martin Buber, *Werke III* (Munich, 1963), 71, quoted in Johann Baptist Metz, "A Short Apology of Narrative," trans. David Smith, in *Why Narrative? Readings in Narrative Theology*, ed. Stanley Hauerwas and L. Gregory Jones (Grand Rapids: Eerdmans, 1989), 253.

36. Robert Jewett, *Saint Paul Returns to the Movies* (Grand Rapids: Eerdmans, 1999), 20.

37. Larry J. Kreitzer, *The New Testament in Fiction and Film: On Reversing the Hermeneutical Flow* (Sheffield: JSOT Press, 1993); Larry J. Kreitzer, *The Old Testament in Fiction and Film: On Reversing the Hermeneutical Flow* (Sheffield: Sheffield Academic Press, 1994).

38. Phillip Yancey, *The Jesus I Never Knew* (Grand Rapids: Zondervan, 1995).

Chapter 5

1. Quoted in Quentin J. Schultze et al., *Dancing in the Dark: Youth, Popular Culture, and the Electronic Media* (Grand Rapids: Eerdmans, 1991), 111.

2. For an early, incisive critique of the movie industry, see William F. Lynch, *The Image Industries* (New York: Sheed & Ward, 1959).

3. See David Bayles and Ted Orland, *Art and Fear: Observations on the Perils (and Rewards) of Artmaking* (Santa Barbara, Calif.: Capra, 1993), 74–77.

4. Tim Wright, "A Conversation with Horton Foote," *Image: A Journal of the Arts & Religion* 20 (summer 1998): 55.

5. Cf. Siegfried Kracauer, *Theory of Film* (New York: Oxford University Press, 1960).

6. "Putting on the *Dogme*," *Time*, 11 October 1999, 84.

7. Cf. Sergei Eisenstein, *Film Form* (New York: Harcourt, Brace, 1949); Ambros Eichenberger, "Approaches to Film Criticism," in *New Image of Religious Film*, ed. John R. May (Kansas City: Sheed & Ward, 1997), 4–5.

8. Aleksandr I. Solzhenitsyn, *East and West*, trans. Alexis Klimoff et al. (New York: Harper & Row, 1980), 3.

9. Richard A. Blake, *Screening America: Reflections on Five Classic Films* (New York: Paulist, 1991), 15. Cf. Ronald Holloway, *Beyond the Image: Approaches to the Religious Dimension in the Cinema* (Geneva: World Council of Churches, 1977), 25; Les Keyser and Barbara Keyser, *Hollywood and the Catholic Church: The Image of Roman Catholicism in American Movies* (Chicago: Loyola University Press, 1984), xiii; John R. May, "Close Encounters: Hollywood and Religion after a Century," *Image: A Journal of the Arts & Religion* 20 (summer 1998): 88.

10. New York: Vintage Books, 1975; quoted in Keyser and Keyser, *Hollywood*, xii.

11. Cf. Lynn Ross-Bryant, *Imagination and the Life of the Spirit: An Introduction to the Study of Religion and Literature* (Chico, Calif.: Scholars Press, 1981), 172.

12. Cf. Giles B. Gunn, "Introduction: Literature and Its Relation to Religion," in *Literature and Religion*, ed. Giles B. Gunn (New York: Harper & Row, 1971), 23.

13. Ibid., 24.

14. Solzhenitsyn, *East and West*, 8.

15. Paul Schrader, *Transcendental Style in Film: Ozu, Bresson, Dreyer* (New York: Da Capo, 1972). The quote is found in Gerardus van der Leeuw, *Sacred and Profane Beauty: The Holy in Art,* trans. David E. Green (Nashville: Abingdon, 1963), 333.

16. Scorsese's quote is used as the epigraph for Clive Marsh and Gaye Ortiz, eds., *Explorations in Theology and Film: Movies and Meaning* (Oxford: Blackwell, 1997), ii.

17. Solzhenitsyn, *East and West*, 6.

18. Robert Gessner, *The Moving Image* (New York: Dutton, 1970), 19, quoted in Thomas Martin, *Images and the Imageless* (Lewisberg: Bucknell University Press, 1981), 159.

19. James M. Wall, *Church and Cinema: A Way of Viewing Film* (Grand Rapids: Eerdmans, 1971), 33.

20. Dorothy Sayers, "Towards a Christian Aesthetic," in *Unpopular Opinions* (New York: Harcourt, Brace, 1947), 39, quoted in Laura Simmons, "Theology Made Interesting: Dorothy L. Sayers as a Lay Theologian" (Ph.D. diss., Fuller Theological Seminary, 1999), 132–33.

21. Mitchell Stephens, *The Rise of the Image, The Fall of the Word* (New York: Oxford University Press, 1998), xi–xii.

22. Schrader, *Transcendental Style*, 123.

23. Mark Swed, "The Transcendent Sounds of 'Kundun,'" *Los Angeles Times*, 9 January 1998, sec. F, p. 12.

24. Cf. Frank Kermode, *A Sense of the Ending: Studies in the Theory of Fiction* (New York: Oxford University Press, 1966).

25. Andrew Greeley, *God in Popular Culture* (Chicago: Thomas More, 1988), 17.

26. Ibid., 252.

Chapter 6

1. Louis Giannetti, *Understanding Movies*, 5th ed. (Englewood Cliffs, N.J.: Prentice Hall, 1990), 300.

2. Frederick Buechner, *Listening to Your Life* (New York: HarperCollins, 1992), 10.

3. Garrison Keillor, quoted by Ken Gire, *Windows of the Soul: Experiencing God in New Ways* (Grand Rapids: Zondervan, 1996), 120.

4. Ibid.

5. Benjamin Svetkey, "Who Killed the Hollywood Screenplay?" *Entertainment Weekly*, 4 October 1996, 32.

6. Ibid., 34.

7. The review of *Fly Away Home* appeared originally in *The Covenant Companion*, May 1997, 27. The review of *Amistad* appeared originally in *The Covenant Companion*, March 1998, 33.

8. Paul Woolf, "Turning toward Home," *Image: A Journal of the Arts & Religion* 20 (summer 1998): 123.

9. Wesley Kort, *Narrative Elements and Religious Meaning* (Philadelphia: Fortress, 1975).

10. Jon Boorstin, *Making Movies Work: Thinking like a Filmmaker* (Los Angeles: Silman-James, 1995), 154.

11. Lynn Ross-Bryant, *Imagination and the Life of the Spirit: An Introduction to the Study of Religion and Literature* (Chico, Calif.: Scholars Press, 1981), 90.

12. Boorstin, *Making Movies*, 65–66.

13. Sergei Eisenstein, *The Film Sense,* trans. and ed. Jay Leyday (New York: Harcourt, Brace & World, 1947), 4, quoted in Roger Kahle and Robert E. Lee, *Popcorn and Parable* (Minneapolis: Augsburg, 1971), 23.

14. See Diane Apostolos-Cappadona, "From Eve to the Virgin and Back Again: The Image of Woman in Contemporary (Religious) Film," in *New Image of Religious Film*, ed. John R. May (Kansas City: Sheed & Ward, 1997), 111–27.

15. An alternate ending was filmed (it is available on the movie's DVD version) that follows the car into the canyon, where it crashes. The realism of the scene was rejected in the editing of the movie, for it destroyed the story's intended message of liberation.

16. Aljean Harmetz, "'Star Wars' Is 10, and Lucas Reflects," *New York Times*, 21 May 1987, 22; quoted in Quentin Schultze, et. al., *Dancing in the Dark: Youth, Popular Culture, and the Electronic Media* (Grand Rapids: Eerdmans, 1991), 128.

17. Harmetz, "'Star Wars,'" 22; quoted in Schultze, *Dancing*, 128–29.

18. For a discussion of Kubrick's use of music, see Vincent Lo Brutto, *Stanley Kubrick: A Biography* (New York: Da Capo, 1997), and Thomas Allen Nelson, *Kubrick: Inside a Film Artist's Maze* (Bloomington: Indiana University Press, 1982).

19. Northrop Frye, *Anatomy of Criticism* (Princeton: Princeton University Press, 1957), 53.

20. Cf. Nathan Scott, *The Broken Center* (New Haven: Yale University Press, 1966), 4.

21. T. S. Eliot, "Religion and Literature," in *Religion and Modern Literature: Essays in Theory and Criticism*, ed. G. B. Tennyson and Edward E. Ericson Jr. (Grand Rapids: Eerdmans, 1975), 25.

22. Walter J. Ong, "Voice as Summons for Belief: Literature, Faith, and the Divided Self," in *Literature and Religion*, ed. Giles B. Gunn (New York: Harper & Row, 1971), 72.

23. Bill Blizek and Ronald Burke, "'The Apostle': An Interview with Robert Duvall," *Journal of Religion and Film* 2.1 (1997): 8.

24. Quoted in Thomas Martin, *Images and the Imageless: A Study in Religious Consciousness and Film* (Lewisburg: Bucknell University Press, 1981), 18. See Norwood Russell Hanson, *Patterns of Discovery: An Inquiry into the Conceptual Foundations of Science* (Cambridge: Cambridge University Press, 1961).

25. Giles Gunn, "Introduction: Literature and Its Relation to Religion," in *Literature and Religion*, ed. Giles Gunn (New York: Harper & Row, 1971), 24.

26. Jon Boorstin, *Making Movies Work: Thinking like a Filmmaker* (Los Angeles: Silman-James, 1995).

27. Robert Jewett, *Saint Paul at the Movies: The Apostle's Dialogue with American Culture* (Louisville: Westminster/John Knox, 1993), 32.

28. Boorstin, *Making Movies*, 162.

29. *Woody Allen on Woody Allen: In Conversation with Stig Bjorkman* (New York: Grove, 1995), 208.

30. Ibid., 225.

31. Ibid., 223.

32. Woody Allen, quoted in Eric Lax, *Woody Allen: A Biography* (New York: Random House, 1991), 28–29.

33. Ibid., 362.

Chapter 7

1. Richard A. Blake, *Screening America: Reflections on Five Classic Films* (New York: Paulist, 1991), 4.

2. Cf. Will Wright, *Six Guns and Society: A Structural Study of the Western* (Berkeley: University of California Press, 1975), 97.

3. Tom Ryall, "Teaching through Genre," *Screen Education* 17 (1975): 27–28, quoted in Peter Hutchings, "Genre Theory and Criticism," in *Approaches to Popular Film*, ed. Joanne Hollows and Mark Jancovich (Manchester: Manchester University Press, 1995), 65–66.

4. Orson Welles, quoted in Louis Giannetti, *Understanding Movies*, 5th ed. (Englewood Cliffs, N.J.: Prentice Hall, 1990), 330.

5. Wright, *Six Guns*, 34.

6. Ibid., 48–49.

7. Jean Renoir, quoted in Blake, *Screening America*, 181.

8. Robert Banks, "The Drama of Salvation in George Steven's *Shane*," in *Explorations in Theology and Film: Movies and Meaning*, ed. Clive Marsh and Gaye Ortiz (Oxford: Blackwell, 1997), 59–72.

9. See Geoffrey Hill, *Illuminating Shadow: The Mythic Power of Film* (Boston: Shambhala, 1992), 118–36.

10. Banks, "The Drama of Salvation," 65.

11. David Bayles and Ted Orland, *Art and Fear: Observations on the Perils (and Rewards) of Artmaking* (Santa Barbara, Calif.: Capra, 1993), 116.

12. Wassily Kandinsky, "Concerning the Spiritual in Art," in *Art, Creativity, and the Sacred: An Anthology in Religion and Art*, ed. Diane Apostolos-Cappadona (New York: Crossroad, 1984), 7 n. 1.

13. It is important not to confuse the director's point of view with the implied narrator. An author's statement on a movie can help one understand what went into the creation of the film, but it can never take the place of the movie itself.

14. Sherman Alexie, quoted by Jeffrey Ressner, "They've Gotta Have It," *Time* 151.25 (29 June 1998).

15. Lester D. Friedman, *The Jewish Image in American Film* (Secaucus, N.J.: Citadel, 1987), 229.

16. *Woody Allen on Woody Allen: In Conversation with Stig Bjorkman* (New York: Grove, 1995), 263.

17. In Woody Allen, *Side Effects* (New York: Random House, 1980).

18. Joel B. Green, "The Death of Jesus: Perspectives from Franco Zeffirelli and Roman History," *Radix* 23.1 (1994): 4.

19. Quoted by Lloyd Baugh, *Imaging the Divine: Jesus and Christ-Figures in Film* (Kansas City: Sheed & Ward, 1997), 73. See William Aldridge, "Franco Zeffirelli on Telling the Story of Christ from Its Real Roots," *Screen International* 48 (7 August 1976): 9.

20. Baugh, *Imaging the Divine*, 83.

21. Jon Boorstin, *Making Movies Work: Thinking like a Filmmaker* (Los Angeles: Silman-James, 1995), 162.

22. Cf., Nora Zamichow, "Psychologists Are Giving Film Therapy Thumbs Up," *Los Angeles Times*, 4 July 1999, sec. A, pp. 1, 12; and Gary Solomon, *The Motion Picture Prescription* (Santa Rosa, Calif.: Aslan, 1995). Solomon reviews two hundred movies "to help you heal life's problems."

23. Kendall Park, N.J.: Fourth Write, 1994.

24. Arnold Penenberg, foreword to *Reel Life/Real Life: A Video Guide for Personal Discovery*, by Mary Ann Horenstein et al. (Kendall Park, N.J.: Fourth Write, 1994).

25. Sarah Anson Vaux, *Finding Meaning at the Movies* (Nashville: Abingdon, 1999), xi, xii.

26. Larry Sturhahn, "*One Flew over the Cuckoo's Nest*: An Interview with Director Milos Forman," *Filmmakers Newsletter* 9.2 (December 1975): 31.

27. Milos Forman and Jan Novak, *Turnaround: A Memoir* (New York: Villard, 1994), 204.

28. John Broder and Katharine Seelye, *International Herald Tribune*, 11 May 1999, p. 2.

29. Quoted in Amy Wallace, "Is Hollywood Pulling Punches?" *Los Angeles Times*, 26 December 1999, Calendar section, pp. 5, 92.

30. Edward R. Murrow, quoted in William F. Lynch, *The Image Industries* (New York: Sheed & Ward, 1959), 37 n. 1.

31. Laura Mulvey, "Visual Pleasure and Narrative Cinema," *Screen* 16.3 (1975): 6–18.

32. Cf. bell hooks, *Black Looks: Race and Representation* (London: Turnaround, 1992), 122–23.

Chapter 8

1. T. S. Eliot, "Religion and Literature," in *Religion and Modern Literature: Essays in Theory and Criticism*, ed. G. B. Tennyson and Edward E. Ericson Jr., (Grand Rapids: Eerdmans, 1975), 21.

2. Cf. Roger Wedell, "Berdyaev and Rothko: Transformative Visions," in *Art, Creativity, and the Sacred: An Anthology in Religion and Art*, ed. Diane Apostolos-Cappadona (New York: Crossroad, 1984), 304.

3. David John Graham, "The Uses of Film in Theology," in *Explorations in Theology and Film: Movies and Meaning*, ed. Clive Marsh and Gaye Ortiz (Oxford: Blackwell, 1997), 41–42.

4. James Wall, *Church and Cinema: A Way of Viewing Film* (Grand Rapids: Eerdmans, 1971), 34.

5. Martin Buber, *I and Thou*, 2d ed. (New York: Scribner's Sons, 1958), 4.

6. Rudolf Otto, *The Idea of the Holy* (New York: Oxford University Press, 1958), 12–40.

7. T. S. Eliot, *The Complete Poems and Plays, 1909–1950* (New York: Harcourt, Brace & World, 1971), 119. Eliot also uses the image in "Triumphal March," stanza one of *Coriolan*, ibid., 86.

8. Wallace Stevens, *Collected Poems* (New York: Knopf, 1955), 209, quoted in Robert N. Bellah, "Transcendence in Contemporary Piety," in *Transcendence*, ed. Herbert W. Richardson and Donald R. Cutler (Boston: Beacon, 1969), 89.

9. Quoted in Roy M. Anker, "Movies and the Mystery of God's Love," *The Banner*, 11 October 1999, 14–17.

10. Peter Berger, *A Rumor of Angels* (Garden City, N.Y.: Doubleday, Anchor, 1970), 57–60.

11. John Updike, "Packed Dirt, Churchgoing, a Dying Cat, a Traded Car," in *Pigeon Feathers and Other Stories* (Greenwich, Conn.: Fawcett, Crest, 1962), 172.

12. Huston Smith, "The Reach and the Grasp: Transcendence Today," in *Transcendence*, ed. Herbert W. Richardson and Donald R. Cutler (Boston: Beacon, 1969), 2.

13. David Hay, *Exploring Inner Space: Scientists and Religious Experience* (London: Mowbray, 1987), 16.

14. Ibid., 207.

15. Wallace Stevens, *Opus Posthumous* (New York: Knopf, 1957), 237, quoted in Robert N. Bellah, "Transcendence in Contemporary Piety," in *Transcendence*, ed. Herbert W. Richardson and Donald R. Cutler (Boston: Beacon, 1969), 86.

16. Nathan Scott Jr., *The Broken Center* (New Haven: Yale University Press, 1966), 204–5.

17. Julius Lester, quoted in Martin Marty, *Context: Martin Marty on Religion and Culture* 28.11 (1 June 1996): 2.

18. Kathleen Norris et al., "Screening Mystery: A Symposium," *Image: A Journal of the Arts & Religion* 20 (summer 1998): 36.

19. Ibid., 41.

20. Paul Schrader, *Transcendental Style in Film: Ozu, Bresson, Dreyer* (New York: Da Capo, 1972), 6.

21. Harvey Cox, "The Purpose of the Grotesque in Fellini's Films," in *Celluloid and Symbols*, ed. John Cooper and Carl Skrade (Philadelphia: Fortress, 1970), 99.

22. Ken Gire, *Windows of the Soul: Experiencing God in New Ways* (Grand Rapids: Zondervan, 1996), 118–19. One of my students related to me that it was the same scene that as a depressed adolescent made him weep as well. The movie was the first "R" rated movie he had seen. He went because his uncle was in the film. And as he followed the struggles of the Richard Gere character, he was both inspired and encouraged.

23. Cf. Michael Bird, "Film as Hierophany," in *Religion in Film*, ed. John R. May and Michael Bird (Knoxville: University of Tennessee Press, 1982), 3–22.

24. Andrew Greeley, *God in Popular Culture* (Chicago: Thomas More, 1988), 245–49.

25. Ibid., 246ff.

26. C. S. Lewis, *The Pilgrim's Regress* (Grand Rapids: Eerdmans, 1958), 171.

27. Greeley, *God*, 250.

28. William Dyrness, "Response to Margaret Miles' Report on Research," unpublished manuscript, 3.

29. Quoted in James Wall, *Hidden Treasures: Searching for God in Modern Culture* (Chicago: Christian Century Press, 1997), 28.

30. Ibid.

31. Cf. Clive Marsh and Gaye Ortiz, "Theology beyond the Modern and the Postmodern: A Future Agenda for Theology and Film," in *Explorations in Theology and Film: Movies and Meaning*, ed. Clive Marsh and Gaye Ortiz (Oxford: Blackwell, 1997), 249.

32. Ernest Ferlita and John R. May, *Film Odyssey: The Art of Film as Search for Meaning* (New York: Paulist, 1976), 14.

33. "Meet Me in Zihuatanejo: A Meditation on Friendship," *The Covenant Companion* 84.9 (September 1995): 12–13, 39.

34. "Has God Gone Hollywood with the Apocalypse?" *The Covenant Companion* 88.1 (January 1999): 22–24.

35. Dietrich Bonhoeffer, *Letters and Papers from Prison,* enlarged ed., ed. Eberhard Bethge (New York: Macmillan, 1972), 193.

36. John Drane, "Making Theology Practical: Three Recent Movies and the Contemporary Spiritual Search" (inaugural lecture as Professor of Practical Theology, University of Aberdeen, Aberdeen, Scotland, 1998).

37. Conrad E. Ostwalt Jr., "Visions of the End: Secular Apocalypse in Recent Hollywood Film," *Journal of Religion and Film* 2.1 (1998): np.

Chapter 9

1. C. S. Lewis, "On Stories," in *Essays Presented to Charles Williams,* ed. C. S. Lewis (Grand Rapids: Eerdmans, 1966), 101.

2. John Ruskin, quoted in John C. Cooper and Carl Skrade, *Celluloid and Symbols* (Philadelphia: Fortress, 1970), 15.

3. Peter Weir, quoted in Sue Mathews, *35mm Dreams* (Ringwood, Victoria, Australia: Penguin, 1984), 102.

4. Ibid., 105.

5. Peter Weir, quoted in Marek Haltof, *Peter Weir: When Cultures Collide* (New York: Twayne, 1996), 28.

6. Ibid., 34.

7. Cf. Sven Birkerts, "Escape from Pleasantville!" *American Graffiti,* 4 November 1998, in *Atlantic Unbound* (www.theatlantic.com, the internet site for *The Atlantic Monthly*).

8. David Glover and Cora Kaplan, "Guns in the House of Culture? Crime Fiction and the Politics of the Popular," in *Cultural Studies,* ed. Lawrence Grossberg, Cary Nelson, and Paula A. Treichle (New York: Routledge, 1992), 213–26. I am indebted to Barry Taylor for pointing out to me this article.

9. Weir, quoted in Mathews, *35mm Dreams,* 98.

10. Ibid., 107.

11. Weir, quoted in Pat McGilligan, "Under Weir and Theroux," *Film Comment* 22 (1986): 25.

12. Weir, quoted in Mathews, *35mm Dreams,* 87.

13. Cf. Haltof, *Peter Weir,* 130.

14. Weir, quoted in Pat McGilligan, "Under Weir," *Film Comment* 22 (1986): 30.

15. I am indebted to one of my students, Chad Pecknold, for pointing out to me the original context for the composition of Gorecki's symphony. He also has provided the English translations of the songs Gorecki uses, as well as a summary of music criticism.

16. Nathan A. Scott Jr., "The Rediscovery of Story in Recent Theology and the Refusal of Story in Recent Literature," in *Art/Literature/Religion: Life on the Borders,* ed. Robert Detweiler (Chico, Calif.: Scholars Press, 1983), 153.

17. Elizabeth Barrett Browning, *Aurora Leigh, and Other Poems* (New York: James Miller, 1866), 263, 265, 266.

18. Sam Keen, *Apology for Wonder* (New York: Harper & Row, 1969), 130.

19. Sam Keen, "My New Carnality," *Psychology Today* 4 (October 1970): 59.

20. Sam Keen, *To a Dancing God* (New York: Harper & Row, 1970), 82–86.

21. Cf. Sam Keen, "Hope in a Posthuman Era," *The Christian Century,* 25 January 1967, 106–9.

22. Keen, *Apology for Wonder,* 188.

23. Rudolf Otto, *The Idea of the Holy* (Oxford: Oxford University Press, 1971), 12–40.

24. T. S. Eliot, *The Complete Poems and Plays, 1909–1950* (New York: Harcourt, Brace & World, 1971), 136.

25. Ibid.

26. Cf. John Updike, "Packed Dirt, Churchgoing, a Dying Cat, a Traded Car," in *Pigeon Feathers and Other Stories* (Greenwich, Conn.: Fawcett, Crest, 1962), 172.

27. Catherine Barsotti and Robert K. Johnston, "Living Dangerously," *The Covenant Companion* 88.11 (November 1999): 29.

28. Cf. Robert Hostetter, "A Controversial 'Witness,'" *The Christian Century*, 10 April 1985, 341–42.

29. C. S. Lewis, *The Silver Chair* (New York: Macmillan, Collier, 1970), 159.

selected bibliography
of theology and film

Adams, Doug. "Theological Expressions through Visual Art Forms." In *Art, Creativity, and the Sacred: An Anthology in Religion and Art*, ed. Diane Apostolos-Cappadona, 311–18. New York: Crossroad, 1984.

Allen, Woody. *Woody Allen on Woody Allen: In Conversation with Stig Bjorkman*. New York: Grove, 1995.

Anker, Roy M. "Movies and the Mystery of God's Love." *The Banner*, 11 October 1999, 14–17.

Apostolos-Cappadona, Diane. "From Eve to the Virgin and Back Again: The Image of Woman in Contemporary (Religious) Film." In *New Image of Religious Film*, ed. John R. May, 111–27. Kansas City: Sheed & Ward, 1997.

———, ed. *Art, Creativity, and the Sacred: An Anthology in Religion and Art*. New York: Crossroad, 1984.

Austin, Ronald. "Editorial Statement: Screening Mystery." *Image: A Journal of the Arts & Religion* 20 (summer 1998): 3–5.

———. "Sacrificing Images: Violence and the Movies." *Image: A Journal of the Arts & Religion* 20 (summer 1998): 23–28.

———, ed. "Screening Mystery: The Religious Imagination in Contemporary Film." *Image: A Journal of the Arts & Religion* 20 (summer 1998).

Baehr, Theodore. "A Cacophony of Prime Time Religions?" In *Religion and Prime Time Television*, ed. Michael Suman, 117–29. Westport, Conn.: Praeger, 1997.

———. *The Media-Wise Family*. Colorado Springs: Chariot Victor, 1998.

Banks, Robert. "The Drama of Salvation in George Stevens's *Shane*." In *Explorations in Theology and Film: Movies and Meaning*, ed. Clive Marsh and Gaye Ortiz, 59–72. Oxford: Blackwell, 1997.

Barthes, Roland. "The Death of the Author." In *Image/Music/Text*, trans. Stephen Heath, 142–48. London: Fontana/Collins, 1977.

Baugh, Lloyd. *Imaging the Divine: Jesus and Christ-Figures in Film*. Kansas City: Sheed & Ward, 1997.

Baxter, John. *The Australian Cinema*. Sydney: Angus & Robertson, Pacific Books, 1970.

Bayles, David, and Ted Orland. *Art and Fear: Observations on the Perils (and Rewards) of Artmaking*. Santa Barbara, Calif.: Capra, 1993.

Bellah, Robert N. "Transcendence in Contemporary Piety." In *Transcendence*, ed. Herbert W. Richardson and Douglas R. Cutler, 85–97. Boston: Beacon, 1969.

Berger, Peter. *A Rumor of Angels*. Garden City, N.Y.: Doubleday, Anchor, 1970.

Beyette, Beverly. "A Modern-Day Schindler Faces the Consequences," *Los Angeles Times*, 19 August 1998, sec. E, p. 1.

Billingsley, K. L. *The Seductive Image: A Christian Critique of the World of Film*. Westchester, Ill.: Crossway, 1989.

Bird, Michael. "Film as Hierophany." In *Religion in Film*, ed. John R. May and Michael Bird, 3–22. Knoxville: University of Tennesee Press, 1982.

Black, Gregory. *The Catholic Crusade against the Movies, 1940–1975*. New York: Cambridge University Press, 1997.

———. *Hollywood Censored: Morality Codes, Catholics, and the Movies*. New York: Cambridge University Press, 1994.

Blake, Richard A. *AfterImage*. Chicago: Loyola University Press, 2000.

———. *Screening America: Reflections on Five Classic Films*. New York: Paulist, 1991.

Blizek, Bill, and Ronald Burke. "'The Apostle': An Interview with Robert Duvall," *Journal of Religion and Film* 2.1 (1997): 8.

Boatwright, Phil. *The Movie Reporter: Know before You Go (Film/Video Reviews from a Christian Perspective)*. Thousand Oaks, Calif.: Central Christian, 1997.

Bobker, Lee R. *Elements of Film*. New York: Harcourt, Brace & World, 1969.

Bonhoeffer, Dietrich. *Ethics*. Ed. Eberhard Bethge. New York: Macmillan, 1955.

———. *Letters and Papers from Prison*. Ed. Eberhard Bethge. Rev. ed. New York: Macmillan, 1967.

Boorstin, Jon. *Making Movies Work: Thinking like a Filmmaker*. Los Angeles: Silman-James, 1995.

Boyd, Malcom. "Theology and the Movies." *Theology Today* 14 (October 1957): 359–75.

Boyum, Joy Gould, and Adrienne Scott. *Film as Film: Critical Responses to Film Art*. Boston: Allyn and Bacon, 1971.

Brown, Robert McAfee. *Persuade Us to Rejoice: The Liberating Power of Fiction*. Louisville: Westminster/John Knox, 1992.

———. *The Pseudonyms of God*. Philadelphia: Westminster, 1972.

Browne, David. "Film, Movies, Meaning." In *Explorations in Theology and Film: Movies and Meaning*, ed. Clive Marsh and Gaye Ortiz, 9–20. Oxford: Blackwell, 1997.

Bryant, M. Darrol. "Cinema, Religion, and Popular Culture." In *Religion in Film*, ed. John R. May and Michael Bird, 101–14. Knoxville: University of Tennesee Press, 1982.

Buber, Martin. *I and Thou*. 2d ed. New York: Scribner's Sons, 1958.

Buechner, Frederick. *Listening to Your Life*. San Francisco: HarperCollins, Harper-SanFrancisco, 1992.

Butler, Ivan. *Religion in the Cinema*. New York: Barnes, 1969.

Butler, John. *TV, Movies, and Morality: A Guide for Catholics*. Huntington, Ind.: Our Sunday Visitor, 1984.

Bywater, Tim, and Thomas Sobchack. *Introduction to Film Criticism: Major Critical Approaches to Narrative Film*. New York: Longman, 1989.

Chetwynd, Josh. "Escaping 'R' Bondage." *USA Today*, 22 November 1999, sec. D, pp. 1, 2.

Connor, Steven. *Postmodernist Culture: An Introduction to Theories of the Contemporary*. Oxford: Blackwell, 1989.

Cook, John W. "Picturing Theology: Martin Luther and Lucas Cranach." In *Art and Religion: Faith, Form and Reform*, ed. Overby Osmund, 22–39. Columbia: University of Missouri, 1986.

Cooper, John C. "The Image of Man in the Recent Cinema." In *Celluloid and Symbols*, ed. John C. Cooper and Carl Skrade, 25–40. Philadelphia: Fortress, 1970.

Cooper, John C., and Carl Skrade, eds. *Celluloid and Symbols*. Philadelphia: Fortress, 1970.

Cootsona, Greg. "Jesus the God of Justice and Compassion in Pasolini's *The Gospel according to Matthew*." *Radix* 23.1 (1994): 8–9, 26.

Coppenger, Mark. "A Christian Perspective on Film." In *The Christian Imagination*, ed. Leland Ryken, 285–302. Grand Rapids: Baker, 1981.

Cox, Harvey. "Feasibility and Fantasy: Sources of Social Transcendence." In *Transcendence*, ed. Herbert W. Richardson and Douglas R. Cutler, 53–63. Boston: Beacon, 1969.

———. "The Purpose of the Grotesque in Fellini's Films." In *Celluloid and Symbols*, ed. John C. Cooper and Carl Skrade, 89–106. Philadelphia: Fortress, 1970.

Crofts, Stephen. "Authorship and Hollywood." *Wide Angle* 5.3 (1982): 16–23.

Culkin, John M. "Film and the Church." In *Communication for Churchmen*, vol. 2, *Television-Radio-Film for Churchmen*, ed. B. F. Jackson Jr. Nashville: Abingdon, 1968.

Cunningham, Cecilia Davis. "Craft: Making and Being." In *Art, Creativity, and the Sacred: An Anthology in Religion and Art*, ed. Diane Apostolos-Cappadona, 8–11. New York: Crossroad, 1984.

De Staebler, Stephen, and Diane Apostolos-Cappadona. "Reflections on Art and the Spirit: A Conversation." In *Art, Creativity, and the Sacred: An Anthology in Religion and Art*, ed. Diane Apostolos-Cappadona, 24–33. New York: Crossroad, 1984.

Detweiler, Robert, ed. *Art/Literature/Religion: Life on the Borders*. Chico, Calif.: Scholars Press, 1983.

Drane, John. "Making Theology Practical: Three Recent Movies and the Contemporary Spiritual Search." Inaugural lecture as professor of practical theology, University of Aberdeen, Aberdeen, Scotland, 1998.

Drew, Donald J. *Images of Man: A Critique of the Contemporary Cinema*. Downers Grove, Ill.: InterVarsity, 1974.

Dykstra, Craig. "The Importance of Stories," *Initiatives in Religion* 2.2 (spring 1993): 1–2.

Dyrness, William. "Response to Margaret Miles' Report on Research." Unpublished manuscript.

Eichenberger, Ambros. "Approaches to Film Criticism." In *New Image of Religious Film*, ed. John R. May, 3–16. Kansas City: Sheed & Ward, 1997.

Eisenstein, Sergei. *The Film Sense*. Trans. and ed. Jay Leyday. New York: Harcourt, Brace & World, 1942.

Eliot, T. S. *The Complete Poems and Plays, 1909–1950*. New York: Harcourt, Brace & World, 1971.

———. "Religion and Literature." In *Religion and Modern Literature: Essays in Theory and Criticism*, ed. G. B. Tennyson and Edward E. Ericson Jr., 21–30. Grand Rapids: Eerdmans, 1975.

Eversole, Finley, ed. *Christian Faith and the Contemporary Arts*. New York: Abingdon, 1962.

Farley, Edward. *Theologia: The Fragmentation and Unity of Theological Education*. Philadelphia: Fortress, 1983.

Ferlita, Ernest. "The Analogy of Action in Film." In *Religion in Film*, ed. John R. May and Michael Bird, 44–58. Knoxville: University of Tennesee Press, 1982.

———. "Film and the Quest for Meaning." In *Religion in Film*, ed. John R. May and Michael Bird, 115–31. Knoxville: University of Tennesee Press, 1982.

Ferlita, Ernest, and John R. May. *Film Odyssey: The Art of Film as Search for Meaning*. New York: Paulist, 1976.

Foote, Horton. "A Conversation with Horton Foote." *Image: A Journal of the Arts & Religion* 20 (summer 1998): 45–57.

Ford, David. "System, Story, Performance: A Proposal about the Role of Narrative in Christian Systematic Theology." In *Why Narrative? Readings in Narrative Theology*, ed. Stanley Hauerwas and L. Gregory Jones, 191–215. Grand Rapids: Eerdmans, 1989.

Forman, Milos, and Jan Novak. *Turnaround: A Memoir*. New York: Villard, 1994.

Friedman, Lester D. *The Jewish Image in American Film*. Secaucus, N.J.: Citadel, 1987.

Frye, Northrop. *Anatomy of Criticism*. Princeton: Princeton University Press, 1957.

Gabler, Neal. *Life the Movie: How Entertainment Conquered Reality*. New York: Knopf, 1998.

Gallagher, Sharon. "Faith in Film." *Radix* 23.1 (1994), 10–11, 27.

———, ed. *Radix* 23.1 (1994).

Garner, Jack, and Bruce Fessier. "Land of the Film." *The Desert Sun*, 18 January 2000, sec. D, p. 3.

Giannetti, Louis. *Understanding Movies*. 5th ed. Englewood Cliffs, N.J.: Prentice Hall, 1990.

Gire, Ken. *Reflections on the Movies: Hearing God in the Unlikeliest of Places*. Colorado Springs: Chariot Victor, 2000.

———. *The Reflective Life: Becoming More Spiritually Sensitive to the Everyday Moments of Life*. Colorado Springs: Chariot Victor, 1998.

———. *Windows of the Soul: Experiencing God in New Ways*. Grand Rapids: Zondervan, 1996.

Girgus, Sam B. *The Films of Woody Allen*. Cambridge: Cambridge University Press, 1993.

Glover, David, and Cora Kaplan. "Guns in the House of Culture? Crime Fiction and the Politics of the Popular." In *Cultural Studies*, ed. Lawrence Grossberg, Cary Nelson, and Paula A. Treichle. New York: Routledge, 1992.

Goldingay, John. "Biblical Narrative and Systematic Theology." In *Between Two Horizons: Spanning New Testament Studies and Systematic Theology*, ed. Joel B. Green and Max Turner, 123–42. Grand Rapids: Eerdmans, 2000.

Graham, David John. "The Uses of Film in Theology." In *Explorations in Theology and Film: Movies and Meaning*, ed. Clive Marsh and Gaye Ortiz, 35–44. Oxford: Blackwell, 1997.

Greeley, Andrew. *God in Popular Culture*. Chicago: Thomas More, 1988.

Green, Joel. "The Death of Jesus: Franco Zeffirelli's Perspective." *Radix* 23.1 (1994), 4–7, 22–24.

Guinness, Os. *Dining with the Devil*. Grand Rapids: Baker, 1993.

Gunn, Giles. "Introduction: Literature and Its Relation to Religion." In *Literature and Religion*, ed. Giles Gunn, 1–33. New York: Harper & Row, 1971.

———, ed. *Literature and Religion*. New York: Harper & Row, 1971.

Haltof, Marek. *Peter Weir: When Cultures Collide*. New York: Twayne, 1996.

Hames, Peter. "Forman." In *Five Filmmakers*, ed. Daniel J. Goulding. Bloomington: Indiana University Press, 1994.

Hamilton, William. "Bergman and Polanski on the Death of God." In *Celluloid and Symbols*, ed. John C. Cooper and Carl Skrade, 61–74. Philadelphia: Fortress, 1970.

Harned, David Baily. *Theology and the Arts*. Philadelphia: Westminster, 1966.

Hasenberg, Peter. "The 'Religious' in Film: From *King of Kings* to *The Fisher King*." In *New Image of Religious Film*, ed. John R. May, 41–56. Kansas City: Sheed & Ward, 1997.

Hauerwas, Stanley, and L. Gregory Jones, eds. *Why Narrative? Readings in Narrative Theology*. Grand Rapids: Eerdmans, 1989.

Hauerwas, Stanley, and William H. Willimon. *Resident Aliens: Life in the Christian Colony*. Nashville: Abingdon, 1989.

Hay, David. *Exploring Inner Space: Scientists and Religious Experience*. London: Mowbray, 1987.

Hill, Geoffrey. *Illuminating Shadow: The Mythic Power of Film*. Boston: Shambhala, 1992.

Holloway, Ronald. *Beyond the Image: Approaches to the Religious Dimension in the Cinema*. Geneva: World Council of Churches, 1977.

Hollows, Joanne, and Mark Jancovich. *Approaches to Popular Film*. Manchester: Manchester University Press, 1995.

hooks, bell. *Black Looks: Race and Representation*. London: Turnaround, 1992.

Horenstein, Mary Ann, Brenda Rigby, Marjorie Flory, and Vicki Gershwin. *Reel Life/Real Life: A Video Guide for Personal Discovery*. Kendall Park, N.J.: Fourth Write, 1994.

Hostetter, Robert. "A Controversial 'Witness.'" *The Christian Century*, 10 April 1985, 341–42.

Howard, David, and Edward Mabley. *The Tools of Screenwriting: A Writer's Guide to the Craft and Elements of a Screenplay*. New York: St. Martin's Press, 1993.

Hulsether, Mark. "Sorting out the Relationships among Christian Values, US Popular Religion, and Hollywood Films." *Religious Studies Review* 25.1 (January 1999): 3–11.

Hurley, Neil P. "Cinematic Transformations of Jesus." In *Religion in Film*, ed. John R. May and Michael Bird, 61–78. Knoxville: University of Tennesee Press, 1982.

———. *Theology through Film*. New York: Harper & Row, 1970.

Jasper, David. "On Systematizing the Unsystematic: A Response." In *Explorations in Theology and Film: Movies and Meaning*, ed. Clive Marsh and Gaye Ortiz, 235–44. Oxford: Blackwell, 1997.

Jewett, Robert. *Saint Paul at the Movies: The Apostle's Dialogue with American Culture*. Louisville: Westminster/John Knox, 1993.

———. *Saint Paul Returns to the Movies: Triumph over Shame*. Grand Rapids: Eerdmans, 1999.

Johnston, Robert K. *The Christian at Play*. Grand Rapids: Eerdmans, 1983.

———. "Christian Theology and Literature: Correlation or Co-Relation?" In *Collection of Papers Celebrating Professor Hiromu Shimizu's Retirement*, ed. Sachiko Yoshida, 12–22. Kyoto: Apollon, 1991.

———. "God in the Midst of Life: The spirit and the Spirit." *Ex auditu* 12 (1996): 76–93.

———. "Image and Content: The Tension in C. S. Lewis' *Chronicles of Narnia*," *Journal of the Evangelical Theological Society* 20 (September 1977): 253–64.

Jones, Beth. "*One Flew over the Cuckoo's Nest*: Mythic Western or Czech Tragicomedy?" Student paper, Fuller Theological Seminary, fall 1996.

Jones, G. William. *Dialogue with the World*. Wilmette, Ill.: Films Incorporated, 1964.

———. *Sunday Night at the Movies*. Richmond: John Knox, 1967.

Kahle, Roger, and Robert E. Lee. *Popcorn and Parable*. Minneapolis: Augsburg, 1971.

Kandinsky, Wassily. "Concerning the Spiritual in Art." In *Art, Creativity, and the Sacred: An Anthology in Religion and Art*, ed. Diane Apostolos-Cappadona, 3–7. New York: Crossroad, 1984.

Kazan, Elia. *Elia Kazan: A Life*. New York: Knopf, 1988.

Keen, Sam. *Apology for Wonder*. New York: Harper & Row, 1969.

———. "Hope in a Posthuman Era." *The Christian Century*, 25 January 1967, 106–9.

———. "My New Carnality." *Psychology Today* 4 (October 1970).

———. *To a Dancing God*. New York: Harper & Row, 1970.

Kenny, Glenn. "Are We There Yet?" *Premiere* (February 1999): 91–95.

Kermode, Frank. *A Sense of the Ending: Studies in the Theory of Fiction*. New York: Oxford University Press, 1966.

Kesey, Ken. *One Flew over the Cuckoo's Nest: Text and Criticism*. Ed. John C. Pratt. New York: Viking, 1973.

Keyser, Les, and Barbara Keyser. *Hollywood and the Catholic Church: The Image of Roman Catholicism in American Movies*. Chicago: Loyola University Press, 1984.

Kitses, Jim. *Horizons West*. Bloomington: Indiana University Press, 1969.

Konzelman, Robert G. *Marquee Ministry: The Movie Theater as Church and Community Forum*. New York: Harper & Row, 1971.

Kopplin, David. "Program Notes (for *The Wind*)," *Los Angeles Philharmonic*, October 1998, 14–17.

Kort, Wesley. *Narrative Elements and Religious Meaning*. Philadelphia: Fortress, 1975.

Kreitzer, Larry J. *The New Testament in Fiction and Film: On Reversing the Hermeneutical Flow*. Sheffield: JSOT Press, 1993.

———. *The Old Testament in Fiction and Film: On Reversing the Hermeneutical Flow*. Sheffield: Sheffield Academic Press, 1994.

Laub-Novak, Karen. "The Art of Deception." In *Art, Creativity, and the Sacred: An Anthology in Religion and Art*, ed. Diane Apostolos-Cappadona, 12–23. New York: Crossroad, 1984.

Lax, Eric. *Woody Allen: A Biography*. New York: Random House, Vantage, 1991.

Lewis, C. S. "On Stories." In *Essays Presented to Charles Williams*, ed. C. S. Lewis. Grand Rapids: Eerdmans, 1966.

———. *The Pilgrim's Regress*. Grand Rapids: Eerdmans, 1958.

———. *The Silver Chair*. New York: Macmillan, Collier, 1970.

———. *Surprised by Joy*. New York: Harcourt, Brace & World, Harvest Books, 1955.

Lewis, R. W. B. "Hold on Hard to the Huckleberry Bushes." In *Religion and Modern Literature: Essays in Theory and Criticism*, ed. G. B. Tennyson and Edward E. Ericson Jr., 55–67. Grand Rapids: Eerdmans, 1975.

Lo Brotto, Vincent. *Stanley Kubrick: A Biography*. New York: Da Capo, 1997.

Lynch, William F. *The Image Industries*. New York: Sheed & Ward, 1959.

MacDonald, Alan. *Films in Close-Up: Getting the Most from Film and Video*. Leicester, England: Inter-Varsity, Frameworks, 1991.

Malone, Peter. "Jesus on Our Screens." In *New Image of Religious Film*, ed. John R. May, 57–71. Kansas City: Sheed & Ward, 1997.

———. *Movie Christs and Antichrists*. New York: Crossroad, 1990.

Marsh, Clive. "Did You Say 'Grace'? Eating in Community in *Babette's Feast*." In *Explorations in Theology and Film: Movies and Meaning*, ed. Clive Marsh and Gaye Ortiz, 207–18. Oxford: Blackwell, 1997.

———. "Film and Theologies of Culture." In *Explorations in Theology and Film: Movies and Meaning*, ed. Clive Marsh and Gaye Ortiz, 21–34. Oxford: Blackwell, 1997.

———. "The Spirituality of *Shirley Valentine*." In *Explorations in Theology and Film: Movies and Meaning*, ed. Clive Marsh and Gaye Ortiz, 193–206. Oxford: Blackwell, 1997.

Marsh, Clive, and Gaye Ortiz. "Theology beyond the Modern and the Postmodern: A Future Agenda for Theology and Film." In *Explorations in Theology and Film: Movies and Meaning*, ed. Clive Marsh and Gaye Ortiz, 245–56. Oxford: Blackwell, 1997.

———, eds. *Explorations in Theology and Film: Movies and Meaning*. Oxford: Blackwell, 1997.

Martin, Joel W., and Conrad E. Ostwalt Jr., *Screening the Sacred: Religion, Myth, and Ideology in Popular American Film*. Boulder, Colo.: Westview, 1995.

Martin, Thomas M. *Images and the Imageless: A Study in Religious Consciousness and Film*. Lewisburg: Bucknell University Press, 1981.

Marty, Martin. *Context: Martin Marty on Religion and Culture* 28.11 (1 June 1996).

Mathews, Sue. *35mm Dreams*. New York: Penguin, 1984.

May, John R. "Close Encounters: Hollywood and Religion after a Century." *Image: A Journal of the Arts & Religion* 20 (summer 1998): 87–100.

———. "Contemporary Theories regarding the Interpretation of Religious Film." In *New Image of Religious Film*, ed. John R. May, 17–40. Kansas City: Sheed & Ward, 1997.

———. "The Demonic in American Cinema." In *Religion in Film*, ed. John R. May and Michael Bird, 79–100. Knoxville: University of Tennesee Press, 1982.

———. "Religion and Film: Recent Contributions to the Continuing Dialogue." In *Critical Review of Books in Religion* 9 (1996): 105–21.

———. "Visual Story and the Religious Interpretation of Film." In *Religion in Film*, ed. John R. May and Michael Bird, 23–43. Knoxville: University of Tennesee Press, 1982.

———, ed. *New Image of Religious Film*. Kansas City: Sheed & Ward, 1997.

May, John R., and Michael Bird, eds. *Religion in Film*. Knoxville: University of Tennesee Press, 1982.

McFarlane, Brian, and Geoff Mayer. *New Australian Cinema: Sources and Parallels in American and British Film*. Cambridge: Cambridge University Press, 1992.

McGilligan, Pat. "Under Weir and Theroux," *Film Comment* 22 (1986): 23–32.

McNulty, Edward. *Visual Parables* (a monthly magazine; view samples from the current issue at www.visualparables.com).

Medved, Michael. "Hollywood Makes Room for Religion." In *Religion and Prime Time Television*, ed. Michael Suman, 111–16. Westport, Conn.: Praeger, 1997.

———. *Hollywood vs. America: Popular Culture and the War on Traditional Values*. New York: HarperCollins, 1992.

———. "Want an Oscar? An 'R' Revs Up Your Chances." *USA Today*, 19 March 1999, sec. A, p. 9.

Metz, Johann Baptist. "A Short Apology of Narrative." In *Why Narrative? Readings in Narrative Theology*, ed. Stanley Hauerwas and L. Gregory Jones, 251–62. Grand Rapids: Eerdmans, 1989.

Miles, Herbert. *Movies and Morals*. Grand Rapids: Zondervan, 1947.

Miles, Margaret. "Report on Research Conducted During 1994–95." Unpublished maunuscript.

———. *Seeing and Believing: Religion and Values in the Movies*. Boston: Beacon, 1996.

———. "What You See Is What You Get": Religion on Prime Time Fiction Television." In *Religion and Prime Time Television*, ed. Michael Suman, 37–46. Westport, Conn.: Praeger, 1997.

Miller, J. Hillis. *Illustration*. Cambridge, Mass.: Harvard University Press, 1992.

Monaco, James. *How to Read a Film*. Rev. ed. New York: Oxford University Press, 1981.

Morris, Michael. "Looking for Reel Religion." *Image: A Journal of the Arts & Religion* 20 (summer 1998): 72–78.

Mulvey, Laura. "Visual Pleasure and Narrative Cinema." *Screen* 16.3 (1975): 6–18.

Murphy, Roland E. "The Kerygma of the Book of Proverbs." *Interpretation* 20 (January 1966): 3–14.

Nelson, John Wiley. *Your God is Alive and Well and Appearing in Popular Culture*. Philadelphia: Westminster, 1976.

Nelson, Thomas Allen. *Kubrick: Inside a Film Artist's Maze*. Bloomington: Indiana University Press, 1982.

Niccol, Andrew. *The Truman Show: The Shooting Script*. New York: Newmarket, 1998.

Niebuhr, H. Richard. *Christ and Culture*. New York: Harper & Row, 1951.

Noll, Mark, Cornelius Plantinga Jr., and David Wells. "Evangelical Theology Today." *Theology Today* 51.4 (1995): 495–507.

O'Meara, Thomas Franklin. "The Aesthetic Dimension in Theology." In *Art, Creativity, and the Sacred: An Anthology in Religion and Art*, ed. Diane Apostolos-Cappadona, 205–18. New York: Crossroad, 1984.

Ong, Walter. "Voice as Summons for Belief: Literature, Faith, and the Divided Self." In *Literature and Religion*, ed. Giles Gunn, 68–86. New York: Harper & Row, 1971.

Ostwalt, Conrad, Jr. "Visions of the End: Secular Apocalypse in Recent Hollywood Film." *Journal of Religion and Film* 2.1 (1998): np.

Otto, Rudolf. *The Idea of the Holy*. New York: Oxford University Press, 1958.

Overby, Osmund, ed. *Art and Religion: Faith, Form and Reform*. Columbia: University of Missouri, 1986.

Packer, J. I. *Knowing God*. Downers Grove, Ill.: InterVarsity, 1973.

Poland, Larry W. *The Last Temptation of Hollywood*. Highland, Calif.: Mastermedia International, 1988.

Postman, Neil. *Amusing Ourselves to Death: Public Discourse in the Age of Show Business*. New York: Penguin, 1985.

Rayner, Jonathan. *The Films of Peter Weir*. New York: Cassell, 1998.

Read, Herbert. *The Redemption of the Robot: My Encounter with Education through Art*. New York: Trident, 1966.

Richardson, Herbert W., and Douglas R. Cutler, eds. *Transcendence*. Boston: Beacon, 1969.

Robinson, W. R., ed. *Man and the Movies*. Baltimore: Penguin, 1969.

Root, Michael. "The Narrative Structure of Soteriology." In *Why Narrative? Readings in Narrative Theology*, ed. Stanley Hauerwas and L. Gregory Jones, 263–78. Grand Rapids: Eerdmans, 1989.

Ross, T. J. *Film and the Liberal Arts*. New York: Holt, Rinehart and Winston, 1970.

Ross-Bryant, Lynn. *Imagination and the Life of the Spirit: An Introduction to the Study of Religion and Literature*. Chico, Calif.: Scholars Press, 1981.

Schaeffer, Franky. *Addicted to Mediocrity: 20th Century Christians and the Arts*. Wheaton, Ill.: Crossway, 1985.

Schillaci, Anthony. "Bergman's Vision of Good and Evil." In *Celluloid and Symbols*, ed. John C. Cooper and Carl Skrade, 75–88. Philadelphia: Fortress, 1970.

Schrader, Paul. *Transcendental Style in Film: Ozu, Bresson, Dreyer*. New York: Da Capo, 1972. (Originally published, Berkeley: University of California Press, 1972)

Schultze, Quentin, Roy M. Anker, et al. *Dancing in the Dark: Youth, Popular Culture, and the Electronic Media*. Grand Rapids: Eerdmans, 1991.

Schweizer, Eduard. *The Holy Spirit*. Philadelphia: Fortress, 1980.

Scott, Bernard Brandon. *Hollywood Dreams and Biblical Stories*. Minneapolis: Fortress, 1994.

Scott, Nathan, Jr. *The Broken Center*. New Haven: Yale University Press, 1966.

———. "The Rediscovery of Story in Recent Theology and the Refusal of Story in Recent Literature." In *Art/Literature/Religion: Life on the Borders*, ed. Robert Detweiler. Chico, Calif.: Scholars Press, 1983.

Shaw, David. "Thumbs Up or Down on Movie Critics?" *Los Angeles Times*, sec. A, pp. 1, 16, 17.

Shiach, Don. *The Films of Peter Weir: Visions of Alternative Realities*. London: Letts, 1993.

Shinn, Roger L. "The Artist as Prophet-Priest of Culture." In *Christian Faith and the Contemporary Arts*, ed. Finley Eversole, 72–79. New York: Abingdon, 1962.

Simmons, Laura. "Theology Made Interesting: Dorothy L. Sayers as a Lay Theologian." Ph.D. diss., Fuller Theological Seminary, 1999.

Sittler, Joseph. *Gravity and Grace*. Minneapolis: Augsburg, 1986.

Sittser, Gerry. *A Grace Disguised*. Grand Rapids: Zondervan, 1996.

Skinner, James. *The Cross and the Cinema: The Legion of Decency and the National Office for Motion Pictures, 1933–1970*. Westport, Conn.: Greenwood, 1993.

Skrade, Carl. "Theology and Films." In *Celluloid and Symbols*, ed. John C. Cooper and Carl Skrade, 1–24. Philadelphia: Fortress, 1970.

Smith, Houston. "The Reach and the Grasp: Transcendence Today." In *Transcendence*, ed. Herbert W. Richardson and Douglas R. Cutler, 1–17. Boston: Beacon, 1969.

Snodgrass, Klyne. "Justification by Grace—to the Doers: An Analysis of the Place of Romans 2 in the Theology of Paul." *New Testament Studies* 32.1 (January 1986): 72–93.

Solomon, Gary. *The Motion Picture Prescription*. Santa Rosa, Calif.: Aslan, 1995.

Solomon, Stanley. *Beyond Formula: American Film Genres*. New York: Harcourt, Brace, Jovanovich, 1976.

Solzhenitsyn, Aleksandr I. *East and West*. Trans. Alexis Klimoff et al. New York: Harper & Row, 1980.

Stassen, Glenn, Diane Yeager, and John Howard Yoder. *Authentic Transformation*. Nashville: Abingdon, 1996.

Stevens, Mitchell. *The Rise of the Image, The Fall of the Word*. New York: Oxford University Press, 1998.

Stevens, Wallace. *Collected Poems*. New York: Knopf, 1955.

Stott, John R. W. *Basic Christianity*. Downers Grove, Ill.: InterVarsity, 1971.

Sturhahn, Larry. "*One Flew over the Cuckoo's Nest*: An Interview with Director Milos Forman." *Filmmakers Newsletter* 9.2 (December 1975): 26–31.

Suman, Michael, ed. *Religion and Prime Time Television*. Westport, Conn.: Praeger, 1997.

Summers, Stanford. *Secular Films and the Church's Ministry*. New York: Seabury, 1969.

Svetkey, Benjamin. "Who Killed the Hollywood Screenplay?" *Entertainment Weekly*, 4 October 1996, 32–39.

Swed, Mark. "The Transcendent Sounds of 'Kundun.'" *Los Angeles Times*, 9 January 1998, sec. F, pp. 12, 14.

Taylor, John V. *The Go-Between God*. Philadelphia: Fortress, 1972.

Telford, William. "Jesus Christ Movie Star: The Depiction of Jesus in the Cinema." In *Explorations in Theology and Film: Movies and Meaning*, ed. Clive Marsh and Gaye Ortiz, 115–40. Oxford: Blackwell, 1997.

Tillich, Paul. "Art and Ultimate Reality." In *Art, Creativity, and the Sacred: An Anthology in Religion and Art*, ed. Diane Apostolos-Cappadona, 219–36. New York: Crossroad, 1984.

———. *On Art and Architecture*. Ed. John Dillenberger and Jane Dillenberger. New York: Crossroad, 1987.

———. *On the Boundary: An Autobiographical Sketch*. New York: Scribner's Sons, 1966.

———. *Systematic Theology*. Vol. 1. Chicago: University of Chicago Press, 1951.

Tompkins, Jane. *West of Everything*. New York: Oxford University Press, 1992.

Updike, John. *The Centaur*. Greenwich, Conn.: Fawcett, Crest, 1962.

———. *In the Beauty of the Lilies*. New York: Knopf, 1996.

————. "Packed Dirt, Churchgoing, a Dying Cat, a Traded Car." In *Pigeon Feathers and Other Stories*. Greenwich, Conn.: Fawcett, Crest, 1962.

Van der Leeuw, Gerardus. *Sacred and Profane Beauty: The Holy in Art*. Trans. David E. Green. Nashville: Abingdon, 1963.

Vaux, Sarah Anson. *Finding Meaning at the Movies*. Nashville: Abingdon, 1999.

Wall, James M. "Biblical Spectaculars and Secular Man." In *Celluloid and Symbols*, ed. John C. Cooper and Carl Skrade, 51–60. Philadelphia: Fortress, 1970.

————. *Church and Cinema: A Way of Viewing Film*. Grand Rapids: Eerdmans, 1971.

————. *Hidden Treasures: Searching for God in Modern Culture*. Chicago: Christian Century Press, 1997.

Wallace, Amy. "Do Movie Ratings Need New Categories?" *Los Angeles Times*, 10 August 1999, sec. F, pp. 1, 4, 5.

————. "Is Hollywood Pulling Punches?" *Los Angeles Times*, 26 December 1999, Calendar section, pp. 5, 92.

————. "'Ryan' Ends Vets' Years of Silence." *Los Angeles Times*, 6 August 1998, sec. A, p. 1.

Walsh, Frank. *Sin and Censorship: The Catholic Church and the Motion Picture Industry*. New Haven: Yale University Press, 1996.

Wedell, Roger. "Berdyaev and Rothko: Transformative Visions." In *Art, Creativity, and the Sacred: An Anthology in Religion and Art*, ed. Diane Apostolos-Cappadona, 304–10. New York: Crossroad, 1984.

Woolf, Paul. "Turning toward Home." *Image: A Journal of the Arts & Religion* 20 (summer 1998): 115–23.

Wright, Will. *Six Guns and Society: A Structural Study of the Western*. Berkeley: University of California Press, 1975.

Yancey, Phillip. *The Jesus I Never Knew*. Grand Rapids: Zondervan, 1995.

Zamichow, Nora. "Psychologists Are Giving Film Therapy Thumbs Up." *Los Angeles Times*, 4 July 1999, sec. A, pp. 1, 12.

Zimmerli, Walther. "The Place and Limit of the Wisdom in the Framework of the Old Testament Theology." *Scottish Journal of Theology* 17 (1964): 146–58.

Zwick, Reinhold. "The Problem of Evil in Contemporary Film." In *New Image of Religious Film*, ed. John R. May, 72–94. Kansas City: Sheed & Ward, 1997.

movies cited

2001: A Space Odyssey (d. Kubrick, 1968) 113–14

Ulee's Gold (d. Nuñez, 1997) 100
Unforgiven (d. Eastwood, 1992) 15
Unmarried Woman, An (d. Mazursky, 1978) 140

Wag the Dog (d. Levinson, 1997) 179
Waterworld (d. Reynolds, 1995) 168
Who's Afraid of Virginia Woolf? (d. Nichols, 1966) 37–38, 55–56
Wild Bunch, The (d. Peckinpah, 1969) 128

Wind, The (d. Sjöström, 1928) 91–92, 215
Witness (d. Weir, 1985) 175, 176, 178, 179–80, 183, 185–86, 188, 208 n. 28
Wizard of Oz, The (d. Fleming, 1939) 107
Working Girl (d. Nichols, 1988) 149–50

Year of Living Dangerously, The (d. Weir, 1982) 43, 175, 176, 177–78, 179, 180, 184, 188, 191, 193–94

Zelig (d. Allen, 1983) 137

subject index

Kandinsky, Wassily 133
Kazan, Elia 24
Kazantzakis, Nikos 44
Keating, John 183–84
Keen, Sam 190–91, 194
Keillor, Garrison 100
Kennedy, John F. 132
Kepler, Johannes 117
Kesey, Ken 120, 141–43
Keyser, Les and Barbara 47
Kierkegaard, S. 91
Kieslowski, Krzysztof 133
King, Martin Luther 132, 190
Klein, Max 178, 183, 186–87, 188, 189, 190, 191, 192
Konzelman, Robert 52
Kort, Wesley 55, 106
Kreitzer, Larry 80, 164
Kubrick, Stanley 113, 114, 133
Kuleshov, Lev 110
Kurosawa, Akira 38, 133
Kwan, Billy 176, 177–78, 184, 193

Ladd, Alan 129
Lamott, Anne 155
landscape 96
Lange, Jessica 22
Lapp, Rachel 180
Lauren, Ralph 23
Lawrence, Martin 147
Lee, Robert 52, 140
Lee, Spike 133
Legion of Decency 35–37, 38
Leigh, Janet 110
Lerner, Jenny 169–70
Lester, Julius 156
Lewis, C. S. 67, 78, 81, 101, 161, 174, 195
Lewis, R. W. B. 50
liberal Protestantism 59

lighting 99, 108, 111
Lindsay, Vachel 32
Lindsey, Hal 171
linear thinking 170
Lishman, Bill 102
literary criticism 50
literature 51, 94–95, 97, 114, 151
longing 67
Lord, Daniel 35
Los Angeles County Museum of Art 88
Los Angeles Philharmonic 87
Los Angeles Times 23, 45
Lucas, George 112–13
Lumière, Louis and Auguste 31, 32
Luther, Martin 75–76, 89
Lutherans 59

MacDonald, George 67
Macquarrie, John 79
McClain, Carl 43
McGill, Tess 149
McLuhan, Marshall 137
McMurphy, Randall 66, 141–43
Malone, Peter 53
Marsh, Clive 164
Martin, Joel 55, 164
Martin, Steve 152
Martin, Thomas 55, 58
Marxist criticism 152
May, John 57, 163
Medved, Michael 38, 46–49
Meili, Christoph 26, 157
Merrik, John 85–86
Michelangelo 87, 97, 133
Miles, Herbert 43
Miles, Margaret 48–49, 64
miracles 68
mise-en-scene 111
montage 110

Morissette, Alanis 45
Motion Picture Association of America 38–39
Motion Picture Producers and Distributors of America (MPPDA) 35
movies. *See also* film
    as collaborative process 133
    as discursive and presentational 152
    form of 109
    on own terms 49, 62
    portrayal of religion 32
    as post-apocalyptic 168
    power of 90
    ratings system 38–39
    as sacramental 77, 97, 161–62
    as self-authenticating 91
    success with public 32
    theological reflection on 85
    value of 64
Mozart, Wolfgang Amadeus 119, 186
Mulvey, Laura 148
Murrow, Edward R. 148
music 96, 97, 106, 108, 113, 186–87
musicals 129
mystery 189, 190–91, 193
mystical images 77
myth 127, 128, 131

narrative 78–82
Native Americans 134–36
nature 178, 181
NC-17 rating 39
Nelson, John Wiley 131
Nichols, Mike 150

Schillaci, Anthony 51
Schiller, J. C. Friedrich
  von 50
Schindler, Oskar 25–26,
  107–8
Schleiermacher, Friedrich
  97
Schrader, Paul 44, 58, 76,
  92–93, 95–96, 158
Scorsese, Martin 43, 44,
  76, 93, 96
Scott, Bernard Brandon
  52, 164
Scott, Nathan 70, 156,
  187
screenwriter 105
screwball comedy 164,
  179
script 105–6
scriptwriter 108, 133
secretary movies 149
secularization 21
  of evil 171–72
seeing 15, 19, 118–19,
  123, 174
Seelye, Katharine 146
"seize the day" 176, 177
sex 15, 33–34, 35, 39,
  114, 173, 190
sexual discrimination 149
sexual orientation 48
Shadvac, Tom 89
Shagwell, Felicity 22
Shakespeare, W. 88, 138
shame 79–80
Shane 129–32, 179–80
Shelton, Ron 76
Shore, Frank 13
Simmons, Jean 22
sin 119
Siskel, Gene 118, 125
Sittler, Joseph 67, 162
Sittser, Catherine 27, 117,
  157, 198 n. 18
Sittser, Gerry 27–28
sixties 175, 176, 181

Sjöström, Victor 91, 92
Skinner, James 35
Sklar, Robert 90
Skrade, Carl 51–52
slow-motion 187
Smith, Kevin 15, 44–45
Snodgrass, Klyne 69
soft-focus 187
Solzhenitsyn, Aleksandr
  90, 91, 93
Sonny 144–46
Sontag, Susan 137
sound 99, 110, 112–13,
  174
Spacek, Sissy 22
special effects 112–13,
  174
Spellman, Cardinal 37
Spielberg, Steven 16, 23,
  26, 60–61, 103,
  133, 146
Spirit 64, 67–70, 188,
  192
spiritual maturity 46
spirituality 14–15, 16, 93,
  192–93
Stephens, Mitchell 95
stereotypes 48, 148,
  149–50
Stevens, George 53,
  130–31
Stevens, Wallace 155,
  156
Stewart, Martha 23
story 14, 64, 78–79,
  82–83, 99–100,
  105, 123, 156–57,
  162, 182
Stott, John R. W. 14
Strauss, Richard 113
studio executives 116
Summers, Stanford 52
Sundance Film Festival
  80, 100, 134
Svetkey, Benjamin
  100–101, 105

Swed, Mark 96
symbols 75

Tanner, Spurgeon 170
Tarantino, Quentin 105,
  146
Taylor, Bruce 13–14
Taylor, John 67
technology 112–13, 170
television 45, 59
telling 174
thematic criticism 115,
  126, 139–41, 150,
  162, 174, 177–78
theological criticism 152,
  163
theological dialogue
  82–83, 163–65
theological imperialism
  49
theological themes
  140–41
theology 14, 16–17, 64,
  79
  as experiential and
    critical 175
  and film 49–50, 54,
    80, 162–65
  ignored by church 63
Thomas à Becket 28–30
Thomas Builds-the-Fire
  134–35
Thoreau, Henry David 15
thriller 127
Tillich, Paul 68, 77–78
Tolstoy, Leo 138
tone. See point of view
tradition 83–84
Trainer, Jack 149
transcendence 57–58,
  92–93, 100,
  154–58
Treves, Sir Frederick 85
truth 70–71, 94, 124

Universal Studios 44

Robert K. Johnston (Ph.D., Duke University) is professor of theology and culture at Fuller Theological Seminary. He is the author or coeditor of several books and a regular film reviewer for *The Covenant Companion*.